SHUDDHI MOVEMENT IN INDIA
(*A Study of its Socio-political Dimensions*)

SHUDDHI MOVEMENT IN INDIA

(A Study of its Socio-political Dimensions)

R.K. GHAI

BL 1215.5
.G 48
1990

Commonwealth Publishers
NEW DELHI-110002
(INDIA)

KANSAS SCHOOL OF RELIGION
UNIVERSITY OF KANSAS
1300 OREAD AVENUE
LAWRENCE, KANSAS 66044

1. Shuddhi movement — India

First Published, 1990

ISBN 81-7169-042-4

© R.K. GHAI

Published by
Commonwealth Publishers
4378/4B, Gali Murari Lal
Ansari Road, New Delhi-110002

Printed at
Gaurav Printers
Maujpur
Delhi-110053

To Indra
My Mother-in-law

Preface

A unique movement, an off-shoot of the reformist zeal of the Hindus to meet the challenge of proselytizing efforts of the Christians, the *shuddhi* movement, according to the generally acceptable view, originated as a defensive social strategy. As it developed, its protagonists and antagonists both from within and without the Hindu society formed perceptions in consonance with the changing political climate of the country. Being demonstrative in nature and marginally affecting the Hindu social structure, the *shuddhi* movement aroused varied and complex responses and reactions encouraging schism within the Hindu society, communal divide and separatist politics. Holistic, conservative, traditional and hierarchical with wide range of graded purity and pollution rituals, as the nature of the Hindu society was, it has been compared with the 'mouse trap with the door turned inside out; one could go out but could not come in.' Therefore, an effort has been made to study the *shuddhi* movement in the perspective of the traditional Hindu social structure and its ethos as well as socio-political milieu of the late nineteenth and early twentieth centuries.

In spite of the fact that the Hindu society was confronted with external challenges and internal pressures, it technically did not institutionalize conversion and reconversion as is practised by the Muslims and Christians. Therefore, the term *shuddhi* was used in ancient times not to denote conversion or reconversion but to the purification process which is a complex graded system of purity and impurity. Secondly, unlike other religious groups, the entry into the caste society placed double burden : one, of entry into the Hindu community, and the second, entry into the caste society. Highly organized as it was the institution of *varna ashrama* caused considerable social problem of acceptance as caste (*jati*) was based on birth and not on social group based on acquired status. Nevertheless, with the emergence of Muslim power in India there has been conversions of the Hindus to Islam. Here it may be mentioned for the proper understanding of the issue that most of the communities which got converted into Islam were semi-agrarian tribal or purely tribal communities which, strictly speaking, were not the caste Hindus or were just marginally so, making effort to enter into the caste Hindu society. However, conversion continued, and the caste society gradually became very rigid.

Again, with the rise of British power in India the conservative and rigid Hindu society and culture came into clash with the dynamic and progressive Western culture. The activities of the missionaries alongwith the Westernization process caused a threat to the very structure of the Hindu society, their life style, and mode of thinking. No doubt, a large number of socio-religious movements began after the contact between the two diametrically opposed cultures in the nineteenth century but it was for Swami Dayanand Saraswati, the founder of the Arya Samaj, who with the Christian missionaries' model desired to stem the conversion. During this period he appeared on the scene of Punjab in 1877 and inaugurated the *shuddhi* movement as a process of reconversion. He and his followers concerned themselves with purification evidently as a defensive mechanism to win back those who had been converted to other religions. To make it rationally explanable Swami Dayanand exploded the basis of caste. With the passage of time the *shuddhi* offered to the Samajists the basis for innovation which would transform Hinduism into a conversion religion, equal institutionally to its competitors. In the early phase of its development we witness tension and resistance within the Hindu society.

But, with the introduction of communal representation in which the number mattered most, the *shuddhi* movement received added impetus and began to be pursued vigorously by the enthusiatic Arya Samajists, leading to serious socio-political implications.

Significant as it is, the *shuddhi* movement, strangely enough, has so far not received the full attention of historians as there is no work of historical scholarship dealing exclusively with it. In this present study an humble attempt has been made to analyse and explain in details the history of the *shuddhi* movement with its socio-political dimensions.

The present study is based on the primary sources. Since most of the original data has been lost during the partition and as such is not available in India, the author, to some extant, has relied upon the secondary records of great importance in delineating the history of the movement.

Although, no effort has been spared to interpret and examine the facts as critically as possible, yet, as E.H. Car writes, "ultimate history we cannot have in this generation...." But if the conclusions arrived at should provoke further thinking on various facets of the movement, this humble attempt shall be considered amply justified.

It is difficult to express adequately my feelings of gratitude to Dr. Satish K. Bajaj, Reader, Department of History, Punjabi University, Patiala, under whose guidance the present work, as a doctoral thesis, was originally undertaken. Always ready to answer my queries patiently, he never left any point unexplained. I am also indebted to Dr. A.C. Arora, Professor of History, Punjabi University for his generoisity and encouragement and to Dr. Gursharan Singh, Head Deptt. of Punjab Historical Studies for his cooperation.

I am equally grateful to the staff of the following institutions for their ungrudging cooperation, courtesy and help: The Bhartiya Hindu Shuddhi Sabha, New Delhi ; The Arya Pratinidhi Sabha, New Delhi; Gurkul Kangri, Hardwar; VVRI, Hoshiarpur; The Nehru Memorial Library, New Delhi; The Arya Pratinidhi Sabha, Punjab. Jalandhar; The National Archieves of India, New Delhi; Punjab State Archieves, Patiala; The Cambridge Brotherhood Library, New Delhi;

Dwarka Dass Library, Chandigarh; Punjab University Library, Chandigarh; Punjabi University Library, Patiala and the Department of Punjab Historical Studies Library, Patiala.

I owe a special and almost inexpressible debt to my wife, Nirmal. Her patience, love and cheerfulness during the travails of my study has always been a source of strength and encouragement. I also express my thanks to my daughter, Gunjan (11) and son, Gaurav (9) for bearing my neglect at the time when they needed my attention the most.

Lastly, I am highly thankful to Mr. B.R. Verma of Commonwealth Publishers, New Delhi for publishing this book in the shortest possible time in an excellent form and to Mr. S.K. Walia of JAICO for his friendly gesture.

R.K. GHAI
PATIALA, PUNJAB

Contents

Preface   *vii*

1. Introduction   1
2. Social Perceptions of Swami Dayanand Saraswati and Genesis of Shuddhi Movement   25
3. Development of Shuddhi Movement: The First Phase (1883-1920)   41
4. Development of Shuddhi Movement: The Second Phase (1920-1947)   83
5. Social Dimensions of Shuddhi Movement   120
6. Political Dimensions of Shuddhi Movement   141
7. Conclusions   155

Appendices

(i) Letters of Ram Bhaj Datt Chaudhri President, All India Bharat Shuddhi Sabha, Gurdaspur   163
(ii) Some cases of Reconversion of individuals and small groups during the years 1929-30   173
(iii) Ten Principles of the Arya Samaj   176
(iv) Objects and Programme of Jat Pat Todak Mandal   178

Bibliography   181
Index   203

1

Introduction

Definition

Etymological study of the word *shuddhi* in its socio-religious context indicates that in the beginning it was used to denote purification.[1] Elaborating it Monier-Williams, one of the greatest authorities on Sanskrit language, defines it as "purity, cleanliness, holiness, freedom from defilement; purification, expiation, cleansing; a particular expiatory rite; it is sometimes given as a name of Durga."[2] Evidently it is a generic term which has various shades but it essentially means the cleansing of one's body from pollution caused by everyday acts through rituals and recitation of the sacred *mantras* (hymns), and in extreme cases through *praschit*.[3] In this sense "the concept is basic to the structure of indigenous traditional thought and practice. One could interpret much of formal

1. Lajpat Rai, *The Arya Samaj : An Account of its Aims, Doctrine and Activities, with a Biographical Sketch of the Founder* (Lahore: Uttar Chand Kapur & Sons, 1932), p. 248.
2. Sir Monier Monier-Williams, *A Sanskrit-English Dictionary* (Oxford : The Clarendon Press, 1872), p. 1014.
3. Prem Ram Uprety, *Religion and Politics in Punjab in the 1920s* (New Delhi: Sterling, 1980), p. 72.

religious life in the context of Indian tradition as the application of techniques with the aim of acquisition, maintenance, and protection of one's own condition of purity—in a predominantly ritual or sacred rather than hygienic or secular sense."[4] In its social context *shuddhi* has been equated with a thermostat device for automatically regulating the social system i.e. the *varnashram*. Ramchandraji Shastri therefore explains it as "the abandonment of prohibited food, separation of contact with low persons, living in one's situation according to *varnashramadharma*."[5] It is in this general sense that the use of the term *shuddhi* can be found in numerous ancient ritual and judicial texts and commentaries.[6] And hence it was not applied in the specific sense of (a) conversion to Hinduism of persons belonging to other religions, (b) reconversion of those who have recently or at a remote period had adopted other religions, and (c) reclamation i.e. raising the status of the so-called depressed classes.[7] But it acquired the specific connotation in the late nineteenth century particularly for the reconversion of the Hindus. J.N. Farquhar writes, "Since a Hindu becomes impure through embracing another religion, the method adopted is to subject those who return to a purification ceremony. Hence the name *shuddhi*, purification."[8] In the almost similar vein, Kenneth W. Jones attempts at defining the term *shuddhi* in its narrowest sense i.e. the word is applied to the "purification of individuals converted to another

---

4. Gene Robert Thursby, "Aspects of Hindu-Muslim Relations in British India : A Study of Arya Samaj Activities, Government of India Policies, and Communal Conflict in the Period 1923-28," Unpublished Ph.D. Dissertation, Duke University, 1972, p. 31.
5. Sriman Mehta Ramchandraji Shastri, *Patiton ki Shuddhi Sanatan Hai* (Shuddhi of the backward classes is ancient) (Lahore : Arya Pradeshik Pratinidhi Sabha, 1908), p. 76.
6. Extensive references could be found in P.V. Kane, *History of Dharmashastra* (Poona: Bhandarkar Oriental Research Institute, 1973), Vol. IV, pp. 117-18, 267-333 and 828-30.
7. *Census of India, 1911*, Punjab Report, p. 148.
8. J.N. Farquhar, *Modern Religious Movement in India* (Delhi : Munshiram Manoharlal, 1967), p. 323.

Introduction 3

religion within their lifetime .... All conversion was, in fact, reconversion, returning an individual to the parent fold of Hinduism."[9] As a ritual *shuddhi*, of course, is as old as Hinduism itself and was an integral part of the Brahminical Hinduism.[10] In this study we are mainly concerned with the 'specific' sense of the term *shuddhi*.

It is generally believed that *shuddhi* as a movement of conversion of people to the fold of Hinduism was inaugurated by Swami Dayanand, the founder of the Arya Samaj. Therefore, it was during the last decade of the nineteenth century, the term came to acquire a more specific meaning, namely, "the incorporation into Hinduism of non-Hindu individuals, groups, or classes of persons by means of ceremonial action and with the intention of extending to them social relations in matters of commensality and marriage."[11] Although the intention in many cases was not fulfilled, but the most notable instances of the practice in the nineteenth century did occur among the Sikhs and the Arya Samajists in the Punjab.[12] In this connection the word *shuddhi* means the reconversion of those people who converted themselves either to the Islam or Christianity.

The word *shuddhi*, however, cannot be equated with the term conversion as understood in the West. There the term conversion applies to a marked change of heart, an emotional regeneration, typically sudden in its advent or consummation, affecting radically the outlook, the inner adjustment and the habits of life of an individual.[13] In a similar sense which is

9. Kenneth W. Jones, "Ham Hindu Nahin : Arya-Sikh Relations, 1877-1905" in *Journal of Asian Studies*, Vol. 32, May 1973, p. 463.
10. Kenneth W. Jones, *Arya Dharm* : *Hindu Consciousness in 19th Century Punjab* (Delhi : Manohar Book Service, 1976), p. 129. (Hereafter quoted as *Arya Dharm*).
11. Gene Robert Thursby, *op. cit.*, p. 31.
12. *Ibid.*
13. E.R.A. Seligman (ed.), *Encyclopaedia of Social Sciences* (New York: The Macmillan Co., 1962), Vol. IV, p. 353.

more psychologically correct, A.D. Knock comments that conversion means "the re-orientation of the soul of the individual, his deliberate turning from indifference or from an earlier form of piety to another, a turning which implies a consciousness that a great change is involved, that the old was wrong and the new is right."[14] According to *Chamber's Encyclopaedia*:[15]

> the term 'conversion' is used in more than one sense. The most important, because it is concerned with the most fundamental change that can take place in any human life, is that in which it denotes the acceptance of an 'other-wordly' or selfish one. This is sometimes regarded as the change from a materialistic to a spiritual attitude to life, and normally involves both a new and intense conviction of the reality of the being of God and a strong sense of obligation to obey His Will.

The aforesaid definitions of conversion refer to the transformation of religious view of an individual which preclude conversion in the context of non-theistic religion such as the Buddhism.

For the purposes of the present study the word *shuddhi* means "a change of fellowship than of conduct or inner life although the latter may in time occur. Conversion on the ideological level can mean little more than acceptance of the decline of Hinduism and the need for its regeneration."[16] But the terms 'conversion' and 're-conversion' which occur in the nineteenth and twentieth centuries are used in the simple non-technical sense to mean the process whereby people move out

---

14. Quoted in G.A. Oddie (ed.), *Religion in South Asia : Religious Conversion and Revival Movements in South Asia in Medieval & Modern Times* (New Delhi : Manohar Book Service, 1977), p. 4.
15. *Chamber's Encyclopaedia* (London : 1959), Vol. VI, p. 92.
16. G.A. Oddie, *op. cit.*, p. 4.

of one religious community and enter into another.[17]

In view of the above definition of *shuddhi* as a means of conversion of an individual into the fold of Hinduism, we may begin our analysis with a pertinent remark of Ganga Prasad Upadhyaya who says, "the Hindu society was, so to speak, a mouse-trap with the door turned inside out. One could go out but could not come in."[18] This assumption appears to be hasty, particularly in the light of Kenneth W. Jones' explanation who believes that *shuddhi* was prevalent in ancient India.[19] These observations make incumbent on a researcher to trace the origin of *shuddhi* in the Indian tradition in order to grasp its relevance, significance, nature and meaning at various points of time in the history of Indian society and culture.

Historical Background

The Hindu social structure has evolved in all its complexities since the period of Indus Valley Civilization. Its basic and the most distinct feature is the caste-system. According to some scholars, it started evolving during the period of Harappan Civilization.[20] It seems that the social structure on the basis of hierarchy, status and power, and purity and pollution was organized in the nature of institutionalized inequality because of marginal surplus which required for the sustenance of society to maintain various occupational groups

17. R K. Ghai, "Genesis of Shuddhi Movement : Its Historical Explanation" in *Punjab History Conference Proceedings*, 17th Session, March 12-14, 1982, p. 247.
18. Ganga Prasad Upadhyaya, *Swami Dayanand's Contribution to Hindu Solidarity* (Allahabad: Arya Samaj, Chowk, 1939), p. 111.
19. Kenneth W. Jones, *Arya Dharm*, p. 129. For similar views, see Sri Ram Sharma, *Conversion and Reconversion to Hinduism during the Muslim Period* (Delhi : All India Shuddhi Sabha, n.d.), p. 1; R.D. Sharma, "The Shuddhi Movement : Origin and Revival" in Swami Satya Prakash Saraswati (ed.), *Dayanand Commemoration Volume* (Ajmer : Paropkarni Sabha, 1983), pp. 197-98.
20. B. Allchin and F.R. Allchin, *Birth of Indian Civilization* : *India and Pakistan before 500 B.C.* (Harmondsworth : Penguin Books, 1968), p. 140.

intact in their positions. The theory of marginal surplus can be applied to the early Aryan Civilization during which the caste-system acquired complex and rigid character. Implicitly referring to this idea, A.R. Desai is of the opinion that the caste-system survived throughout the ancient as well as in the medieval period due to "the low level of economic existence of the Indian people. The pre-capitalist economy on which it rested was primarily based on village autarchy, the absence of appreciable development of exchange relations, and extremely weak and meagre means of transport."[21] It is evident from the fact that during the Vedic period developed the Brahminical tradition and entire range of rituals and practices which is designated as by scholars 'the sacred tradition'. However, in the sixth and fifth centuries B.C. two great systems of religious faith and philosophy appeared in north-east India viz., Jainism and Buddhism. An important and well established system at that time was the Vedic form of Brahminism which had been making steady progress in north India since the time of the *Rigveda*.[22] Large areas of north-east India were still free from the influence of Brahminism in the age of the Buddha and Vardhaman Mahavira. It may, however, be pointed out that both religions were missionary faiths whereas the Brahminical Hinduism was not.[23]

The Vedic form of Brahminism was not a universal religion; that is to say, its doctrines were neither acceptable nor open to all the men and women. Even the much praised doctrines of the *Upanisads*[24] were meant only for the circle of

21. A.R. Desai, *Social Background of Indian Nationalism* (Bombay: Popular Prakashan, 1981-82), p. 247.
22. Lalmani Joshi, *Studies in the Buddhistic Culture of India* (*During the 7th and 8th Centuries A.D.*) (Delhi: Motilal Banarasidas, 1967), pp. 1-12.
23. Donald Eugene Smith (ed.), *South Asian Politics and Religion* (Princeton: Princeton University Press, 1966), p. 6.
24. The word *Upanisad* means 'secret', or 'confidential'. One could learn the mysteries and doctrines of Vedic Brahminism only by sitting at the feet of the learned Brahman teacher. L.M. Joshi (ed.), *History of the Punjab* (Patiala: Punjabi University, 1977), Vol. I, Introduction.

the initiates. The knowledge of the technique of performing sacrificial ritual (*yajna*) was a monopoly of the priestly class of Brahmans. This knowledge was sacred as well as secret and it was not generally imparted to the Ksatriyas, Vaisyas and Sudras. Initiation (*diksa*) in traditional Brahminical fold of society was known but it was not open to all persons. The Brahmans thus could not convert any one else to their 'sacred tradition.'

There was yet another difficulty inherent in the traditional Brahminical Hindu religion which stood in the way of conversion and universalization. The scheme of four classes, the *varna-vyavastha* with its rigid list of obligations, duties, rights and privileges, prescribed for the members of each *varna*, left no room for converting the outsiders to Hinduism.[25] One had to be born a Brahman or Ksatriya; an outsider who was neither a Brahman, nor a Ksatriya, nor a Vaisya, could not become a member of any of these classes under ordinary conditions.[26] When *varna* degenerated into caste or *jati*, the socio-religious scheme hardened, and the doors of orthodox Brahminism were closed for all those who were outside the purview of the *varna-vyavastha*.[27]

It is significant to note that no ceremonies or rituals are found in *Dharmasashtras* for converting people to Brahminical Hinduism. But it does not mean that there was no cultural assimilation or Aryanization. It is a known fact that in the ancient period a number of foreign tribes came to India and were gradually assimilated by the indigenous people. Some of these foreign tribes established their own strong monarchies in India. The Greeks, the Hunas, the Sakas and the Kusanas forcibly achieved the position of Ksatriyas of some sort by becoming rulers over the territories in which the members of

25. Munshi Ram Jijyasu and Rama Deva, *The Arya Samaj and its Detractors* : *A Vindication* (Gurukul Kangri: 1910), p. 13.
26. *Ibid.*
27. Richard Lannoy, *The Speaking Tree* : *A Study of Indian Culture and Society* (London: Oxford Press, 1971), p. 142.

the Brahminical classes lived. They were never formally converted by Brahminical priest;[28] but they themselves adopted Brahminical religious and social customs and thus became Brahminised or Hinduised.[29]

It may here be mentioned that the conversion of the Hindus into the fold of Buddhism and Jainism was not conversion in a strictly technical sense of the term for two reasons. One, these religions did not transform the style of life and mode of thinking of the people of India. And secondly, the thoughts of these two religions were absorbed into the Hindu religious philosophy and life. By virtue of this process the *shuddhi* or conversion lost its relevance as far as Indian society was concerned. They tended only to loosen the grip of Brahminical rituals on the society.

With the decline of Buddhism the conversion movement took a new turn under the Muslim rule. The Hindu society became very conservative and rigid as the *shuddhi* began to be denoted as the ritualistic purification process of a large number of impurities and pollutions of temporary nature. The advent of Muslim rule in India brought a distinct religion with a universal view of its own and with missionary zeal. The Muslims used force, persuasion and all other means to convert the Indians.[30] The lure of high posts or feudatory gains secured to Islam, during the Muslim rule, many high-caste Hindus. Kenneth W. Jones observes, "The cultural contact between the Islamic world and Hindu tradition created an

---

28. Sri Ram Sharma, "Swami Dayanand and Shuddhi", Unpublished article in the possession of Professor Bhawani Lal Bharti, Head, Swami Dayanand Chair, Panjab University, Chandigarh, p. 2.
29. Richard Lannoy, *op. cit.*, p. 178. The upward mobility of the lower caste cannot be equated with *shuddhi*. It was a definite kind of social change as has been described by M.N. Srinivas while using the term 'Sanskritization'. *Social Change in Modern India* (Bombay: Orient Longmans Ltd., 1982), p. 6.
30. Vishwa Prakash, *Life and Teachings of Swami Dayanand* (Allahabad: Kala Press, 1935), pp. 156-57.

historical situation similar to that of the nineteenth century. The Hindus, who participated in this Muslim world, learned Persian and adjusted to a foreign culture, created new forms of identity, and new concepts of self."[31] But by far the majority of converts, who entered the fold of Islam through persuasion of missionaries, belonged to lower castes or classes of Hindus and the tribal communities to whom the religion of Arabia at once brought that social equality which Hinduism had denied them from the time immemorial.[32] The caste system played a great role here also. The lower castes were looked down upon by the Brahmans; they were not allowed to come near the 'twice-born'. To all caste Hindus the untouchables were a source of pollution; their touch defiled, and the infection had to be removed by purificatory rites which usually included ceremonial washing.[33] In South India their mere propinquity was considered to cause defilement and they had therefore to be settled outside a village inhabited by the caste Hindus.[34] So strong was the hold of caste on the people that when at last a vigorous onslaught was made against it, it was from the lower castes and the untouchables themselves and not from the higher castes that the most vigorous opposition proceeded. Those Brahnans who performed priestly functions naturally resisted, but, on the whole it is believed by some scholars, the lower the caste the more conservative it would be. The reason appears to be very simple. The caste discipline was far stricter among the lower castes not because they desired to maintain the strangulating caste structure but because the fear of being outcasted was more intense. The whole system, moreover, was hollowed by *dharma*, divinely instituted and was therefore considered as unalterable.[35] The caste system, in

31. Kenneth W. Jones, *Arya Dharm*, p. 2.
32. R.C. Majumdar (ed.), *History and Culture of Indian People* (Bombay: Bharatiya Vidya Bhavan, 1965), Vol. X, Part II, p. 140.
33. K.L. Seshagiri Rao (ed.), *Hinduism* (Patiala: Punjabi University, 1969), p. 57.
34. *Arya*, May 1936, pp. 31-32.
35. J.N. Farquhar, *op. cit.*, pp. 395-96.

fact, escorted the Hindu society everywhere and in all circumstances.

Living under many social disabilities, the low caste Hindus were vulnerable to conversion programme of the Muslims. Metaphorically speaking, as a knife goes into a melon without much efforts, so did Islam penetrate into these castes with little persuasion. Islam was adopted by families or groups of families or communities or part thereof who were regarded as outcaste in the Hindu society because of their profession, or because they had lost caste under the Muslim government.[36]

If on the one hand there was a strong conservative reaction to the conversion of Hindus as due to it the Hindu society tended to defend itself by making a cacoon of caste system to defend themselves,[37] the reponse to the changing socio-cultural phenomenon in the form of Bhakti Movement against the Brahminical hold is sometimes analysed in Weberian terms as in spite of being religious in tone and temper, it universally condemned caste hierarchy and division which to some degree, loosened the hold of caste on the Indian social system. Nevertheless it did not radically change the Indian society. By and large the caste was retained as an essential part of social organization, of course, permitting people for greater interaction without impinging upon the social structure.

In the wake of declining Mughal Empire and the foreign invasions of Nadir Shah and Ahmad Shah Abdali, the Indian political structure got destabilised as in the process it provided opportunities to the indigenous regional power such as the Marathas, the Nizams of Hyderabad, Haider Ali and Tipu Sultan of Mysore, Nawabs of Oudh and Bengal, Sikhs in the

36. R.K. Ghai, "Religious Conversions in the Punjab, 1849-1914", Unpublished M. Phil. Dissertation, Punjabi University, Patiala, 1980, pp. 123-31.
37. G.S. Ghurye, *Social Tensions in India* (Bombay: Popular Prakashan, 1968), p. 242.

Punjab and host of others to establish their independent authorities. Alongwith them the European powers such as the French and the British also ran for the race to acquire political base in India in order to secure their trade. This period of political instability was one of the most crucial phase in the social history of India. Confronted with rampant immorality, tyranny and corruption, the Indian society degenerated to such an extent that religious bigotry, superstition, irrational and inhuman beliefs and practices such as *sati*, infanticide, human sacrifice so on and so forth became cardinal principles of the Indian value system. Politically divided, socially degenerated, economically exploited and religiously steeped into ignorance, India in a short period of less than sixty years after 1757 lay lacerated and prostrate before the British might. The British conquest of India is the most significant development in the history of India for it unleashed many great developments which laid the foundation of modern Indian society.

Due to the impact of British policies, the Indian society began to undergo radical social changes such as the destruction of village autarchy, creation of proprietary rights in land, the steady industrialization leading to urbanization and rapid means of transportation, accompanied by the introduction of comprehensive land revenue system, development of market economy, introduction of money economy, increase in population and exodus of mass population from villages to cities and proliferation of professions led to the formation of new property relations, decline of indigenous industry and impoverishment of the masses. However, the British conquest created necessities as well as economic opportunities which led the Indian people to adopt new professions, thus dissolving the rigidity of social structure.[38] The urbanization process created great mobility and forced people of various castes and communities to work together ignoring the caste and communal divisions. The introduction of new legal system,

---

38. B.B. Misra, *The Indian Middle Classes: Their Growth in Modern Times* (London: Oxford University Press, 1961), p. 15.

hierarchy of courts, administrative institutions loosened the hold of caste and in the process caste gradually became a voluntary association.[39] A.R. Desai remarks, "This horizontal division on new class lines increasingly weakened the old vertical caste lines,"[40] but did not lead to the destruction of traditional society as caste and communal division continued to survive. It has been observed that the structure of Indian society was modified but not remoulded by the British policies in India.[41] Hence our intention is simply to suggest that the ritualistic basis for the existence of caste system disappeared. It, as G.S. Ghurye suggests, began to evolve on the lines of caste associations in the urban areas.[42] In fact, with the advent of the British rule in India and consequent introduction of new values such as rationalism, individualism and liberalism accompanied by new socio-economic and administrative policies, the traditional Indian society came under tremendous pressures because it eroded the basic values of Indian tradition. Under the impact of Western ideas, supremacy of reason over faith and supremacy of individual conscience over outside authority were established. The accumulative effect of these changes on the Indian society was that the individual began to move up or down in the social scale according to his circumstances.[43]

The impact of the British policies and Western ideas crystallized the challenge posed by the Western culture including that of the Christian missionaries to the Indian society which presented a highly complex spectrum of socio-religious institutions. If, on the one hand, there were highly developed philosophies and the sciences as discovered by the Orientalists to show

39. *Ibid.*
40. A.R. Desai, *op. cit.*, pp. 349-50.
41. D. Kumar, "Caste and Landless in South India" in *Comparative Study in Society and History*, Vol. IV, 1961-62, Hague, 1962, p. 363.
42. G.S. Ghurye, *op. cit.*, p. 299. Also see, M.N. Srinivas, *op. cit.*, p. 70.
43. B.B. Misra, *op. cit.*, pp. 15-16.

that Indian civilization had reached a high watermark, there were, on the other hand, also large number of religious sects with variety of gods and goddesses imbued with the philosophy of animism, and accompanied by abominable social customs such as polygamy, child-marriage, infanticide, *sati*, human sacrifice, untouchability so on and so forth. Shocked to witness such customs, the Utilitarians, inspired by the ideas of Jeremy Bentham who refuted the assertions of the Orientalists, took great pains to show that the Indian society was backward rather barbarous and therefore required to be reformed radically on the principles of Utilitarianism.[44] The Evanglicals on the other hand sought to change India by converting Indians to Christianity and also through the spread of education. They believed that the dynamic qualities of Christianity and the Western culture would shake the roots of ancient Hindu religion and philosophy.

However, the conservative and tradition-bound Indian society sharply reacted to the over-zealous Christian missionary propaganda as it posed a serious challenge to the age-old customs, beliefs and tradition. Persuading the English East India Company to withdraw its official support to the 'heathen practices', as is evident from the memorandum presented by them to the Government of Bombay in 1839,[45] the Christian missionaries, in collusion with the bureaucracy, attacked the socio-religious institutions of the Indians and condemned them as false and primitive.[46] Not only this, they "denounced in the schools and market places, the heathen scriptures, the

44. Eric Stokes, *The English Utilitarians and India* (London: Oxford University Press, 1963), p. xiv.
45. Among other things, the memorandum included objections against the participation of Government officials (in their official capacity) at Hindu and Muslim festivals, the inscription of 'Sri' on public documents, the firing of salutes by the troops and the use of regimental bands in the processions of Hindu and Muslim festivals. R.C. Majumdar, *op. cit.*, p. 153.
46. Ganga Prasad Upadhyaya, *The Arya Samaj and Christianity* (Allahabad: Arya Samaj, Chowk, 1931), p. 13.

Quran, the *Shastras*, and the *Granth* and condemned, as false guides in morals and religion, the *Bhagats, Sufis, Sadhus* and *Mahants*."[47] The Christian missionaries not only condemned their scriptures but also resorted to more subtle and direct methods to spread Christianity and gain converts.[48] Christianity being the religion of the ruling class, the missionaries were encouraged by them in their proselytizing work.[49]

During their first eighty years in India, the Christian missionaries were presented with two rather unique opportunities which they decided to take advantage of and which had a great influence upon their history. The first of these was the demand made by high caste urban Indians for the Western education in the English language so that they might be qualified for entrance into government service or the legal, medical, engineering or teaching professions.[50] The educational work gave the missionaries prominence and influence out of all proportion to their numbers.[51] The second opportunity was created by the widespread desire among the lower castes to better their lot and improve their status either by making themselves more respectable in traditional Hindu terms or by

47. John Clark Archer, *The Sikhs* (Princeton: Princeton University Press, 1946), p. 266. Also see Emmett Davis, *Press and Politics in British Western Punjab, 1836-1947* (Delhi: Academic Publications, 1983), p. 65.
48. Rafiq-i-Hind, December 31, 1892 in *Selections from the Vernacular Newspapers published in the Punjab, 1893*, p. 5. (Hereafter quoted as *SVNP*).
49. "Sir Henry Lawrence, the Head of the Board of Administration in the Punjab in his letter to welcome to the Missionaries and his subscription of Rs. 500 a year to the Mission, showed the importance which he attached to the work in which they were engaged." Rev. Robert Clark, *A Brief Account of Thirty Years of Missionary Work of the Church Missionary Society in the Punjab and Sindh, 1852-1882* (Lahore, 1883), pp. 4-5.
50. John C.B. Webster, *Christian Community and Change in Nineteenth Century North India* (Delhi: Macmillan Company of India, 1976), p. 53.
51. *Census of India, 1868*, Punjab Report, p. 22.

converting *en masse* to any religion or sect which ensured equality of man.[52] The former process has been described as 'Sanskritization' by M.N. Srinivas.[53] Since this process was rather difficult due to the opposition of orthodox Hindus, the lower castes selected the latter course i.e. to convert themselves *en masse*.[54]

Assisted by the factors such as employment avenues, the establishment of Christian colonies, rampant illiteracy of the Indian people and their economic conditions the Christian missionaries achieved a considerable success[55] which is evident from the Census accounts. In 1891, Indian Christians numbered 19,547, and in 1901 it rose to 37,980.[56] But after 1901 the increase had been more than maintained, and the Census of 1921 shows 315,031, or an increase of 295,484, since 1891.[57] Upto 1901, the total number of Christian community

---

52. Pundit Shanker Nath, *Duty Towards Our Depressed Brethren* (n.p., n. pub., 1926), pp. 8-9.

53. 'Sanskritization' is the process by which a "low Hindu caste, or tribal, or other group, changes its customs, ritual, ideology, and way of life in the direction of a high, and frequently, 'twice-born' caste." M. N. Srinivas, *op. cit.*, p. 6.

    In this connection an example of a Chamar Conference held in 1914 in a village in the Karnal district of the Punjab at which resolutions were passed to the effect that 'no Chamar should eat anything cooked by a non-Hindu and that every Chamar should regard the protection of the cow as his first duty, could be mentioned. For reference, see *Observer*, March 7, 1914 in *SVNP, 1914*, p. 272.

54. In the early stages, the Christian missionaries did not make the large number of converts they had hoped for except among the untouchables, some of whom they were successful in converting *en masse*. For reference see Shyamala Bhatia, "Social Change and Politics in the Punjab 1898-1901", Unpublished Ph.D. Thesis, Delhi University, 1984, p. 216.

55. Om Parkash Pursharthy, *Bharat Me Bhiunkar Ishai Sheduntur* (Delhi: Sarvdeshik Press, n.d.), p. 1.

56. *Census of India, 1901*, Punjab Report, p. 158.

57. *Census of India, 1921*, Punjab and Delhi Report, p. 188.

in India rose to 2,923,241, of whom 2,664,313 were native converts.[58]

The conversions and attacks on the Indian religions created apprehension in the minds of Indians that Christianity might engulf the whole of India.[59] Besides this, several official measures like the abolition of the practices of *sati*, infanticide, child-marriage and passing of the Widows' Remarriage Act, 1856, though aimed at social reform, filled the minds of the orthodox Indians with suspicion. The change in the law of property inheritance,[60] thereby preventing a convert from losing his estate, was considered to be a violation of the Indian tradition. The onslaught of Westernization also began to encroach upon the centuries-old spiritualism of the East. The following observation of Macaulay, who had been a member of William Bentinck's Council, is illuminating in this respect:[61]

> European science, astronomy and surgery were all opposed to the teachings of the *Brahmans*. The mysticism and symbolism of the East were fading before Western materialism. The telegraph and railway were looked upon askance as magical and diabolical agencies.

There was a common belief that under the pretext of introducing reforms, the English were actually trying to strike at the very roots of Indian culture and civilization.[62] In the

58. *Census of India, 1901*, India Report, p. 387.
59. *Vedic Magazine and Gurukula Samachar*, Vol. 11, No. 4, 1908-09, p. 2. Also see, Jatinder Sandhu, "British Rule and Cultural Adjustment in the late Nineteenth Century Punjab", in *Punjab History Conference Proceedings*, 19th Session, March 1985, p. 329. Also see P.E. Roberts, *History of British India under the Company and the Crown* (Oxford : Clarendon Press, 1921), p. 364.
60. The Religious Disabilities Act was passed in 1856, according to which a Hindu convert could not be deprived of inheriting his ancestral property. Previously, a convert from Hinduism was not allowed to inherit his ancestral property.
61. Quoted in P.E. Roberts, *op. cit.*, p. 364.
62. Ganga Prasad Upadhyaya, *The Arya Samaj and Christianity*, pp. 14-15.

words of G.N. Singh "the aggressive European innovations had roused the conservative and orthodox instincts of the people."[63] Thus any attempt of the English at introducing reforms or innovations was regarded as an effort to Europeanize or Christianize them. Their suspicion was justified as is testified by the statement of Mr. Mangles, Chairman of the Directors of the East India Company, which he made in the House of Commons in 1857 :[64]

> Providence has entrusted the extensive empire of Hindustan to England, in order that the banner of Christ should wave triumphant from one end of India to the other. Everyone must exert all his dilatoriness on any account in continuing in the country the grand work of making India Christian.

However, the public reaction discussed above was simultaneously accompanied by favourable response. In this context the introduction of English education proved to be a catalyst. The new educational system based on liberalism, individualism and rationalism infused new vigour and spirit of independence in the Indian youth. With "freshness, energy and initiative," there was "a growing desire to defend Hinduism, and increasing confidence in its defensibility."[65] Though primarily literary in content and designed to serve the Indian bureaucracy, the new education opened the flood-gate of Western thought and Western literature and in the process imparted a rational outlook of understanding the Indian religious practices, myths, symbols and traditional beliefs which stimulated the Indian mind to a new concept of life and explore the possibilities of evolving a new socio-religious vision compatible with Western science and rational thought and Indian tradition as well.[66] In the light of this new knowledge, the evil customs in Hindu

63. G.N. Singh, *Landmarks in Indian Constitutional and National Development* (Banaras, 1930), p. 65.
64. Quoted in P.C. Joshi (ed.), *Rebellion 1857 : A Symposium* (New Delhi: People's Publishing House, 1957), p. 154.
65. J.N. Farquhar, *op. cit.*, pp. 25-26.
66. Lajpat Rai, *op. cit.*, p. 139.

society began to lose their significance[67] as the traditional beliefs and faiths began to be judged on reason instead of orthodox superstitions. The age-long apathy and inertia was removed by a new zeal of reformation. The total impact was that it gave new values, like nationalism, spirit of scientific enquiries in the field of social and religious institutions, freedom of action and freedom of thought, which brought about changes in traditional beliefs and pattern of the Hindus. The supremacy of reason over faith, of individual conscience over outside authority resulted in its wake the new conceptions of social justice and political rights.[68] Inspired by the new vision and new ideology, the educated Indian youths, unlike the orthodox Hindus, became liberal and rational in their outlook. They rose above religious fanaticism and tried to analyse the causes which were responsible for their social and cultural degeneration. They thought that the values of the East and the West, instead of coming into conflict with one another, should make a happy and harmonious blending. They tried to evolve a synthesis between the fast spreading Western ideas and India's glorious past. Thus the English education as well as the contact with the West could be regarded as an essential prelude to the resurgence of social and religious reform movements.[69]

One of the most significant socio-religious movements was the Brahmo Samaj. Its founder Raja Ram Mohan Roy[70] may rightly be regarded as the pioneer[71] of "the first organized

67. D.S. Sarma, *Hinduism Through the Ages* (Bombay : Bharatiya Vidya Bhavan, 1973), p. 61.
68. Charles H. Heimsath, "Rammohun Roy and Social Reform" in V.C. Joshi (ed.), *Rammohun Roy and the Process of Modernization in India* (Delhi : Vikas Publishing House, 1975), p. 151.
69. J.N. Farquhar, *The Crown of Hinduism* (London: Oxford University Press, 1915), p. 150.
70. David Kopf, *The Brahmo Samaj and the Shaping of the Modern Indian Mind* (New Jersey : Princeton University Press, 1979), p. xiii.
71. Raja Ram Mohan Roy is remembered as the 'Pole Star of Indian Awakening'. For detail see, Nemai Sadhan Bose, *Indian Awakening and Bengal* (Calcutta : F.K.L. Mukhopadhyay, 1976), p. 27.

effort made by the educated Indians to reform the Hindu way of life and the Hindu social system."[72] The movement aimed at purifying Hinduism by rejecting the dogmas and superstitions of religion, as it was then practised and in the process freeing the Hindus from the Brahminical domination[73] and evil practices like idol-worship, child-marriage, infanticide, *sati*, *purdah* and caste system, and paving the way for moral and social reconstruction of Hindu society. Thus the Brahmo Samaj did what orthodox Hinduism was powerless to do.[74]

After the death of Ram Mohan Roy, there arose a schism between orthodox and the radical wings of the Brahmo Samaj, the one led by Devendra Nath Tagore and the other led by Keshab Chandra Sen.[75] Whereas Devendra Nath Tagore wanted "to keep the movement as much as possible on the old lines of reverence for the ancient Hindu scriptures,"[76] Keshab Chandra Sen and his followers intended to broaden the basis of Brahmoism, with a view to make it more comprehensive and universal in appeal. The Brahmo Samaj under the leadership of Devendra Nath Tagore began to be known as the Adi Brahmo Samaj and the other group, led by Keshab Chandra Sen, assumed the title of the Brahmo Samaj of India.[77]

The Brahmo Samaj as a religious faith remained confined to a few as it was "too intellectual, too unrelated to the tradition of Hinduism, too deeply imbued with modern ideas

72. S. Natrajan, *A Century of Social Reform in India* (Bombay: Asia Publishing House, 1962), Foreword.
73. *Ibid.*, pp. 25-32.
74. E. Thompson and G. Garrett, *Rise and Fulfilment of British Rule in India* (Allahabad: Central Book Depot, 1969), p. 310. Also see N. Gerald Barrier, "Muslim Politics in the Punjab, 1870-1890" in *The Panjab Past and Present*, Vol. V, Part I, April 1971, p. 86.
75. K.P. Karunakaran, *Religion and Political Awakening in India* (Meerut: Meenakashi Prakashan, 1966), p. 45.
76. R.C. Majumdar, *op. cit.*, p. 102.
77. J.N. Farquhar, *Modern Religious Movements in India*, pp. 29-31.

to have any great effect on the people as a whole."[78] Although Ram Mohan Roy and his followers often found themselves drawn into religious controversies and were charged with misinterpreting the sacred texts[79] yet its importance in the history of socio-religious movements in India cannot be minimised as it "was the first important intellectual movement, which spread the ideas of rationalism and enlightenment in modern India."[80] Raja Ram Mohan Roy attacked the multiplicity of creeds, replacing superstition and polytheism by intellectualised principles of cosmic causality. He expounded his ideas in accordance with the principles of Western logical thought and thus initiated a historical movement of universalization to transform Hinduism into a unified monotheistic religion.

Raja Ram Mohan Roy sought to model himself on the Protestant Reformation. Though his efforts to institutionalise and organize his movement on the pattern of the Christian Church mark the beginning of modern intellectual life in India yet he or Brahmo Samaj seem to have made no attempt to bring the masses into the movement as he rejected the popular religious forms.[81] Moreover, though a great defender of Hinduism who reformed and reoriented it to meet the contemporary challenge, Raja Ram Mohan Roy was a suspect for his close association with the Christians and also was alleged to have married a Muslim lady.[82] It may also be pointed out that the successors of Raja Ram Mohan Roy, particularly Devendra Nath Tagore and Keshab Chandra Sen injected a fair degree of mysticism and emotional devotionalism in the Brahmo Samaj alongwith Upanishadic rationalism which was

78. K.M. Panikkar, *A Survey of Indian History* (Bombay: Asia Publishing House, 1962), p. 215.
79. Nemai Sadhan Bose, *op. cit.*, p. 105.
80. K.P. Karunakaran, *op. cit.*, p. 50.
81. Sumit Sarkar, "Rammohan Roy and the Break with the Past" in V.C. Joshi, *op. cit.*, pp. 46-48.
82. A.R. Salahuddin Ahmad, "Rammohan Roy and His Contemporaries" in *Ibid.*, pp. 96-97.

not palatable to an average Indian mind. That is why the Prarthana Sabha and Arya Samaj while encouraging the ideals of Brahmo Samaj i.e. "individuals' break with popular practices" avoided "a sharp rationalistic break with customary religion."[83] Consequently the Brahmo Samaj found itself "semi-isolated from the rest of the society,"[84] as it represented "a direct challenge to orthodox Hinduism." And the Brahmos were viewed as "apostates who had forshaken the faith of their ancestors."[85] Similarly, Swami Vivekanand and Aurobindo reinterpreted the *Upanishads* and *Vedanta* to establish neo-Hinduism. These movements presented a rational challenge to the Christianity enhancing the estimation of Hinduism at spiritual plane.

As opposed to the rationalistic interpretation of Hinduism by Raja Ram Mohan Roy and Vivekanand, the Arya Samaj had no faith in foreign ideals and foreign language. It resorted to traditional ideas and symbols which were closer to the hearts of people to activate the masses. It had deep roots in the traditional religious culture. There is no doubt that politicization preceded alongwith social and religious reforms since the time of Raja Ram Mohan Roy. But the Indian masses could not grasp the complex rational approach of neo-Hinduism as it bore no relation to the social situation. At the time of Swami Dayanand the Muslim movement under Sir Sayyed Ahmad Khan and Wahabi leaders, though distinct in character, developed on the line of reassertion of doctrinal purity and communal solidarity. On the rocks of this assertion floundered the process of universalization resulting in a "change in the nature of place of religion in communalism."[86] Religion became a matter of mere appearance as people were not "really concerned with the substance of religion, religion having

---

83. Charles H. Heimsath, *op. cit.*, p. 155.
84. *Ibid*.
85. Kenneth W. Jones, *Arya Dharm*, p. 17.
86. Louis Dumont & D. Pocock (ed.), *Contribution to Indian Sociology* (Paris : The Hague, 1969), Vol. VII, p. 45.

become the sign of their being distinct."[87] Therefore, the attempt of Swami Dayanand can be grasped more clearly from the social and political angles rather than religious. His religious ideas are more designed to establish a social organization of the Hindus having distinct identity. Hence we may describe Dayanand as the propounder of 'Hindu nationalism'— the term may appear contradictory but it certainly helps in explaining the tendencies of the Hindus and Muslims as separate from each other.

The tradition-bound Indian society particularly the Hindus were not willing to break with the past. This is evident from the two major developments which more or less preceded the establishment of Arya Samaj. One, the Wahabi movement among the Muslims, the Kuka movement among the Sikhs and the Sanatan Dharm movement among the Hindus, were indigenously inspired reactions to the spread of Western culture and Christianity.[88] Two, a large number of local revolts since the days of Warren Hasting upto 1876 were resistance movements of the Indian traditional society to the Western onslaughts.[89] These evidences of the resistance of the tribal and semi-agrarian tribal societies clearly indicate that it was difficult to harmonise the primary loyalties to the caste tribes or religions with the superior political organization of the British. Moreover, it shows that the Indian masses apprehended threat to their religion and social structures from the Britishers. Therefore,

---

87. *Ibid.*
88. B.B. Misra, *The Indian Political Parties* (Delhi: Oxford University Press, 1976), p. 52. Here the author equates the Kuka movement with the Arya Samaj as both these movements appear to him as puretical, revivalists and politically opposed to the British rule. For other works on Kuka movement, see Fauja Singh, *Kuka Movement* (Delhi: Motilal Banarsidass, 1965); and Ganda Singh, "Was the Kuka (Namdhari) Movement a Rebellion against the British Government?" in *The Panjab Past and Present*, Vol. VIII, Part II, October 1974, pp. 325-41.
89. Allamah Fazle Haq, "The Study of the War of Independence 1857-58" in the *Journal of the Pakistan Historical Society*, Vol. V, Part I, January 1957, p. 29.

wherever the community kinship relations still survived those societies presented violent opposition to the British and it is evident in the revolt of 1857.[90]

In the third quarter of the nineteenth century, Bankim Chandra Chatterjee celebrated these resistance movements in his *Anand Marg*. His writings are imbued with the religious fervour. We also discern another set of social movements which were indigenously inspired, having religious and ethical base, and unlike the aforesaid movements, they were non-violent. To cite a few we may refer to Dev Samaj, Radha Swami, Nirankari etc. etc. These movements form a perspective to the emergence of Arya Samaj for the latter derived its spirit from almost all of them. Its religious and social content can be traced to the Brahmo Samaj; its sources of inspiration can be linked up with the ancient Indian tradition and its spirit of meeting the challenge of Christianity is quite identical with the political resistance movements minus the violence. Its leaders belonged to the petty bourgeoisie which formed catalystic agents of Westernization and Aryanization (Hinduization).

In this general perspective we may reproduce the argument built up by Kenneth W. Jones in his book *Arya Dharm* as a specific illustration of the growing dichotomy and increasing awareness of the need to defend the Hindu tradition.[91] Explaining various trends emerging in Punjab among the Hindus he asserts that there were forces of continuity and change simultaneously operating on the psyche of the Hindu masses. In the beginning, the orthodoxy i.e. the Sanatanists resisted the forces of change and generated counter-pressures to defend their faith. The major argument was that only a true Hindu could provide protection to Hinduism. A true Hindu was a Sanatanist who defended the tradition as it prevailed at that time with all its ritualism and symbols of orthodox Hinduism. In the face of external and internal

90. P.C. Joshi (ed.), *op. cit.*, pp. 119-157.
91. Kenneth W. Jones, *Arya Dharm*, pp. 1-29.

challenges it was "a self-defensive strategy," yet aggressive. In defence of Hindu orthodoxy, its foremost leader Shraddha Ram Phillauri criticised the Brahmos, Christians and Muslims and went to the extent of purifying the Hindus who had been lost to the faith. Although his efforts of conversion were later condemned by the Sanatanists themselves, it provides an illustration of the fact that the Hindus were confronted with tremendous pressure from the Christians and Muslims.[92] While on the other hand, the Brahmos and the liberal Hindus responded favourably to the Western culture for the modernization of Hinduism. These two divergent trends— as reaction and response to Western culture created "milieu of intellectual and psychological ferment" to which Swami Dayanand Saraswati provided "the catalyst for a coalescence of this ferment, a channelling of unrest into organizational action directed at transforming Hinduism into a faith capable of commanding the respect and commitment of a culturally lost generation."[93]

92. Sriman Mehta Ramchandraji Shastri, *op. cit.*, p. 14.
93. Kenneth W. Jones, *Arya Dharm*, p. 29.

2

Social Perceptions of Swami Dayanand Saraswati and Genesis of Shuddhi Movement

The social perceptions of Swami Dayanand concretise the social reality as was prevailing during his times. Emerging from within the Indian traditions, the life of Swami Dayanand itself is a testimony of the resilience of Indian tradition and society. Therefore the greatest resistance to change emanated from within the Hindu society itself. Although there had been constant change in the Indian society since ancient times, there was built-in resistance to change due to certain peculiar characteristics of the Hindu society such as traditionalism, continuity and highly ritualised and brahaminised social system. The behaviour of Indian masses was controlled by the caste system and holistic dharm i.e. the religious principles which always thwarted the secular ambitions of the Indians. These characteristics of the Hindu society got further consolidated during the medieval period despite the fact that there was Bhakti Movement which, to a certain degree, released the regression. Nevertheless, as the Bhakti Movement was more religious in tone and temper than social, the medieval socio-religious movements could not bring into play radical forces for the transformation of the Indian society. In the late eighteenth and early nineteenth centuries, and to a certain degree, upto the present times the Indian masses have remained traditional and conservative as is evident from the hold of rituals, beliefs and customs on them. They have survived through the institutionalised solidarity of prosperous caste associations. Highly ritualised and hierarchical, the caste society was sustained by such a thought and conviction of the Indian masses in "mechanical efficiency of spirituality," rites or mystical exercises with absolute authority of the 'Word', unitary thought, rebirth and casualty and the concept of *maya*. Richard Lannoy believes that the Indian cultural tradition denied an individual or a group "of the possibility of ameliorating the human condition" or mastering the hostile environment. The author concludes, "since the individual cannot essentially alter the course of history, acquiescence in the hierarchy of power and wealth, and legitimization of ambitious war-lords as quasi-divine protectors of the millennialist *dharm*, form an integral part of this attitude towards and desire to escape from the terror of time, to preserve the immediacy of a non-sequential unified-field awareness."[1]

From the contemporary Hindu society infected by the multiplicity of sects, beliefs and faiths based on a large number of religious scriptures, Swami Dayanand witnessed absolute lack of individual morality and social ethics. Whether he was in Gujrat or in rural Doab or in Punjab, he was shocked to witness the total deterioration of the Hindu society. Consequently, so great was the resistance that even the firebrand, Swami Dayanand had to, in later years of his life, either absorb certain fundamentalism in his preachings or keep quite against some of the criticism levelled by the Hindu orthodox scholars.[2] This was the cause of the limited success of Swami

---

1. Richard Lannoy, *The Speaking Tree: A Study of Indian Culture and Society* (London: Oxford University Press, 1971), pp. 292-93.
2. J.F. Seunarine, *Reconversion to Hinduism Through Suddhi* (Madras: The Christian Literature Society, 1977), pp. 13-15.

Dayanand and Arya Samaj in areas such as Banaras, Gujrat, Bombay and Rajputana where the society was dominated by the Hindu orthodoxy from which, according to Jordens, Punjab was free. Being in minority there was "that communal gravitational pull" which brought actual cohesion among the Punjabi Hindus.[3]

Confronted with volatile social ecology, Swami Dayanand, the founder of the Arya Samaj and the *shuddhi* movement, was bound to contemplate and react for he displayed certain qualities of a rebel from his early childhood. It is believed, of course, with a certain degree of uncertainty, Mool Shanker, the original name of Swami Dayanand, who refused to divulge his birth place and ancestry, was born in 1824 at Tankara near Morvi in Kathiawar, Gujrat in the family of Karsanji. From the later autobiographical writings of Dayanand and the researches conducted by scholars, it is evident that his father was authoritarian, strong willed and orthodox Shavite Brahman[4] of high pedigree deeply rooted in the Brahminical tradition. The Kathiawar Brahmans of that period were closely linked "to the traditional ancient Sanskrit roots of Hinduism and to the ancient glory of Kathiawar history," observes Jordens.[5]

Descending from such parents it was natural, presumes Bawa Chhajju Singh, that he should have the immutable resolve of his father and possess a "heart embracing the whole world in its circle of sympathy."[6] Precocious child, Mool Shanker began to feel vexed with the problems of life, death, ritualism, and salvation at an early age. He was of stern and rebellious mood who often "showed an unwillingness to accept

3. J.T.F. Jordens, *Swami Dayanand Saraswati, His Life and Ideas* (Delhi: Oxford University Press, 1979), p. 160.
4. Yudhisthir Mimamshak, *Poona Pravachana arthat Upadesh-Manjari* (Delhi, 1969), Introduction.
5. J.T.F. Jordens, *op. cit.*, p. 9.
6. Bawa Chhajju Singh: *Life and Teachings of Swami Dayanand Saraswati* (New Delhi, Jan Gyan Prakashan, 1971), pp. 1-2.

both his family's plans for his future and orthodox Hinduism."[7] Much against the wishes of his father to grow into the family tradition, Mool Shanker came into conflict with his father when he was just 14 years of age and finally renounced his house at the age of 22 to escape marriage. He became a wandering *sanaysi*, a renouncer in search of personal salvation. For fourteen years the youth from Kathiawar wandered in search of a true guru. But to his utter disappointment and dismay he came across many holymen in the Himalayas as well as plains, discovering many new dimensions of Hinduism, but none could satisfy his pragmatic rationalism, till he met Swami Virjanand Saraswati, a blind ascetic from the Punjab at Mathura in November 1860. His association with Swami Virjanand, a great Sanskrit and Vedic scholar, dispelled his scepticism and reimposed his faith in the *Vedas* and God. With the newly acquired fundamental beliefs from his guru Dayanand combined his own reaction to Hinduism which he had formed on the basis of his "intimate contact with the chaotic reality of Hinduism" in Mathura. Jordens writes, "here in Mathura, he was physically immersed in the thick of it for nearly three years, and the living Hindu devotee was right under his eyes all the time."[8] Dayanand realised that the "degeneration of Hinduism is fundamentally connected with the proliferation and influence of 'spurious' works of a sectarian nature giving rise to numerous sects, accompanied by a parallel neglect of the real sources of Hinduism, the books of the *rishis*."[9] Showing deep concern for Hinduism and for the Hindus, Swami Dayanand developed the idea that regeneration of Hinduism was possible by cultivating the faith of the Hindus in the *Vedas* which were, in his opinion, the real source of Hinduism. It is here at Mathura that 'The Luther of India' resurrected. When Swami Dayanand took leave of his guru in 1863, "he gave as guru *dakshina* (a departing gift) the

7. Kenneth W. Jones, *Arya Dharm: Hindu Consciousness in 19th Century Punjab* (Delhi: Manohar Book Service, 1976), p. 30-31. (Hereafter quoted as *Arya Dharm*).
8. J.T.F. Jordens, *op. cit.*, p. 34.
9. *Ibid.*, p. 38.

promise to reform Hinduism"[10] and spread the Vedic faith. To fulfil this promise he travelled almost whole of India preaching the message of the *Vedas*. He declared that the *Vedas* were the infallible and inexhaustible source of all knowledge.[11] He exhorted the Hindus to seek inspiration from their glorious past and study the Vedic culture. He held several *shastrarths* (religious debates), with numerous contemporary pundits, Christian priests and scholars at different places of northern and western India, and soon he began to be recognized as a profound scholar of *Shastras* all over India.[12] With vast experience of associations with the traditional elite of Hinduism and conservative masses of north India, Swami Dayanand was exposed to the Adi Brahmos who were spearheading a newly emerging movement of Hinduism to counteract Westernization of Bengal society. He met historians, philosophers, missionaries, social reformers of variety of shades which had definite influence on his ideas. Nevertheless, he maintained the view that the Hindu religion and culture was superior if only it is based on the Vedic studies.[13] His interaction with men like Devendra Nath, Akshaykumar Datt, Keshab Chander Sen, Vidya Sagar and a host of others wrought a transformation in his outlook. It is presumed by scholars that he must have been impressed by "a fascinating spectrum of different mixtures in their conceptions of Hinduism, of religious reform, and of social reform ranging from the conservative orthodox to the agnostic,"[14] and "by the extreme individualism of the Calcutta intelligentsia....Their conceptions of the essence of Hinduism, the sources of true religion, and the implementation of religious reform, were amazingly divergent. Perhaps there was only one conviction

10. Kenneth W. Jones, *Arya Dharm*, p. 31.
11. A.R. Desai, *Social Background of Indian Nationalism* (Bombay: Popular Prakashan, 1966), p. 290.
12. Har Bilas Sarda, *Life of Dayanand Saraswati, World Teacher* (Ajmer: Vedic Yantralaya, 1946), pp. 61-62.
13. Bhagwandatta (ed.), *Rishi Dayanand Saraswati ke Patra Aur Vigyapan* (Amritsar: Ram Lal Kapur Trust, 1955), p. 127.
14. Quotes given below from J.T.F. Jordens, *op. cit.*, pp. 88, 91.

they all shared : denial that the *Vedas* presented the unique and definitive revelation." Again he must have been influenced by the deep concern of the Calcutta intelligentia "about the state of Hindu society, its cultural degradation, its religious enslavement, and its political insensitivity." It may be added that in Calcutta "for the first time he learned to see Hinduism in the context of other religions, especially Christianity and Islam, and to affirm its radical superiority." His sojourn in Calcutta is significant for three reasons: one, his idea of forming a Sabha acquired a maturity as he became aware of the basic weakness of the Brahmo Samaj which had split up in three parts; second, on the advice of Keshab Chander Sen, he began to use Hindi in his speeches in order to reach out to the masses, and lastly, again on the advice of Keshab Chander Sen he changed his robes in order to become acceptable to people including women.[15]

After his visit to Calcutta he penned *Satyarth Prakash*, a comprehensive document of his ideas and experiences. As the purpose of our study is not to explain the intricate doctrinal aspect of Dayanand's philosophy, here an attempt would be made to study his major ideas and assumptions which provide a perspective to the origins of the *shuddhi* movement. Believing that the *Vedas* were eternal, unalterable, infallible, divine, he asserted that the Vedic religion alone was true and universal. He held that "the Aryans were the chosen people, the Vedas the chosen gospel, and India the chosen land."[16] Thus by providing a base to his entire gamut of social thought he rejected the whole scriptural superstructure of Hinduism that had emerged after the *Vedas*. This included the Indian tradition on which the social system of the nineteenth century was based. It is interesting to note that by providing such a steel-frame to his ideas, he criticised the emergence of Jainism,

15. According to Kenneth W. Jones, "Dayanand still retained the inner aspects of *sanyasi* and adhered to all his earlier vows." *Arya Dharm*, p. 34 f.
16. Tara Chand, *History of the Freedom Movement in India* (Delhi: Government of India, 1967), Vol. II, pp. 422-23.

Social Perceptions of Swami Dayanand Saraswati 31

Buddhism and a large number of sects and institutions intimately connected with the current practices of Hinduism such as the caste system, *sati*, *purdah*, polygamy, infanticide, ritualism etc. etc. And in the process, he emphasised the significance of moral, ethical and enlightened man. Jordens has aptly remarked that the essence of his social ethics was based on two key principles i.e. "knowledge is the key to right action, and action constitutes the very nobility of free man."[17] According to Swami Dayanand, "Man's freedom is the greatest gift of God's mercy,"[18] and "Nothing is known properly without the virtue of wisdom, and wisdom is impossible without effort."[19] He liberated the individual from superstitions, ritualism, miracles, pilgrimages and rigidity of social customs and practices as he in his *Satyarth Prakash* makes a savage indictment of all these aspects of Hinduism.[20] Then he provides a historical perspective to his ideas proving that man during the Vedic age was moral, ethical, enlightened, free and active. Swami Dayanand himself had never accepted outside authority except the authority of knowledge which lay in the *Vedas* and in the man himself. The creation of a man free from external authority whether of caste, sect, scriptures, customs or of any human being was his ultimate aim.

Swami Dayanand was of the opinion that centuries of worship of false gods and political subjugation of men to inferior culture and civilization, the foreign rule of a thousand years had sapped the strength and undermined the morale of Indians. To liberate man from mental servitude and to make him realise his degradation and ignorance and help him to recover his strength, self-confidence and a will to break the fetters that bound him and regain his spiritual, social, and

17. J.T.F. Jordens, *op. cit.*, p. 104.
18. Dayanand Saraswati, *Satyarth Prakash*, (Banaras: Star Press, 1875), 1st edition p. 252.
19. *Ibid.*, p. 291.
20. Ganga Prasad Upadhyaya, *The Light of Truth*, English Translation of *Swami Dayanand's Satyarth Prakash* (Allahabad: Kala Press, 1956), p. 392.

political freedom, Swami Dayanand established the Arya Samaj and emphasised the significance of education in dispelling ignorance, the root cause of India's degeneration and he gave access to education to all human beings irrespective of caste, colour, creed and sex and gave a new interpretation of the caste system.[21] Rejecting birth as the basis of caste, he asserted that quality and merit should determine the caste of an individual.[22] Thus he rejected the rigidity of caste and allowed social mobility upward and downward in the caste hierarchy according to the qualities and merit of the persons and dispensed with the purity and pollution concept associated with it. Retorting to the objection of the Hindus against accepting food from the lower castes, Dayanand said that the food is spoiled by dirt or by tainted money that procures it.[23]

Being acutely conscious of the highly orthodox society which he intended changing and the anglicised behaviour of the Brahmo as a cause of their failure to reach the masses, Swami Dayanand secured his newly established movement for social change within the parameters of Hindu society to which he gave new name—The Arya Samaj. It may be said with a certain degree of plausibility that in doing so he might have been influenced by his own past experience i.e. his training within the traditional Hindu system and also to the opposition and resistance by the orthodox society of the Doab and the Punjab. In Punjab particularly he was opposed by the orthodox Brahmans. "The amount of obloquy and persecution to which Swami Dayanand was exposed in his lifetime may be gathered from the fact that numerous attempts were made on

21. According to James Reid Graham, "To achieve reform of Indian Society Dayanand advocated state reclassification of the people on the basis of *gun*, *karma* and *swabhav*." "The Arya Samaj as a Reformation in Hinduism with Special Reference to Caste", Unpublished Ph. D. Dissertation, Yale University, 1942, p. 1.
22. Lajpat Rai, *A History of the Arya Samaj* (Bombay: Orient Longman, 1967), pp 53, 84.
23. Lekhram, *Maharshi Dayanand Saraswati ka Jivan Charitra*, tr. by Kaviraj Raghunandansingh 'Nirmal' and ed. by Pandit Harischandra Vidyalankar (Delhi, 1972), p. 129.

his life by the orthodox Hindus; assassins were hired to kill him; missiles were thrown at him during his lectures and disputations; he was called a hired emissary of the Christians, an apostate, an atheist, and so on."[24] Wherever he visited, the orthodox Brahmans under the leadership of Pandit Shraddha Ram Phillouri followed him condemning and blaming him as an apostate of the Hindu religion. In Rawalpindi their efforts kept many people away from the lectures;[25] in Gujrat they prevented him from founding a local Samaj; and in Multan the newly founded Samaj mustered only a few members.[26]

The Genesis of Shuddhi

After liberating man from the past traditions, moulding and recreating a new dynamic and liberated individual by demolishing the walls of separatism, allowing social mobility vertically (horizontal mobility being already there) and dissolving social rigidity, it was natural for Swami Dayanand to reform and consolidate Hindu society by establishing *shuddhi*, a process of ritual purification to destroy the walls of hierarchical separatism and imparting man active and cosmic qualities to develop his capabilities.[27] It was an institutional framework more or less similar to the Christian missionaries and justified ritual purification i.e. *shuddhi* for the consolidation of the Hindu society. First of all, he rejected the use of the word Hindu in favour of 'Arya' because the word Hindu was a later innovation and with the passage of time had acquired a specific meaning embracing the entire post-Vedic socio-religious tradition. Secondly, Swami Dayanand asserted that the Vedic society was free from all such evils which were existing during his time, and the man was free. This implies

---

24. Lajpat Rai, *op. cit.*, p. 65. Also see Kenneth W. Jones, *Arya Dharm*, p. 40.
25. Ghasiram, *Maharshi Dayananda Saraswati ke Jivan Charit* (Ajmer: Propakarni Sabha, 1957), Vol. II, p. 76.
26. *Ibid.*, p. 101.
27. James Reid Graham, *op. cit.*, p. 517.

that the rigidity of Indian social system emerged later due to the growing Brahminical traditions.

Later scholars and historians such as Har Bilas Sarda,[28] P.V. Kane,[29] and Sri Ram Sharma[30] have developed the argument that the institution of *shuddhi* can be traced back to the ancient times. Imparting historical perspective, it is asserted that for centuries a large number of races of peoples of foreign origin had been continually coming to India before the Muslims, and were absorbed into Hinduism.[31] Basing their assertion on a popular Vedic injunction i.e. 'make the whole world Aryan', they argued that the ancient Aryans had tremendous zeal for Aryanizing people as they did with the Dravidians, the Greeks, the Sakas, the Kushans, the Huns and various other tribes.[32] P.V. Kane on the authority of *Dewala Smriti* and *Agni Purana* refers to the existence of the institution of conversion under the name *Vratyastoma*,[33] but it was with the advent of Islam the reverse process started and the Hindus began to be converted. Gradually as the caste system became rigid, there appeared an unwillingness to take back into Hinduism the

---

28. Har Bilas Sarda (ed.), *Dayanand Commemoration Volume*, (Ajmer: Vedic Yantralaya, 1933), p. 179.
29. P.V. Kane, *History of Dharmshastra* (Poona: Bhandarkar Oriental Research Institute, 1973), Vol. IV, pp. 267-333.
30. Sri Ram Sharma, "Swami Dayanand and Shuddhi", Unpublished article in the possession of Dr. Bhawani Lal Bharti, Head, Swami Dayanand Chair, Panjab University, Chandigarh, p. 1.
31. Richard Lannoy, *op. cit.*, p. 178.
32. *Ibid.*, p. 179.
33. P.V. Kane, *op. cit.*, pp. 267-333. Explaining the meaning of *Vratyastoma*, Rameshwar G. Ojha writes, *Vratya* is one of the most interesting words in the history of ancient Indian society. The accepted meaning of this word is "fallen from *Vrata*", i.e. degraded on account of neglecting the duties of one's *Varna*. *Vratya* popularly denotes a person who neglects sacraments; in short, neglect of Vedic Samskaras accounted for one being a *Vratya*. "Vratyastoma" (Readmission into Hinduism of the Depressed and Fallen Classes) in Har Bilas Sarda, *Dayanand Commemoration Volume*, p. 169.

people who had been converted. On the authority of Al Beruni who came to India in the 12th century, it was argued that the Hindu society had become so rigid that if a high caste Hindu took food at the hands of a non-Hindu, he became impure and contaminated for ever.[34] From this an obvious conclusion is drawn that from the 12th century onwards or even earlier the reconversion though not altogether given up, had become a very rare phenomenon.[35] Consequently, thousands of Hindus were converted to Islam and Christianity,[36] many among them were still clinging to the Hindu institution. On account of petty pollution many Hindus had to leave the fold of their religion.[37] Illustrating this, Sri Ram Sharma writes :[38]

> The younger Sheshadari in Bombay was pronounced to have lost the status of a Hindu because he had lived for a day or two with his minor elder brother whom the missionaries had succeeded in converting to Christianity.

He fusther adds :[39]

> Even leaders like Bal Gangadhar Tilak and Mahadev Gobind Ranade might have been lost to Hinduism in the later half of the nineteenth century if they had not undergone purificatory ceremony. Their sin had been that they had allowed the Christian organiser of a prize giving function in the Mission School to offer them cups

34. Edward C. Sachau (ed.), *Alberuni's India: An Account of the Religion, Philosophy, Literature, Geography, Chronology, Astronomy, Customs, Laws and Astrology of India about A.D. 1030* (Delhi: S. Chand & Co., 1964), Vol. II, pp. 136-37.
35. Kenneth W. Jones, *Arya Dharm*, p. 179.
36. Har Bilas Sarda, *Dayanand Commemoration Volume*, p. 179.
37. J.T.F. Jordens, "Reconversion to Hinduism, the Shuddhi of the Arya Samaj" in G.A. Oddie (ed.), *Religion in South Asia: Religious Conversion and Revival Movements in South Asia in Medieval and Modern Times* (New Delhi: Manohar Book Service, 1977), pp. 145-46.
38. Sri Ram Sharma, *op. cit.*, p. 1.
39. *Ibid.*

of tea; they had not touched the cup much less partaken the tea in it.

The Arya Patrika refers to many cases with a view to establish that a large number of Hindus were driven into the fold of Christianity and Islam because at some occasion they inadvertently or by the force of circumstances became victims of petty pollutions and were excommunicated.[40] In view of this it was argued that almost all religions of the world keep their doors open to 'newcomers' to their faith. Islam and Christianity were proselytizing religions in India and Hinduism was fast losing some of its members to both. This explains why Rameshwar G. Ojha writes :[41]

> In the last quarter of the nineteenth century, Maharshi Dayananda Saraswati stressed the revival of the ancient *Vratyastoma* under the guise of *shuddhi*, a term so easily intelligible to a man in the street. *Shuddhi* movement will ever remain as an eternal monument of Swami Dayananda's foresight and his invaluable services to Hindus as a great social reformer. It has gone a great way towards the regeneration, and re-admission into the Vedic Dharma, of thousands and thousands of such Hindus, whose ancestors under the stress of circumstances in centuries gone by, had to take shelter under the banners of Islam and Christianity.

On the basis of the assumption that the *shuddhi* existed in ancient India these scholars not only attempt at providing a

---

40. *The Arya Patrika* of August 22, 1885 at p. 4 quotes that "a Kayastha ... had been excommunicated and treated as a Muhammadan some time ago on account of his living and eating with Muhammadans." The same paper of October 31, 1885 at pp. 4-5 mentions the case of a Brahman who had fallen ill in Quetta and had been obliged to eat from a Muhammadan's hand was excommunicated from the *biradari*. Yet another example of excommunication of a man of Khatri tribe by the name of Badhao, who had become Muhaommadan in the state of intoxication is quoted by the same paper of October 5, 1886, p. 4.

41. Rameshwar G. Ojha, *op. cit.*, p. 179.

historical justification for the revival of the institution of *shuddhi* but also offer an implicit suggestion that there was a need to stem the rot from within the social body of the Hindus.

Reiterating our argument of the previous chapter, it may be said that the word *shuddhi* was a familiar one in India and referred to a system of religious rites for the purposes of purification. A large number of purification rituals had been evolved to remove pollution due to daily routine, touch, eating of food etc. etc.[42] But a ritualised system of conversion of an outsider into the fold of Hinduism did not exist. It was Swami Dayanand who turned his attention to *shuddhi* as a process of reconversion.[43] It is believed that the question of *shuddhi* for the first time arose during Swami Dayanand's visit to Punjab in 1877.[44] During next two years rather upto the end of Swami Dayanand's life only few cases of *shuddhi* have been noticed. In Jullundur, six months after his arrival in the Punjab, he reconverted a Hindu who had become a Christian.[45] Kharak Singh, who was born a Sikh then became a Hindu, and was consequently baptized by Rev. Robert Clark of Amritsar,

42. For detail, see Richard Lannoy, *op. cit.*, pp. 145-56.
43. Sri Ram Sharma, *op. cit.*, p. 2.
44. The reasons being "The Christian missionaries introduced into the Punjab a spirit of religious combativeness, not in the accidental manner which was always inherent in India . . . but in a much more premediated manner. Proselytizing was the normal activity of the missionary and religious strife the inevitable result," writes Kenneth W. Jones. "The Arya Samaj in the Punjab: A Study of Social Reformation and Religious Revivalism, 1877-1902," Unpublished Ph. D. Dissertation, University of California, Berkeley, 1966, p. 21.
45. Lekhram, *op. cit.*, p. 371. Also see Ghasiram, *op. cit.*, p. 71; Prithvi Singh Azad, *Arya Samaj ka Digh Darshan* (Jullundur: Arya Pratinidhi Sabha, Punjab, n.d.), p. 20.

became an Arya on meeting the Swami.[46] One Ramsharan, a Brahman of Ludhiana, who was teaching in a Mission School and was about to be converted to Christianity, abandoned his idea on meeting Swami Dayanand.[47] Later on, in Dehra Dun, in 1879, he reconverted a born Muslim, Muhammad Umar, giving him the name of Alakhdhari.[48] In all these cases it is significant to note that the word *shuddhi* was not used nor the ceremonies connected with it were used as they had not been evolved. Besides these individual cases, there are a few instances which establish that any person could be admitted to the fold of Hinduism if he promised to lead the life according to the dictates of the *Vedas*. Moreover, he, through his speeches, impressed many probable converts to Christianity to remain within the Hindu fold and in the process stemmed the tide of Christianity. At Amritsar, about 40 Hindu students under the influence of Christian propaganda had almost become unbaptized Christians, who on listening to Swami Dayanand's preachings did not desert to Christianity. There are instances showing that a few European Christians also adopted Hinduism under the influence of Swami Dayanand. For instance, John Montgomery Hamilton, a Police Inspector changed his name to Sukh Lal.[49] Martin Luther, a teacher working in Christian Orphanage was also converted to

---

46. Har Bilas Sarda, *Life of Dayananda Saraswati*, pp. 196-98. According to him, Kharak Singh or Khadasingh was brought to Swami Dayanand by Babu Gyansingh. Impressed by the latter, he became his follower and began to preach Vedic Dharm. He also married his two daughters to the Aryas. He also mentions that many persons who had become Christians were reconverted much against the wishes of Rev. Barring. However, he makes no mention of a *shuddhi* ceremony, only that "Khadasingh began to preach Vedic Dharm." Also see James Reid Graham, *op. cit.*, p. 201; Sri Ram Sharma, *op. cit.*, p. 2; and C.F. Andrews, *In North India* (London, 1908), p. 139.

47. Satyakethu Vidyalankar and Haridutt Vidyalankar, *Arya Samaj ka Itihas* (Delhi: Ajai Printer, 1984), Vol. I, p. 617.

48. *Ibid*, p. 619. Also see *Arya Gazette*, November 23, 1882, p. 5; Ghasiram, *op. cit.*, p. 171.

49. Sri Ram Sharma, *op. cit.*, p. 2.

Hinduism.[50] A Christian lady with her two children was converted on August 26, 1883 at Ajmer.[51]

The evidences of conversion during the lifetime of Swami Dayanand being few in number has given the impression to scholars that the movement did not make much progress in early stage[52] nor was *shuddhi* a 'major issue' for Swami Dayanand.[53] Nevertheless, it has been viewed as an humble beginning, a preparatory stage[54] which "lessened the sense of impotence, and signified a new world in which Hindus could fight to maintain themselves and their religion."[55] It goes to the credit of Swami Dayanand, acknowledges J.T.F. Jordens, of proclaiming "the principle that reconversion was the right procedure, a principle the Arya Samaj would later fully put into practice."[56] From a principle it developed into a movement ever enlarging its scope and proliferating its dimensions.[57]

The *shuddhi*, a process of purifying an individual and making him again acceptable to his caste fellows, was first realised to retain Hindus who had been converted to either Christianity or Islam.[58] In due course of time, it was extended to those whose ancestors had been converted, and finally, to those who had never been Hindus at all and whose ancestors

50. *Arya Samachar*, September 3, 1883, p. 4.
51. *Arya Samaj ka Itihas*, p. 619.
52. Rameshwar G. Ojha, *op. cit.*, p. 179.
53. J.T.F. Jordens, *Reconversion to Hinduism*, p. 147.
54. *Arya Pratinidhi Sabha Panjab ka Sachitra Itihas*, published by Arya Pratinidhi Sabha, Punjab (Lahore, 1992 Bik.), p. 401.
55. Kenneth W. Jones, *Arya Dharm*, p. 133.
56. J.T F. Jordens, *Reconversion to Hinduism*, p. 147.
57. Bawa Chhajju Singh, *op. cit.*, Introduction. Also see Chamupati, *Glimpses of Dayanand* (Delhi: Sharada Mandir Ltd., 1937), p. 95.
58. V.K. Vashishtha, "Arya Samaj Movement in Rajasthan during the Nineteenth Century" in S.C. Malik (ed.), *Dissent, Protest and Reform in Indian Civilization* (Simla: Indian Institute of Advanced Study, 1977), p. 232.

had not been Hindus.[59] thus giving Hinduism an institution of conversion which it had not traditionally possessed.[60] Once it had become possible to purify a foreigner or a Hindu whose family had been converted centuries before, the Arya Samajist thought it prudent to purify the members of the outcastes and raise their status to the level of the caste Hindus.[61] Surely, if one can purify an Englishman or an American, then one can purify a *Bhangi* or a *Chamar*. This concept of caste reform through *shuddhi* was to come later and perhaps the full implications of it were never realised.

In the end, we may draw two major points of conclusion. One, that there is no clear cut evidence as to when and how the *shuddhi* movement originated but the social ideas of Swami Dayanand amply demonstrate that it was their natural outcome which was adopted with zeal and enthusiasm by the Punjabi Arya Samajists. Secondly, during the lifetime of Swami Dayanand we do not find that the *shuddhi* was adopted seriously by him perhaps because his primary concern was to create such institution which could positively help in the regeneration of Hinduism within. Moreover, it may also be surmised, as pragmatic and rational Swami Dayanand was, that he did not wish to touch such issues which could bring Arya Samaj movement into conflict with other communities. Perhaps, he was also aware of the fact that such converts could not be accepted in the fold of Hinduism so long as the Hindu mind and ethos were not liberalised.

59. Diwan Chand, *The Arya Samaj: What it is and What it Stands for* (Lahore: Arya Pratinidhi Sabha, 1942), p. 99.
60. Kenneth W. Jones, "Communalism in the Punjab: The Arya Samaj Contribution" in *Journal of Asian Studies*, Vol. 28, 1968-69, p. 53. Also see Munshi Rama Jijyasu and Rama Deva, *The Arya Samaj and Its Detractors, A Vindication* (Hardwar: Gurukul Kangri, 1910 A.D.), p. 14; and John C.B. Webster (ed.), *Popular Religion in the Punjab Today* (Delhi: I.S.P.C.K., 1974), p. 5.
61. Ganga Prasad Upadhyaya, *The Arya Samaj and Islam* (Allahabad: Arya Samaj, Chowk, 1933), p. 10.

3

Development of Shuddhi Movement: The First Phase (1883-1920)

After its genesis, the *shuddhi* movement witnessed a rapid development more due to favourable social ferment at the national and regional levels. Growth of education, press, means of transportation and communication, the policy of racism and communalism, emergence of middle classes, demand for the introduction of representative institution and the rise of neo-Hinduism collectively initiated a process of modernising the tradition and evolution of Indian as well as communal identity. In this respect we may refer to the fact that the Hindu minority in Punjab was confronted with two proselytizing religions—Islam and Christianity. As it has already been noticed that the Christian missionaries adopted subtle and dubious[1] means to propagate Christianity, the educated Hindus

1. To get more converts from Hinduism, the Christians even offered their daughters for marriage. The *Himala* of Rawalpindi warned such marriages of Hindus with European ladies with the remarks that the "Hindus in their present state of degeneration should not contact marriages with European ladies who are far in advance of them in wealth, education & C." June 16, 1893 in *Selection from Vernacular Newspapers published in the Punjab*, p. 320. (Hereafter quoted as *SVNP*).

of Punjab apprehended a serious threat to their religion due to the increasing number of the converts from the lower castes to Christianity.[2]

Reporting on the response of the Hindus, particularly the Arya Samajists, *Regenerator of Arya Varta* in as early as 1883 clearly conveys the anxiety of the Hindus of the Punjab over the activities of the Christian missionaries and their desire to devise a "counter force to counteract the pernicious and unhealthy influence of the Christian doctrine."[3] The growing group consciousness of the English educated Hindus[4] were now ready to utilize institutional innovations as defensive and reformative strategies such as the Arya Samaj centres, educational institutions, the Arya Pratinidhi Sabha,[5] and for the promotion of cohesion and identity among the Hindus, the institution of *shuddhi* received their special attention. From among them we may refer to Pandit Guru Datta[6],

---

2. Bhawani Lal Bhartiya, *Arya Samaj Ateet ki Uplabdhian Tatha Bhavisha ke Prashin* (Jullundur: Arya Pratinidhi Sabha, Punjab, 1978), p. 160.

3. *Regenerator of Arya Varta*, September 3, 1883, p. 3.

4. Kenneth W. Jones, *Arya Dharm, Hindu Consciousness in 19th Century Punjab* (New Delhi: Manohar Book Service, 1976), p. 61. (Hereafter quoted as *Arya Dharm*).

5. Arya Pratinidhi Sabha, Punjab was established in 1885 in Guru Datta Bhavan, Lahore. It was followed by Arya Pratinidhi Sabha, United Provinces on December 29, 1886. Within a period of a decade afterwards, a galaxy of Arya Pratinidhi Sabhas were established at various places in India. For their full account, see Arya Directory (Delhi: Sarvdeshik Arya Pratinidhi Sabha, 1998 Vik.), pp. 43, 47, 53-54, 60-61, 65, 67, 70-71, 74-75, 77 and 80. Also see *The Arya Patrika*, December 7, 1886, pp. 7-8.

6. For a brief biography of Guru Datta's life, see Guru Datt, *Wisdom of the Rishi or Works of Pt. Gurudatta Vidyarthi M.A.* (Delhi: Sarvdeshik Pustakalaya, n.d.), pp. i-vi.

Lala Hans Raj,[7] Pandit Lekh Ram,[8] Lala Lajpat Rai,[9] and Lala Munshi Ram (later known as Swami Shraddhanand)[10] who took leading part in the *shuddhi* movement and made it a force to reckon with. But caught in a peculiar situation, the educated and enthusiastic Arya elite found itself in a dilemma. They were confronted with internal resistance and rigidity in their effort to expand the ranks of Hinduism as conversion neither was in the tradition of Hinduism nor was it acceptable to the psyche of the Hindus. Externally the activities of the Christian missionaries and Muslim priestly efforts threatened to make them a gradually depleting minority. They began to view it as a major weakness.[11] Commenting upon the situation, *The Arya Patrika* writes:[12]

> The absence of proselytism in Hindu society is certainly a very important drawback in the way of its reform. No increase can now take place in the number of the Hindus and even persons gone out of their society cannot enter it without undergoing a set of ceremonies to submit to which would reflect volumes of discredit upon an educated person.

Finding no other alternative, the Arya Samajists, alongwith the development of institutional infrastructure began to evolve *shuddhi* as a part of the Arya Samaj movement.

7. For his life sketch, see Sri Ram Sharma, *Mahatma Hansraj: Maker of the Modern Punjab* (Jullundur: Arya Pradeshik Pratinidhi Sabha, 1965), pp. 1-8.
8. For his detailed biography, see Swami Shraddhanand, *Dharmvir Pandit Lekh Ram, Jivan-Charitra* (Jullundur: Arya Pradeshik Sabha, n.d.). Also see Ram Chandra Javed, *Arya Samaj ke Maha Purush* (Jullundur, University Publishers, n.d.).
9. For reference, see Lajpat Rai, *Lajpat Rai Autobiographical Writings* ed. by Vijay Chandra Joshi (Delhi: University Publishers, 1965).
10. For a brief biography, see M.R. Jambunathan (ed.), *Swami Shraddhanand* (Bombay: Bharatiya Vidya Bhavan, 1961).
11. B.M. Sharma, *Swami Dayanand* (Lucknow: The Upper India Publishing House, 1933), p. 124.
12. *The Arya Patrika*, September 14, 1886, pp. 2-3.

The history of the *shuddhi* movement of the Arya Samaj after the death of its founder has been divided into three phases. According to Diwan Chand:[13]

> In the first stage, the Arya Samaj was on the defensive. Its main aim was to prevent conversion of Hindus to Islam and Christianity. In the second stage, an attempt was made also to reconvert those who had forshaken Hinduism and embraced Islam and Christianity. In the third and final stage, to these activities was added the conversion of born Muslims and Christians.

But from the point of view of its social and political dimensions, the history of the *shuddhi* movement for the purposes of present study has been divided into two main periods i.e. from 1883 to 1920 during which it primarily remained a social movement and from 1920 to 1947, the phase signifying the assumption of political overtones.

In its earliest form *shuddhi* was aimed at reconverting Hindus from either Christianity or Islam. Later, under the leadership of Munshi Ram its area was "broadened to include the conversion of non-Hindus and even those whose ancestors had never been Hindus."[14] Also, it was used as an institution for caste reform. However, this concept of caste reform through *shuddhi* was to come later and perhaps without realising its social implications.[15]

Tracing the history of the *shuddhi* movement since the year 1884, after the death of its founder Swami Dayanand,

---

13. Diwan Chand, *The Arya Samaj: What it is and What it Stands for* (Lahore: Arya Pradeshik Pratinidhi Sabha, 1942), p. 99.
14. Kenneth W. Jones, "The Arya Samaj in the Punjab: A Study of Social Reform and Religious Revivalism, 1877-1902," Unpublished Ph. D. Thesis, University of California, Berkeley, 1966, p. 138. (Hereafter quoted as *The Arya Samaj in the Punjab*).
15. James Reid Graham, "The Arya Samaj as a Reformation in Hinduism with special reference to Caste," Unpublished Ph. D. Dissertation, Yale University, 1942, p. 460.

Development of Shuddhi Movement

we find numerous references to the *shuddhi* ceremonies scattered over in the pages of the Punjab Arya Samaj journals. An analysis of these cases makes a very interesting and significant reading. Married couples,[16] individuals including women[17] were reconverted and were taken into the fold of Hinduism. There are four redeeming features: one, all these cases are stray, isolated and individual cases[18] indicating no trend or

16. "On the twentieth of April 1884, a married couple who had gone to Mohammadanism was purified and restored to the rights of Hinduism on going through the penances enjoined by the Shastras. The couple consists of a Rajput and his wife. She was born a Hindu but by lodging with a Mussalman Khansama, lost her caste. Subsequently, the Rajput finding her a Hindu, married her...." *Arya Magazine*, June 1894, p. 86.
17. "The Rawalpindi Arya Samaj purified a goldsmith woman who had become a Mohammadan and had her readmitted to caste." *The Arya Patrika*, October 4, 1886, p. 4.
18. "On Sunday May 4th, 1884 a boy, Hari Chand, who on April 16th under the influence of *bhang* took bread from Mohammadans and lost caste was also purified and restored to his former position in society by going through the fasts and japs according to Manu Laws." *Arya Magazine*, June 1884, p. 86.

The *Aryan Samachar* of Meerut tells of "two Hindus named Bhagwan Das and Bhagwan Deen of Jabalpur who had become Christians, now became Hindus through the Arya Samaj in Allahabad. They were made to perform certain penances on the banks of the Triveni (confluence of the Gangas and Jumna)... and Bhagwan Das who had been reclaimed has been taken back by his *biradri*." *Arya Magazine*, October 1884, p. 171.

"A Kayasth from Rawalpindi named Krishna Lal who had been excommunicated and treated as a Mohammadan for his having lived with Mohammadans and who wished to be restored to Hinduism was regained through the efforts of the Rawalpindi Arya Samaj. In a meeting on August 16th all the persons present including many 'raises' (leaders) of the city and members of Sukhdayak and Singh Sabhas ate the sweetmeats distributed by Krishna Lal with his own hands." *The Arya Patrika*, August 22, 1885, p. 4.

"Nathu Mal ate when sick at the hands of Mohammadans in Quetta. He admitted this when he came to his home in Gujranwala (Punjab). He was excommunicated and the orthodox pundit sent

((Contd.)

movement; two, in all these cases the persons who sought reconversion were anxious to return to the Hindu fold; three, in all the cases the persons were lost to Hinduism either inadvertently or by force of circumstances as they violated the social norms and consequently became impure; and four, the movement confined to major urban centres of Punjab like Rawalpindi, Gujranwala and Amritsar.[19]

For 1884 the *Arya Magazine* reported that 39 people had been newly reclaimed from Christianity,[20] and in the following years it was reported in *The Arya Patrika* that 55 persons had been purified.[21] Though not very large in number these events mark a new era in the history of Hinduism. The Editor of *The Arya Patrika*, in commenting on the purification of converts in Amritsar and elsewhere, remarks:[22]

> The Amritsar Arya Samaj has taken the lead in this matter, and Hindu society must be grateful to that Samaj.

---

him to the Ganges to perform *Praschit* ceremony for one month. But on his return the *biradari* did not accept him. He struggled on for three years, and then appealed to the Gujranwala Arya Samaj. The latter took steps and called a meeting of leading Hindus in Gujranwala to explain why he had broken caste; they then took water and sweets from his hand. It was a great success for the Arya Samaj." *Ibid.*, October 31, 1885, p. 5.

"Ganga Prasad, who had become a Mohammadan at the age of eight comes to Simla. The Arya Samaj reconverted him to Hinduism. A meeting of Hindus including Brahmans and Kayasths was held. The Pundit said he could be reclaimed and taken back into caste after undergoing *praschit*. Some of the people, especially the Kayasthas disagreed . . . . He is going to Arya Samaj meetings regularly and is about to start for Hardwar to undergo *praschit* appointed by the Pundits." *Ibid.*, August 10, 1886, p. 4.

19. James Reid Graham, *op. cit.*, p. 457.
20. *Arya Magazine*, August 1884, p. 131.
21. *The Arya Patrika*, October 5, 1886, p. 2.
22. *Ibid.*, August 22, 1885, p. 4.

Very much is due in this direction to Pundit Tulsi Ram of Amritsar, who takes deep interest in Hindu society and deeply aware of the necessity of this reform, carries it into practices.

As regards the rituals connected with *shuddhi*, the standard ceremonies were not evolved by Swami Dayanand. Consequently uptil 1889, the Arya Samaj used Brahmans and traditional ceremonies to perform *shuddhi* unmindful of the fact that it was contrary to its basic tenets.[23] The traditional method can be explained by the event narrated in the *Diary* of Swami Shraddhanand of February 5, 1889 on the question of reconversion of one named Ramgopal:[24]

> It was now 2 o'clock and at 4 a meeting of the Antaranga Sabha (Executive Committee) was held. The main business was the consideration of the reconversion of Ramgopal who was for some time a Mussalman. The Sabha proved nervous and, instead of taking the lead, sent him away to Amritsar...the Amritsar Arya Samaj was under the influence of a Pandit by name Nathuram. Having extracted Dakshinas (offerings of cash) from fallen men, he used to direct them to Hardwar where, after bath, they would get themselves purified by taking water made holy with cow dung by paying Rs. 5-4-0.

After a few years of purifying people according to the orthodox requirements and then sending them for a second purification on the banks of the Ganges, certain members of the Samaj began to protest against the type of purificatory ceremonies employed. As early as 1888, they found contradiction between the principles which the Arya Samaj propagated and the ritualistic system of the *praschit*. It was viewed as surrender to the latter, emanating from the position

---

23. Kenneth W. Jones, "Communalism in the Punjab: The Arya Samaj Contribution" in *Journal of Asian Studies*, Vol. 28, 1968-69, pp. 47-48. (Hereafter quoted as *Communalism in the Punjab*).
24. Quoted in M.R. Jambunathan, *op. cit.*, p. 111.

of weakness of the Arya Samaj. The following longish quotation from *The Arya Patrika* testifies to the facts. It states:[25]

> Do Aryas hold the *Praschit* ceremony of Hindus? Do they insist on the eating of cow-dung, paying of vists to the Ganges and feeding of the Brahmans? Such *Praschit* is degrading and a true Arya would never bow down to such unmeaning ceremonies and their selfish advocates, the Brahmans. Why have any *Praschit*? It was not for those who have become degraded and not merely because of matters relating to food. Hindus became Aryas without purification.
>
> The Arya Samaj is strong enough to get Hindu converts back to Hinduism, but owing to its weakness it has had to compromise with Hinduism and accept the process of *Praschit*. This state of things has continued and I am sorry the Arya Samaj has not been able to wield so much influence as to transform even Hindu converts without asking help from the Hindus by way of *Praschit*. But this must not be allowed to continue. The Arya Samaj must in time make *Praschit* a purifying institution instead of allowing it to continue in its present degraded state.

So the built-in resistance of the orthodox Hindu society took five years of agitation of the radical Arya Samajists to get purificatory ceremonies changed in 1893. The new system however was a radical one. But for some time a part of the earlier system of *praschit* also continued. Where the Samajists had been following the ceremonies prescribed by *Manu* they substituted it with the new ones; namely the ceremony of tonsure, or cutting of hair, the offering of the *Hom*, or fire-sacrifice, investment of a sacred thread,[26]

25. *The Arya Patrika*, August 21, 1888, p. 5.
26. According to Lala Lajpat Rai, "The sacred thread occupies an important place in the eyes of the high caste Hindus. To invest the lower classes with the sacred thread is to raise them, at once in their own estimate." P. Nagar, *Lala Lajpat Rai: The Man and His Ideas* (Delhi: Manohar Book Service, 1977), p. 232.

and the learning of the sacred *Gayatri Mantra*,[27] explanation of the Ten Principles of the Arya Samaj, and finally distribution of sweets (*sherbat*) by the converts to all the present.[28] *The Tribune* mentions one instance of *shuddhi* in 1893 of a newly purified Hindu who distribuled sweets to all the present which were accepted by all without any fear of their *biradri*.[29] However, the Samaj employed both their own ceremonies and a trip to Hardwar for orthodox purification. But with the passage of time the Samaj stopped sending purified persons to the Ganges for a second purification at the hand of orthodox priests.[30] Apparently, having made a beginning in purification ceremonies with the leaders of orthodoxy, the Arya Samajists now felt themselves powerful enough to dispense with their help.

Since the basic pre-condition for the success of the *shuddhi* movement was the transformation of the attitude of the highly conservative society of the Hindus, it required tremendous patience, hard work, persuasion to loosen the rigid social structure to accept the converted members. The structured social relationship continuing for centuries and governing all aspects of social life of the Hindus not only countered the threat of excommunication for being polluted by dining with the converts but the Arya Samajists themselves were so conservative that they refused to socially accept new entrants to the ranks of Hindus. In December 1889, it was reported that "fifteen Arya Samajists of Moradabad were outcasted by the members of the orthodox community on the offences of drinking Ganges water from Christians who had

---

27. The *Gayatri Mantra* is a prayer recited by all Hindus in their daily worship. Drawn from the *Rig Veda*, it could be learned and used only by members of the three upper *varnas*, the Brahmans, Kshatriyas, and Vaishyas. Under no circumstances should it or any other section of the sacred *Vedas* be taught to Sudras, outcastes, or non-Hindus. Kenneth W. Jones, *Arya Dharm*, p. 133 f.
28. James Reid Graham, *op. cit.*, pp. 463-65.
29. *The Tribune*, February 18, 1893, p. 4.
30. One Muslim convert was purified by the Montgomery Arya Samaj in which *praschit* was performed but the trip to Hardwar was eliminated. *Ibid.*, May 28, 1893, p. 5.

become Hindus again."[31] This was the case of Moradabad where the Hindus were more conservative than in Punjab. But in Punjab there were powerful caste *biradris*. Afraid of being excommunicated by the *biradris*, some of Arya Samajists were not willing to have social relationship with the converts,[32] instead proposed that they might be organized into separate groups thus eliminating the necessity of social relationship.[33] Exhorting the members of Arya Samaj against succumbing to the caste *biradris*' pressure, the Editor of *The Arya Patrika* writes: "the hours of trial has come. We have said the *Vedas* were for all. People are coming to us. Will we receive them? We are afraid the *biradri* will excommunicate us."[34] The fact that the Arya Samajists had not broken away with their orthodox caste brotherhood, it was this early realization as an obstacle to the carrying on of a *shuddhi* programme as well as of other types of reforms. Confronted with a highly rigid hierarchical, regimented, structured and conservative society, the path of the Arya Samaj was not easy when it set out on the task of restoring to caste the persons who had gone out of Hinduism into other religions.

This implied that the Arya Samaj accepted in the beginning the traditional ceremonies, and rituals of conversion as a tactical measure of blunting the opposition of the tradition-bound classes. But it was apparent that the "ceremonies which might satisfy a Pandit in Hardwar or the local Arya Samaj did not mean automatic readmission to caste privileges."[35] To encounter this kind of caste attitude the Samaj adopted the strategy of persuasion and public ceremonies. The latter strategy was a demonstration to give shock realisation to the people and assurance to the converts

31. *The Arya Patrika*, December 10, 1889, p. 4.
32. *Ibid.*, April 17, 1897, p. 6. Also see Lajpat Rai, *The Arya Samaj: An Account of Its Aims, Doctrine and Activities, with a Biographical Sketch of the Founder* (Lahore: Uttar Chand Kapur and Sons, 1932), p. 251.
33. James Reid Graham, *op. cit.*, p. 463.
34. *The Arya Patrika*, April 17, 1897, p. 6.
35. Kenneth W. Jones, *Arya Dharm*, p. 133.

that they had been duly accepted in the Hindu society. Therefore, whenever possible, the Arya Samajists sponsored a meeting of reconciliation in which the newly purified would distribute food and all would eat, signifying his acceptance in the Hindu society. The story of Ganga Pershad, a Young Kayastha, who had been converted to Islam, illustrates the method of reacceptance:[36]

> On the 26th ultimo, some of the relatives of Ganga Pershad gave a dinner party to which they invited about 60 representatives of the various communities. The proceedings were opened by Swami Ishwara Nand Saraswati who recited a good many mantras from the Vedas and performed the ceremony of Hom. After the meals were served Ganga Pershad (was) sanctified and blessed. The dinner being over Swami Ishwara Nand and others made very eloquent speeches and impressed upon the minds of their audience the supreme importance of doing away with the baneful custom of not allowing our "wandering away friends" to rejoin our fold and they no doubt succeeded in proving to the satisfaction of all that this custom was undermining our social strength. With usual thanks to the President the party dispersed leaving the priest to cry in the wilderness.

Till 1893 the task of purification of the converts was being performed by individual initiative and drive. It was in that year that organized effort was made and a special Shuddhi Sabha at Lahore was established.[37] The contemporary accounts indicate that although a number of Arya Samajists of the 'College Party' like Lala Hans Raj, Lala Lal Chand and Lala

---

36. *The Arya Patrika*, July 26, 1887, p. 4.

37. The Lahore Shuddhi Sabha was established by Dr. Jai Singh on April 17, 1893, with the object of "reclaiming those Sikhs and Hindus who had apostalized themselves by contracting alliances with Muslim men or women." Jagjit Singh, *Singh Sabha Lahir* (Amritsar: Lahore Book Shop, 2nd Edition, 1974), p. 50.

Lajpat Rai[38] were members of this Sabha, the Sikhs were the real controlling power of its destinies. Bhai Basant Singh of the Singh Sabha, Lahore[39] was at its head, and occasionally it was referred to as the Sikh Shuddhi Sabha.[40] One of its important but irritating features was the obligation on the part of those Muslims seeking restoration to Hinduism or Sikhism to eat pork. It was based on the simple principle of convenience which was being applied by the Muslims who insisted on eating beef by the Hindu and Sikh converts. "If the eating of beef could transform a Hindu into a Muslim, they argued, by a similar logic the eating of pork would signify the return of a Muslim to Hinduism or Sikhism," writes Kenneth W. Jones.[41] Moreover, this also indicates the predominant influence of the Sikhs on the *shuddhi* movement because they were in large number meat-eaters and had developd definite taboos, like the Muslims, with regard to *jhataka* and *halal*.[42] However the *shuddhi* work remained a

38. Kenneth W. Jones, "Ham Hindu Nahin: Arya-Sikh Relations, 1877-1905" in *Journal of Asian Studies*, Vol. 32, May 1977, p. 664. (Hereafter quoted as *Ham Hindu Nahin*).
39. The first Singh Sabha was founded in Amritsar in 1873. This Sabha was largely concerned with defending Sikhism from Hindu and Christian criticism. In 1879 the Lahore Singh Sabha was organised with the goals of social reform, education and religious revivalism. These Singh Sabhas, which cooperated with the Arya Samaj, were associated with the Lahore movement. For reference, see Khushwant Singh, *A History of the Sikhs* (Princeton : Princeton University Press, 1966), Vol. II, pp. 141-44. Also see Harbans Singh, *The Heritage of the Sikhs* (Bombay : Asia Publishing House, 1964), pp. 146-47.
40. *Sri Guru Singh Sabha Gazette*, Lahore, No. 4, September 2, 1893, p. 7.
41. Kenneth W. Jones, *Ham Hindu Nahin*, p. 465.
42. According to Khalsa Rehat Maryada, *Jhataka* means to kill an animal with one stroke of the sword. For reference, see Kahan Singh Nabha, *Encyclopaedia of Sikh Literature* (Patiala: Language Department, Punjab, 1960), p. 406.
Halai, according to Shariat is the meat of an animal slaughtered according to Muslim rites. For reference, see *Standard Persian Dictionary* (Allahabad: Ram Narain Lal Beni Madho, 1931), p. 235.

joint venture of the reformed Sikhs of Gujranwala and the Arya Samaj during the year 1893-94. They succeeded in purifying "lost Sikhs and Hindus in Gujranwala and the surrounding area."[43] The 'pork-test' was perhaps the cause of much unfavourable comment by the Hindus and the Muslims alike.[44] The militant but vegetarian Aryas not only withdrew their support from the Shuddhi Sabha, Lahore but also condemned them for degenerating Hinduism.[45] Even some conservative Sikhs did not appreciate this idea of 'pork-test' as it was apprehended to lead to communal strife in the Punjab, a Muslim majority province.[46]

The same pork eating by the converts was one of the causes of the vertical split in 1893 between the 'College Party' and the 'Mahatma Party' in the Arya Samaj itself.[47] The 'Mahatmas', or the militants led by Lala Munshi Ram and Pandit Lekh Ram wanted, besides other things, to desist the Arya Samajists from meat eating.[48] But the 'College Party' opposed these ideas.[49] The bitterness generated in this quarrel entered into a debate on various dimensions of the problem, including that of the proper ways and means of restoring converts to Hinduism. The 'College Party' charged the 'Mahatmas' of being unwilling to help in the restoration of the purified ones to Hinduism because they had been unwilling to cooperate with the newly formed Shuddhi Sabha. The 'Mahatmas', on the other hand, condemned the 'College Party' for collaborating with the Lahore Shuddhi Sabha, which was

43. *The Tribune*, February 18, 1893, p. 4. Also see *Ibid.*, April 8, 1893, p. 4; January 24, 1894, p. 4; March 14, 1894, p. 4; and August 18, 1894, p. 4.
44. *The Arya Patrika*, July 4, 1896, p. 5.
45. *Sat Dharm Pracharak*, January 8, 1897, in *SVNP, 1897*, p. 40.
46. The *Singh Sahai* of Amritsar published a letter of one Bawa Sarmukh Singh stating "the action of Lahore Shuddhi Sabha in openly making the Muhammadans eat pork is calculated to lead a religious disturbance." March 12, 1895 in *SVNP, 1895*, p. 162.
47. *Sat Dharm Pracharak*, August 20, 1897 in *SVNP, 1897*, 766.
48. K.N. Kapur, *Swami Shraddhanand* (Jullundur: Arya Pratinidhi Sabha, Punjab, 1978), pp. 28-29.
49. *Ibid.*, p. 29.

sponsoring the 'pork-test' and other unscriptural ceremonies as well as renewing the old practices of sending converts to the Ganges for purification.[50] Supporting the ideas of the 'Mahatmas', the Editor of *The Arya Patrika* writes:[51]

> What does this unholy alliance of the 'Cultured' with the Sikh Shuddhi Movement mean? These gentlemen say they are Aryas though they seceded years ago. But it is the Arya Samaj that gets the credit for embittering the relations of Hindus and Mussalmans; it is all the fault of the 'Cultured' (intellectuals of 'College Party').

It further adds:

> The 'Cultured' should cease to call themselves Arya or else cut off their connection with the Shuddhi Movement. The Arya Samaj has nothing to do with the Shuddhi Movement and will not be involved with the 'Cultured' section.

The 'Mahatmas' however continued the purification work along the reformed lines,[52] i.e. *shuddhi* of the converts without 'pork-test' and sending them again to the Ganges. They called on all the Arya Samajists to break off all connections with the Shuddhi Sabha, Lahore.

The division in the Samaj members in 1893 had but little effect on the work of purification as the Arya Samaj wing of the 'College Party' and the Singh Sabha of Gujranwala continued their collaborative efforts to perform *shuddhis*.[53] Reporting on their collaboration in the *shuddhi* work, *The Tribune* writes that on February 15, 1893 a young Sikh boy who had embraced Islam due to his love with a Mussalman woman was reconverted by the Singh Sabha, Gujranwala and

---

50. James Reid Graham, *op. cit.*, p. 467.
51. *The Arya Patrika*, August 29, 1896, p. 10.
52. *Ibid.*, December 26, 1896, p. 6.
53. Kenneth W. Jones, *The Arya Samaj in the Punjab*, p. 200.

the local Arya Samaj.[54] In April 1893, the Singh Sabha and Arya Samaj of Gujranwala again joined forces and brought back into the fold of Hinduism a man who had turned Mussalman about seven months ago.[55] A Hindu named Nehal Chand and his wife, who had become Christians, some time ago, were 'purified' by the unified efforts of the Arya Samaj and Singh Sabha on March 12, 1894,[56] and on August 10, 1894 a Hindu woman of Hafizabad was purified again by the Singh Sabha and Arya Samaj.[57] In 1895, seven *shuddhis* were reported and these were performed jointly by the Arya Samaj and the Singh Sabha of Gujranwala.[58] In 1896, the number of reported *shuddhis* in the newspapers had risen to 12, five of which were performed by the Shuddhi Sabha, Lahore.[59] This was probably not the total number of *shuddhis* performed and only tends to give an indication of the increased frequency of purifications. A Report of the Arya Pratinidhi Sabha, Punjab states that fifteen *shuddhis* were reported in Samaj papers and that there might have been between twenty to thirty *shuddhis* in all during the last twelve months.[60]

However, some differences of opinion arose between the Singh Sabha and the Arya Samaj as the converts were to join either the ranks of Hindus or Sikhs. In the beginning a kind of tacit compromise was reached on the question whether a convert would be a Hindu or a Sikh after conversion. It was understood that in the case of a reconvert being Sikh previously he would be readmitted to Sikhism. Similar practice was adopted in the case of Hindus. But this was not always the practice.

The number of *shuddhis* continued to mount with an increase in 1896 to over 200. In order to account for this

54. *The Tribune*, February 18, 1893, p. 4.
55. *Ibid.*, April 8, 1893, p. 4.
56. *Ibid.*, March 14, 1894, p. 4.
57. *Ibid.*, August 18, 1894, p. 4.
58. *Ibid.*, April 8, 1896, p. 4.
59. *Ibid.*
60. *Arya Pratinidhi Sabha, Punjab Report, 1895-96*, p. 30.

increase we must examine the changing nature of the reconversions. Perusal of *The Tribune* files of the years 1894-96 clearly shows that originally the first reconverts were individuals or small families, and often persons who had been converted to Christianity or Islam for only a short time.[61] On Aug. 31, 1896, however, a major change occurred which revolutionized the institution of *shuddhi*. At the village of Madhopur (Gurdaspur district), the Lahore Shuddhi Sabha purified a family of over two hundred outcaste Sikhs.[62] The great great-grandfather of this family had lived with a Muslim woman and as a result was excommunicated. His descendents, living together in a village, had been outcasted by the Sikh community ever since. The ceremony was attended by about one hundred Sikhs, Khatris, Brahmans and Aroras who joined the reconverts in a common meal at the close of the ceremony.[63] This was the first mass reconversion performed in the Punjab and it marked as well the transition from *shuddhi* as an institution for the reconversion of Hindus from Islam or Christianity to *shuddhi* as a method for raising outcaste groups to the level of the 'pure' or 'twice-born' Hindus.

Another aspect of *shuddhi* which became evident during these years, was a growing number of couples who sought purification in order to regularize their marriages. A Sikh who had married a low caste Hindu and then was excommunicated was reaccepted after he and his wife went through

61. In 1894, two men were purified in one ceremony held in Gujranwala and sponsored by the local Arya Samaj. In July 1895, another dual ceremony was held and in the same month three Muslims were reconverted at one time in a purification ceremony sponsored by the Lahore Shuddhi Sabha. The members included in a single ceremony continued to increase. In April, 1896, the Shuddhi Sabha reclaimed five persons including a woman at one time, and in July, a group of nine. For reference, see *The Tribune*, January 24, 1894, p. 4; June 8, 1895, p. 4; July 27, 1895, p. 4; April 8, 1896, p. 4; and July 7, 1896, p. 4.
62. *Ibid.*, September 2, 1896, p. 4.
63. *Ibid.*

the *shuddhi* ceremony.⁶⁴ In another such case, a girl who had been converted to Islam was purified and married to the Hindu with whom she had been living. In 1897, a similar case concerning a Muslim girl and a Hindu boy was settled through recourse to *shuddhi*.⁶⁵ In this way inter-caste and inter-community marriages could be regularized and accepted through *shuddhi*. In the years to come the Arya Samaj provided a way for many young couples to marry against the opposition of their family, caste or community.

From the increase in the number of converts it may not be construed that all opposition to the *shuddhi* movement had disappeared or even had lapsed into sullen silence. In fact with the growth of the *shuddhi* movement many of its social dimensions came to the surface in the form of criticism. The *shuddhi* was opposed by both the orthodox Hindus and the members of other religions against whom it was primarily aimed at. Expressing the reaction of the conservatives, the *Akhbar-i-Am* condemned the Shuddhi Sabha for eating with the outcastes and the Muslims who had been purified and joined Sikhism.⁶⁶ A part of the criticism also appeared in *The Tribune*. However, these opinions were easily outweighed by those who approved of the reconversion.⁶⁷ Perhaps, the most significant sign of approval was registered when a group of orthodox pundits at Hissar themselves purified a Rajput who had been a Muslim for two years.⁶⁸ This more than any other single instance indicates the beginning of acceptance of *shuddhi* by the orthodox Hindus.

The intensification of efforts in Vedic *prachar* and in *shuddhi* generated a corresponding increase in communal tension. Relations between the Hindus and the Christians

---

64. *Ibid.*, July 14, 1895, p. 4.
65. *Ibid.*, October 12, 1895, p. 4 and March 6, 1897, p. 4.
66. *Akhbar-i-Am*, April 18, 1895 in *SVNP, 1895*, p. 162.
67. *The Tribune*, June 22, 1895, p. 4; january 22, 1896, p. 4; August 5, 1896, p. 4.
68. *Ibid.*, December 23, 1896, p. 4.

continued to be strained, and those between the Hindus and the Muslims steadily deteriorated. The activities of the Arya Samaj, as well as of the militant Muslim groups and the Christian missionaries, contributed to this increasingly polarized atmosphere. Not all segments of communities were alienated from each other, but the general tone of the province was one of gradually worsening off inter-communal relations causing the communal strife between the Hindus and the Muslims in 1897. Though it did not tear the fabric of intimate relationship between these two communities[69] yet it led to the murder of Pandit Lekh Ram which was reported on the day it occurred i.e. on March 6, 1897, in a Lahore newspaper, the *Punjab Samachar*. Four persons were killed in Lahore and Lala Ralla Ram, the founder of the National High School at Peshawar and a prominent Arya Samajist, was also reported murdered.[70] Probably, it was the first serious communal riot in the Punjab during the British rule which was not only a symptom of communal divide in Punjab but also its consequence. Throughout the provice particularly in Lahore, the murder of Pandit Lekh Ram caused panic amongst the Hindus of the central Punjab. Realising the need to put up a united front against the Muslims, the Hindu organizations including the splinter groups of the Arya Samaj got united which is evident from the fact that the condolence meetings to mourn the death of Pandit Lekh Ram held at various cities by the local Arya Samajists were attended by other Hindu organizations. On March 9, 1897, about 2,000 persons attended a large meeting held in Rawalpindi. The gathering consisted of representatives of the Arya Samaj, the Singh Sabha, and the Sanathan Dharm Sabha, among others. In this meeting Rs. 400 were collected for Lekh Ram's widow and mother.[71] The murder of Pandit Lekh Ram no doubt elevated the position of Arya Samaj as the foremost organization of the

---

69. Kenneth, W. Jones, *The Arya Samaj in the Punjab*, p. 220.
70. However, *The Tribune* refuted it and reported that he was only assaulted. March 10, 1897, pp. 2-4.
71. *Ibid.*, March 13, 1897, p. 5.

Hindus. It became a symbol and a cause, especially for the militant faction within the *shuddhi* movement.[72]

Inspired by the sacrifice of Pandit Lekh Ram and having received the general approval of the Hindu masses, the Arya Samaj consolidated its position and undertook extensive work of purification. Thus the *shuddhi* movement entered into a new phase. The Arya Samaj enrolled several *updeshaks* (missionaries) and sent them to different parts of India to do the missionary work. These missionaries were quite active in the Kashmir State in the North, and in Hyderabad in the South. In both these places they confronted many difficulties from the local officials.[73] In 1899, a new area of potential missionary work attracted the attention of Punjabi Arya Samajists, this was in Madras Province. The Shanars, a group of toddy-tapers in South India, were being converted to Islam which generated fanaticism and strong feeling resulting in communal riots in Tinnevelly and other areas of Madras Province. The *Arya Gazette* of July 13, 1899, reported these events and called for the immediate despatch of Arya Samaj missionaries to reconvert the Shanars to Hinduism.[74] By the following month several missionaries had left for Madras in order to 'save' the Shanars. This step was opposed by the members of the Anjuman-i-Islam of Lahore who despatched a Maulvi to aid in the conversion of the Shanars to Islam.[75]

Though this initial attempt to spread Samajic doctrine and new Samaj innovation of *shuddhi* to South apparently failed due to the vehement opposition of the Hindu orthodoxy there,[76] yet the precedent was created and in later years the Samaj renewed its efforts to expand into the Southern part of

72. Kenneth W. Jones, *The Arya Samaj in the Punjab*, p. 229.
73. *Sat Dharm Pracharak*, June 23, 1899 in *SVNP, 1899*, p. 363.
74. *Arya Gazette*, July 13, 1899 in *SVNP*, 1899, p. 408. Also see *Sat Dharm Parcharak*, August 4, 1899 in *Ibid.*, p. 456.
75. *Wakil*, August 14, 1899 in *SVNP*, p. 471.
76. *Sanathan Dharm Gazette*, October 31, 1899 in *SVNP, 1899*, p. 664.

India, particularly during the Moplah uprising in the 1920s, and later in Hyderabad State.

By the year 1897, the *shuddhi* movement did not remain merely as a defensive strategy to check the proselytizing activities of the Christians in which it had, of course, been successful, at least, it is what *The Arya Patrika* believed. It mentions:[77]

> The Arya Samaj has dealt a most fatal blow to the interests of the Missionaries, by disabusing the native mind of these wrong and pernicious ideas which it has been the constant endeavour of the Missionaries, to instil into it, ever since they set their foot upon Indian soil.

Thereafter, it underwent a radical change which is clear from the fact that from this year onwards the *shuddhi* movement became an agency for the consolidation of Hindu society. As a process of consolidation, the *shuddhi* became a comprehensive three dimensional strategy, to undertake the *shuddhi* activities of purifying the low caste and converting people from other religions, to propagate the Arya doctrines and to undertake philanthropic activities. The Arya Samajists were sent all over India to stem the proselytizing activities of the Christians by persuading the Hindus to reform Hindu society from within.

One of the strategies which was generally employed by the Christian missionaries was that famines which were frequent in the second half of the nineteenth century used to cause large scale mortality. As a result, a large number of orphans used to be given shelter by the Christian missionaries with a view to convert them to Christianity. Seeing the danger of losing so many children from the Hindu fold, the Arya Samaj launched their own rescue operations. As early as 1877 Swami Dayanand had established a Hindu Orphanage at Ferozepur Cantt.[78] Their number in Punjab had increased to

77. *The Arya Patrika*, July, 26, 1887, pp. 1-2.
78. *Arya Directory*, p. 185.

four by the year 1897. But their primary aim was to train boys and girls[79] facilitating their settlement in life and also removing the attraction of conversion to Christianity. Nearly one thousand orphans had been settled by that year.[80] This movement was revived in 1899 in which Lala Lajpat Rai played a prominent role. "Under the leadership of Lala Lajpat Rai the Hindu Orphan Relief movement was started, mostly to take care of Hindu children left without any means of support," writes Sri Ram Sharma.[81] So far the only non-official agency then available to help the Government in its humanitarian work was the Christian missionaries. Thus "the sight of Hindu children passing into the hands of Christians, presumably to be reared in their faith, attracted the notice of the Arya Samajists in the Punjab."[82] The Arya Samaj was thus the first non-Christian private agency which started a non-official movement for the relief of distress caused by famine.[83] This activity of humanitarian work brought the Christian missionaries and the Arya Samaj into direct conflict, for both had identical aim of converting the distressed persons thus saving them from going to the alien faith. The Arya Samajists' antipathy came to light when during the famine of 1899-1900 they were outweighed in the famine relief work in Rajputana, the Central Provinces, Bombay, Kathiawar and the parts of the Punjab by the government and Christian missionaries. Even Lala Lajpat Rai admits this when he writes:[84]

> The missionaries were fighting a noble battle, and it was not for us to start an agitation against them in Rajputana; nor had we the means and strength to do so even had we the mind to try. We made no secret of our concern at the conversion of a large number of our co-religionists to an alien faith, and we tried to arouse

79. Lajpat Rai, *The Arya Samaj*, p. 238.
80. Kenneth W. Jones, *The Arya Samaj in the Punjab*, p. 239.
81. Sri Ram Sharma, *Mahatma Hansraj*, p. 104.
82. Ibid.
83. Lajpat Rai, *The Arya Samaj*, p. 239.
84. *Ibid.*, pp. 241-42. Also see Sri Ram Sharma, *op. cit.*, p. 105.

attention to it here and there; but we soon found that this negative work alone would not suffice, and that it was not likely to bear fruit, even in Native States, much less in British territory. To save even a few hundred, we must be prepared to bring them to the Punjab, where they were to find sufficient food and clothing to keep them going till the end of the famine.

There is no doubt that the Arya Samajists followed the same device as the Christian missionaries in meeting the demands of the famine stricken people. The young members of the Samaj, particularly of the Punjab worked hard to help the needy persons. They were able to bring back more than seventeen hundred orphans to the Punjab, as local arrangements in Rajasthan proved improper and inadequate.[85] About the work done by the Arya missionaries, the remarks of Lala Lajpat Rai are worth mentioning:[86]

> Thanks to the Almighty whose grace and mercy was our own support. . . . The best acknowledgments of the Hindu community are due to those young men (most of our agents were young and honorary) who risked their lives in this noble undertaking, because it was no easy matter to travel in search of orphans in Rajputana and the Central Provinces, where not only was there a terrible scarcity of food and water, but where cholera and fever were raging. Conceive of a young Panjabi Hindu travelling on camels day and night in search of orphans in tracts devastated by famine, where neither good food nor wholesome water was to be had for miles and miles together. Add to this the fear of pestilence and the anxiety of having left behind wives and children. Add also their anxiety to spend as little as possible on their own comfort, with the knowledge that the funds at their disposal and at the disposal of those who had deputed them were so small as to make economy a

---

85. James Reid Graham, *op. cit.*, pp. 413-14.
86. Lajpat Rai, *The Arya Samaj*, p. 245.

strict necessity. Yes, blessed are those who faced all these privations boldly and worked under these difficulties with a religious sense of duty to help the little ones of their community in the time of dire calamity.

This remarkable operation of famine relief work put the Arya Samaj on the map as an organization that could rival the Christians in philanthropic work. Although it did not entail any *shuddhi* activity, it did influence its development in some ways.[87] It helped the Arya Samaj to realise that they were now strong enough to cope with them. Since a large number of the orphans came from the lower strata of Hindu society, the outcastes, it drew the Samaj's attention to their lot. So whereas the Arya Samaj leaders were busy looking after the victims of famine and establishing orphanages at far off places, they were also engaged in other social activities for the welfare of the Hindus especially the depressed classes. Commenting upon this Lajpat Rai writes: "The philanthropic work of the Arya Samaj is not, however, confined to famine relief, but includes various kinds of social service. In times of pestilence it organizes medical relief, nursing the sick, and helping in the disposal of the dead."[88]

The Arya missionaries demonstrated the spirit of devotion and dedication on the occasions of festivals. Lala Munshi Ram, himself a missionary, reports with tremendous sense of satisfaction that:[89]

> Dassera at Jullunder was a grand success.... Near the Ram Leela Tank (the present Gandhi Mandap) we had pitched our tents. It was strange to see Bhakta Ram, Headmaster of the Local Mission High school, who was then the Vice-President of the Arya Samaj, driving one of

---

87. *Ibid.*, p. 247.
88. *Ibid.* Also see *Home Deptt. Poll. Deposit*, No. 7, November 1908, p. 9 (NAI).
89. M.R. Jambunathan, *op. cit.*, p. 78.

the pegs of the tent into the ground and holding in his hand an "OM" flag. Intense propagand was carried on there on behalf of the Arya Samaj. . . . Even the sons of Zamindars and Sowcars who were wasting their lives in vice were moved by our lectures. The two or three Hindu boys who were attending Christian lectures also came of their own accord to our camp. That year's Christian propaganda was a distinct failure.

The Arya Samaj was especially successful in stemming the tide of conversion of the urban middle classes to the Christianity primarily due to its educational policy. Confronted with the dilemma posed by the Western education which offered employment opportunities and as such economic security and attracted young men to be influenced by it, the problem was however successfully solved by establishing Dayanand Anglo-Vedic Schools which not only promised deliverance from a painful choice of leaving one's religion but opened the path of a new future—a future of economic expansion with a degree of cultural security. About its success, *The Arya Patrika* writes:[90]

There was a time when the faith of all educated Hindus in their own religion had been shaken. Many through ignorance embraced Christianity and many others were ready to follow them. But thanks to God that the tide has now turned, and in these days it is a very rare occurrence to see an educated Hindu embracing Christianity or Muhammadanism. The educated Hindus have now learned that the religion of their forefathers is founded on solid rock of truth.

Of course, by the closing years of the nineteenth century, the Arya Samaj did succeed in stemming the tide of conversion among the Hindu elites and the educated ones.[91] But it dismally failed to prevent a wholesale exodus of the outcastes

---

90. *The Arya Patrika*, April 13, 1886, p. 5.
91. *Census of India, 1901*, India Report, p. 393.

from Hinduism to Christianity. Their hope was rudely schocked by the *Census Reports for 1891*. In the years 1881-1891, the Christian missionaries managed to increase the number of Indian Christians in the Punjab by over fourfold, and in Sialkot District alone the Christian convert community literally exploded from 253 in 1881 to 9,711 in 1891, an increase of over 3,000 per cent.[92] This increase was due to the 'mass movement' among the *chamars* (leather workers), *chuhras* (a sweeper community in the Punjab) and Lal Bagis (also a sweeber community in U.P.) who were converted and were still being converted to Christianity *en masse* in order to improve their social status and in particular to remove the stigma of untouchability.[93]

The Arya Samaj from the very beginning vehemently opposed caste system based on the idea of birth and had propagated against the treatment of outcaste Hindus. But the caste prejudices were primarily responsible for the conversion of millions of Hindus, asserts Vishwa Prakash, first to Islam and then to Christanity. He comments:[94]

> For ten centuries, Hinduism was a prey to foreign religions. Muhammadans came and conquered this country. Later they began their conversion work. By threats of life, or baits of officialdom they succeeded in converting more than a quarter of the Hindu population. When English came to this country they brought Christian missionaries in their lap. These Christian missionaries were educated people and they had a sufficient backing from their countries. They obtained very little success amongst the educated classes, so they shifted their energies to the people of lower strata of society. Untouchables and hill tribes were converted to

92. *Census of India, 1891*, Punjab Report, pp. xxxliv, 97.
93. John C.B. Webster, *The Christian Community and Change in Nineteenth Century North India* (Delhi: Macmillan Company of India, 1976), p. 62.
94. Vishwa Prakash, *Life and Teachings of Swami Dayanand* (Allahabad: Kala Press, 1935), pp. 155-56.

their faith. But what for Hinduism? Hinduism was not a proselytizing religion. It could easily lose its own men, but no one could be brought back into its fold. Swami Dayanand saw that this was the weakest point of Hindus. A society, however large it may be, will surely be extinct from the face of the earth, if it allows its people to go away, but does not allow others to come in. So he opened the portals wide, he began the conversion work (*shuddhi*) which was taken up by his disciples and today it is settled fact that Hinduism has become a proselytizing religion.

In January 1899, the *Arya Musafir* printed an extensive article attacking the caste system as one of the erroneous elements of orthodox Hinduism, classing it with idol worship and the *srāddha*[95] and the issue sparked off when attempt was made to raise the traditional social status of the *Mazhabi* Sikhs.[96] Highlighting the importance of the problem, *The Arya Patrika* offers pertinent observations:[97]

> There is one point in connection with the caste system upon which I wish to address you most particularly. This consists in our practising a very bad moral tyranny upon a sect of our countrymen—who happen to believe in the same God as the other Hindus do, and recognize the same Scriptures as others do. I, of course, allude to the *Mazhabi* Sikhs. You know, gentlemen, the view in which the generality of *Mazhabi* Sikhs is held by us. A Mahummadan may touch up and even share our bed but the very touch of a *Mazhabi* Sikh pollutes a Hindu; and his shadow even spoils the person of a Hindu.

95. *Srāddha* means an entire body of rituals and domestic ceremonies connected with the propitiation of the dead. For detailed reference, see K.L. Seshagiri Rao, *The Concept of Sraddha* (in the Brahmanas, Upanisads and the Gita) (Patiala: Roy Publishers, 1971), p. 2.
96. Literally *Mazhabi* Sikh means an untouchable Sikh. *Census of India, 1921*, Punjab and Delhi Report, p. 184.
97. *The Arya Patrika*, April 27, 1886, p. 4.

And again:[98]

> It is said that these people number about 70,000. If they be taken in, they will form a valuable acquisition to the ranks of the Hindu society. Reformers who are justly declaiming against the tyranny of the caste are requested to consider this question seriously. All our social organizations in the Punjab should take up the question, and prepare the minds of the generality of the people (Hindus) for receiving the *Mazhabi* Sikhs into their midst. I am very glad to see, that several spirited gentlemen connected with the Arya Samaj are contemplating to take some steps in the matter; and as the question is really of great importance it should be taken up right earnest by the Arya Samaj, which on account of its being a national movement.

The missionary spirit of idealism was countered by pragmatism. *The Arya Patrika* again raised some relative questions in the form of introspection. It writes:[99]

> Even in the matter of converting people from other religions we Aryas are subject to the Hindus. They would not allow us to drink water or take food from Mohammadans or Christians. Of course, we are not to dine with those who eat meat or drink wine....Hindus of different provinces will not eat together; some Hindu customs are superstitious. Can the Aryas root out these without severing the connection in important matters from the Hindus? Experience answers in negative. Jullundur could not take in the Rahtias.

98. *Ibid.*
99. *Ibid.*, June 9, 1900, p. 5. The first group of Rahtias had sought admission to the Jalandhar Arya Samaj for a whole year but without success. Ganda Singh (ed.), *Bhagat Lakshman Singh: Autobiography* (Calcutta: The Sikh Cultural Centre, 1965), p. 163.

It reiterates:[100]

> How can we expect converts from non-Hindus unless we mix with them and think them members of any society? There is the necessity of severing our connection with Hinduism and having a society of our own which may shatter from every creed.

Even the Lahore Shuddhi Sabha noted in one of its *Proceedings* that "the time has not yet come for admitting *Mazhabi*, *Chamars* and Muhammadans...."[101] But most of the Aryas were in favour of admitting the lower castes into a full caste status for, in their opinion, "it is the obligation of the Arya Samaj to admit those of lower caste even at the risk of offending many; otherwise the Vedic cosmopolitanism is meaningless."[102]

After about two years' debate on the question of converting lower castes, particularly the Rahtias, the *Mazhabi* Sikhs belonging to the profession of weavers and coblers,[103] distributed in the districts of Lahore, Jalandhar, Hoshiarpur, the Arya Pratinidhi Sabha, Punjab[104] took a decision of purifying them.[105] The Aryas particularly the members belonging to the younger generation undertook the task of *shuddhi* in right earnest.[106] It may be pointed out that the Rahtias had been seeking readmission in the Sikh fold for sometime but no action was taken up. In June 1899, they came to Mahatma Munshi Ram who tried his best to get his "proposals to purify the Rahtias by the Jullundur Samaj Committee" passed.[107] But

---

100. *The Arya Patrika*, September 15, 1900, pp. 10-11.
101. *Singh Sahai*, March 12, 1895 in *AVNP, 1895*, p. 162.
102. *The Arya Patrika*, May 12, 1900, p. 5.
103. *Census of India, 1911*, Punjab Report, p. 150.
104. The Arya Pratinidhi Sabha, Punjab was, as has been earlier stated, established in 1885 at Lahore. Mahatma Munshi Ram (Swami Shraddhanand) and Lala Devraj played a leading role in purifying the Rahtias at Jalandhar. *Arya Directory*, p. 191.
105. *Census of India, 1911*, Punjab Report, p. 150.
106. *Ibid.*
107. Bhimsena Vidyalankar, *Arya Pratinidhi Sabha Punjab ka Sachitar Itihas* (Lahore: Arya Pratinidhi Sabha, Punjab, 1935), p. 210.

due to persistent opposition of the Aryas, he could not get the Rahtias admitted, as it was argued that their interest in seeking conversion was simply for the elevation of social status and not for the interest in the Vedic religion or learning.[108] Reacting sharply to this, the Editor of *The Arya Patrika* writes:[109]

> I have met some of them and have conversed with them personally. I found them sincere believers in the tenets of the Divine Faith and ardent admirers of the Maharishi. Their earnestness and sincerity may be judged from the fact that in spite of the refusal of the Jullundur Arya Samaj to admit them to its fold, they are perfectly ready to get their heads shaved. And is it sinful to desire a rise in social status?

However, in spite of the opposition of the orthodox Hindus as well as by the Sikhs and the Muslims, the Rahtias were purified by the Lahore branch of the Arya Samaj.[110] It is interesting to note that despite their being co-religionists the initiation ceremonies adopted to convert them were the same as those used in the case of non-Hindus such as the Mulims and Christians. The sacred thread ceremony and the recitation of sacred *Gayatri mantra* were used in the purification of low caste. There was a strong reaction to the procedure of admitting low castes. There was a considerable tension[111] as some of the Arya Samajists were excommunicated for participating in the ceremony and eating at "the hands of Rahtias admitted to the Arya Samaj at Lyallpur."[112] Similar purifica-

108. *Ibid.*
109. *The Arya Patrika*, May 12, 1900, p. 8.
110. Pundit Shunker Nath, *Duty Towards Our Depressed Brethren* (1926), p. 10. Also see *SVNP*, *1900*, p. 304.
111. There was a rumour in *The Tribune* that the "Sikhs had massacred the Jullundur Aryas and that Munshiram was admitted in hospital in a critical condition." For reference, see June 1900 in *SVNP*, *1900*, p. 332.
112. *The Arya Patrika*, August 4, 1900, p. 8. Also see *Vedic Magazine and Gurukula Samachar*, Vol. IV, No. 1, 1910-11, p. 50.

tion ceremoies were held at Lahore then at Jalandhar[113] and Ropar in August and September 1900 respectively.[114]

Large scale conversion of the Rahtias by the Arya Samaj enhanced its prestige and recognition as the leading institution for elevating the caste status of the members of the lower caste and as such it began to attract men of other lower castes.[115] After the Rahtias about 200 Ramdasias[116] (generally *chuhras* and *chamars* by caste) were purified in the districts of Jalandhar and Hoshiarpur, and in parts of Patiala.[117] It was followed by the Ods, a group of untouchable caste, whom the Multan Arya Samaj successfully purified in 1901-02.[118] Writing about their descent, Sir Denzil Ibbetson says:[119]

> The Od or Odh is a wandering tribe whose proper home appears to be Western Hindustan and Rajputana; at least the Ods of the Panjab usually hail from those parts. They are vagrants, wandering about with their families in search of employment on earthwork. They will not as a rule take petty jobs, but prefer small contracts on roads, canals, railways, and they like, or will build a house of adobe, and dig a tank, or even a well. . . . They eat anything and everything, and though not unfrequently Musalmans, especially in the west, are always outcaste. . . . They claim descent from one Bhagirat. . . .

113. *Ibid.*, August 25, 1900, p. 7.
114. *Ibid.*, September 29, 1900, p. 5.
115. But it created many difficulties for the Rahtias. They had not only to face the wrath of the villagers but excommunication from their *biradari*. *The Khalsa Akhbar*, June 22, 1900, p. 5.
116. *Census of India, 1900*, Punjab Report, p. 150. Sir Denzil Ibbetson writes that "in the north and centre of the Eastern Plains a very considerable number of Chamars have embraced the Sikh religion. These men are called Ramdasia after Guru Ram Das. . . ."*Panjab Castes* (Lahore : Government Printing Press, Punjab, 1916), p. 300.
117. *Ibid.*
118. James Reid Graham, *op. cit.*, p. 493.
119. Sir Denzil Ibbetson, *op. cit.*, p. 275.

Development of Shuddhi Movement

Till the reappearance of Bhagirat they will, they say, remain outcastes. They are said to claim Rajput or Kshatriya origin and to come from Marwar. They worship Rama and Siva.

The movement of purification of the Ods spread to other districts of Punjab and about 23,000 of them were purified in the districts of Multan, Lyallpur, Montgomery. Jhang and Muzaffargarh during the first decade of the present century.[120]

Next came Meghs, also a low-caste group of the Punjab. Sir Denzil Ibbetson reports:[121]

The Meg or as he is called in Rawalpindi Meng, is the Chamar of the tract immediately below the Jammu hills. But he appears to be of a slightly better standing than the Chamar; and this superiority is doubtless owing to the fact that the Meg is a weaver as well as a worker in leather. ... They seem at present to be almost confined to the upper valleys of the Ravi and Chanab, and their stronghold is the sub-montane portion of Sialkot lying between these two rivers. They are practically all Hindus.

The purification of the first batch of Ods had not set completed "when another problem of greater magnitude (the Shuddhi of the Meghs) almost forced itself upon the attention of the

---

120. The Ods were generally belonged to both Hindu and Muslim communities. Their numbers as mentioned in various *Census* reports are given below :

Caste	1881	1891	1901	1911	1921	1931
Od Hindu	11,540	12,316	17,911	20,375	18,282	19,583
Od Muslim	4,065	10,082	8,174	11,170	10,192	13,041

The figures indicate more than 3 hundred per cent increase in the Muslim Ods and only seventy per cent among the Hindus. This was primarily due to the conversion efforts of the Arya Samaj. *Census of India, 1931*, Punjab Report, p. 350.

121. Sir Denzil Ibbetson, *op. cit.*, p. 333.

72   Shuddhi Movement in India

Arya Samaj."[122] Starting on March 14, 1903 the task of converting the Meghs like that of Ods proved hazardous and magnitudenous. It took six years of effective campaigning of the Arya Samaj during which they were confronted with social boycott and occasional violence to purify not less than 36,000 Meghs.[123] Reacting sharply to the purification of the Meghs of Pattansen in Sialkot district, the Rajputs "attacked the poor Bhagats (the name which was given to the Meghs after their purification) in their houses, armed with 'lathies', beat them severely and ordered them to leave either the Aryan religion or the village."[124] Again, writing about the stiff opposition of the conservative Hindus to the purification of Meghs, the Secretary, Sanatan Dharm Sabha, Sialkot wrote that "the Hindus, however, would not admit the whilom Meghs into their society, and the latter received a beating at the first Kahar shop they entered to take food. They are, therefore, worse off now."[125] This is a clear indication of the inter-caste rivalry stimulated by the Arya *shuddhi* campaign.[126] But in spite of the stiff opposition of the orthodox Hindus, Muslims and Christians, the *shuddhi* work of the Arya Samaj went successfully in respect of Meghs especially. The Arya Samajists not only purified the Meghs but also opened few schools to educate them, for, they thought, "the work of raising the social status of the Meghs could not be effectively done without improving their minds by giving them education."[127] It is interesting to note that the Sialkot Arya Samaj especially under the command of Swami Satyananda Saraswati, who

122. *Census of India, 1911*, Punjab Report, p. 150.
123. Ganga Ram and Charu Dass, *The Upliftment Movement at Sialkot Punjab : A Brief Report of the Working of the Arya Megh Uddhar Sabha* (Aryan Mission for the Uplift of the Megh Untouchables) *Sialkot, Punjab* (Calcutta: A.C. Sarkar, 1915), p. 12. *Arya*, Lahore, June 1924 at p. 17 mentions that in Jammu about 50,000 Meghs were purified.
124. Kenneth W. Jones, *The Arya Samaj in the Punjab*, p. 214.
125. *Bharat Partap*, May 1903 in *SVNP, 1903*, p. 182.
126. Bhimsena Vidyalankar, *op. cit.*, p. 211.
127. Ganga Ram and Charu Dass, *op. cit.*, p. 21.

performed the purification ceremony of 200 Meghs, alone borne the expenses of *shuddhi* movement for more than nine years. But when in 1912 its work, both educational and religious, assumed "such proportions as to render it impossible for the Sialkot Arya Samaj to meet its demands unless helped by the public at large,"[128] the Executive Committee of the Sialkot Arya Samaj resolved on April 21, 1912 to entrust this work to the Arya Megh Uddhar Sabha i.e. Aryan Mission for the uplift of the Megh untouchables, which the latter did it successfully by opening atleast seven technical and non-technical schools for the boys of these untouchables.

During the same period the *shuddhi* of groups low in the social scale and half-Muslim, half-Hindu in Sindh was undertaken by the Sukkar Arya Samaj. As an illustration we may cite the example of the Sheikhs of Larkana in Sindh who were all converted Hindu Brahmans. They included Nehrus, Kitchlews, Bedis.[129] As the names of the groups signify, they were one of the groups low in the social status who were originally Hindus and who were partially made into Muslims but who never fully became Muslims in social and religious conduct. The occasion of purification lasted three days, from 9th to 11th July, 1905 with some degree of opposition. Explaining the opposition to the *shuddhi* ceremony, James Reid Graham writes:[130]

128. *Ibid.*, p. 22.
129. Based on information furnished by Lala Ram Dass, President, All India Dayanand Salvation Mission, Hoshiarpur in one of his interview with the author. According to him, "They were converted during Nasir-ud-din, the Mughal Emperor's regime." He further added that "Sheikh Abdulla of Kashmir was one of the descendents of Brahmans. These Sheikhs were reconverted at the time of Maharaja Ranbir Singh of J & K who is said to have got a *fatwa* from the Pandits of Benaras that these Sheikhs could be reconverted." Also see *The Arya Patrika*, August 5, 1905, p. 5.
130. James Reid Graham, *op. cit.*, p. 495.

The *shuddhi* which was to have been done on the 10th was done on the 11th due to the opposition of the local panchayat. . . . The *shuddhi* was given on the 11th with all the solemnity and grandeur it deserved, the converts one and all wearing yellow *dhotis*. The male members were purified in the *mandap* (or tent) and the female at their houses.

Among such people, who were half-Hindus and half-Muslims, the Arya Samaj carried on the work of *shuddhi* in several areas. We may refer to the Soubrai Labanas of Ludhiana in Punjab and Maiwaris of Ajmer in Rajastan.[131]

Similarly, the Arya Samaj leadership purified the Jats numbering about 30,000[132] to the status of *Dwija* (twice-born) in the districts of Karnal, Gurgaon, Rohtak, Delhi, Hissar, Ambala and in the Patiala, Nabha and Jind States.[133] These Jats had been for centuries formed peripheral castes of the Hindu society and were now anxious to enter into the caste hierarchy of the Hindus.

The Arya Samaj outside Punjab was also very active in the *shuddhi* work. In U.P. in 1902, the *shuddhi* ceremony of 130 men and women of lower caste was performed at Bharthana (Etawah). These persons were once Rajputs and through the great efforts of one Pandit Bhagwandin arrangements for weddings of many of them were made then and there among Rajputs. During the same year, in the village Kapura of Mainpuri district, 375 persons who had embraced Islam over 200 years ago, were taken back in the Aryan fold.[134]

131. *Arya Messenger*, July 4, 1902, p. 8.
132. *Census of India, 1911*, Punjab Report, p. 149.
133. *Ibid*.
134. Radhey Shyam Pareek, *Contribution of Arya Samaj in the Making of Modern India, 1875-1947* (Delhi: Sarvdeshik Arya Pratinidhi Sabha, 1973), pp. 155-56.

Development of Shuddhi Movement

Writing about the increase in the members of the Arya Samaj in the U.P., a Census Report says that the number of Aryas of this province grew from 65,572 in 1901 to 131,638 in 1911 due to *shuddhi* movement.[135]

Between 1907 and 1911, 722 persons of the Kabirpanthi sect (*chamar* by caste and weavers by profession) were elevated to higher social status by the Arya Samaj in 49 villages of the Hoshiarpur and Kangra districts[136] mainly by the effects of one Lala Devi Chand and Hoshiarpur Shuddhi Sabha.[137]

The Arya Samaj had to face considerable opposition when they purified about 10,000 Vaishists at Nathanshah (Sind) in 1911. The *Arya Directory* reports that Aryas who participated in this purification ceremony were excommunicated. It further reports that the *yogyopavit* of one of the convert was taken off and a permanent sign of *yogyopavit* was presented with hot iron rod.[138]

Since numbers had become a significant factor in the wake of the Act of 1909 which granted communal representation to Muslims, the Arya Samaj took keen interest in converting the Muslim Rajputs who had only recently changed their faith and were retaining many of the Hindu social and religious practices in their life and culture. The Samaj leaders particularly Choudhry Ram Bhaj Dutt and Pandit Bhoj Dutt carried on their *shuddhi* campaign among the Rajputs of the

---

135. *Census of India, 1911*, United Provinces Report, p. 105.
136. *Census of India, 1911*, Punjab Report, p. 152.
137. It is interesting to note that Lala Ram Dass of Dayanand Salvation Mission, Hoshiarpur was one of the members of the Kabirpanthi sect who were purified. According to him, after the purification, these untouchables became touchables and were considered as the members of the Arya Samaj. He became a member of Parliament and one another person, Prithi Chand Azad, who was also a Kabirpanthi achieved a high position in Hindu Samaj.
138. *Arya Directory*, p. 191.

United Provinces, Central Provinces and Baroda[139] by establishing Rajput Shuddhi Sabha in 1909 at Agra[140] to convert Muslim Rajputs. Reclaiming these lost Kshatriyas was considered as an event of great significance as this addition was viewed as a part of the process of consolidation of the Hindus and "moral victory of incalculable significance."[141] Though this Sabha remained in existence upto 1911 only but this society claimed to have converted 1100 neo-Muslim Rajputs from 1909 to 1911,[142] in the districts of Mainpuri, Hardoi and Shahjahanpur of the United Provinces.[143]

The conversion of Dumnas of Gurdaspur and Kashmir in Punjab and the hill tracts of the United Provinces was taken up by Choudhry Ram Bhaj Dutt. Writing about Dumna caste, Sir Denzil Ibbetson reports:[144]

> The Dumna, called also Domra, and even Dum in Chamba, is the Chuhra of the hills proper, and is also found in large numbers in the sub-montane districts of Hushyarpur and Gurdaspur. Like the Chuhra of the

139. *Census of India, 1911*, Baroda Report, p. 56.
140. Swami Chidanand Saraswati, "Shuddhi ka Naya Daur" in *Shradhanand*, November 1954, p. 5. Also see *Arya Directory*, p. 196.
141. Kenneth W. Jones, *Arya Dharm*, p. 304.
142. Swami Chidanand Saraswati, *op. cit.*, p. 5.
143. However, the *Census of India, 1921*, United Provinces Report, p. 134 suggests that "On a single day 370 such Rajputs were converted to Aryaism. In three years, between 1907 and 1910, this society claims to have converted 1,052 Muslman Rajputs." It may be pointed out that scholars like Lajpat Rai, *The Arya Samaj*, p. 249, James Reid Graham, *op. cit.*, pp. 505-06 and Kenneth W. Jones, *Arya Dharm*, p. 304 have cited this source in support of their argument. As far as the conversion of the Muslim Rajputs is concerned, their number however does not differ much from those given by the Arya Samaj sources. But the *Census Report* erroneously suggests that Rajput Shuddhi Sabha started its work of converting the Muslim Rajputs in 1907 instead of 1909.
144. Sir Denzil Ibbetson, *op. cit.*, pp. 333-24.

plains he is something more than a scavenger; but whereas the Chuhra works chiefly in grass, the Dumna adds to this occupation the trade of working in bamboo, a material not available to the Chuhra. ... The Dumna appears hardly ever to become Musalman or Sikh, and is classed as Hindu, though being an outcaste he is not allowed to draw water from wells used by the ordinary Hindu population.

The Dumna is often called Dum in other parts of India, as in Chamba; and is regarded by Hindus as the type of uncleanness.

According to a Census Report:[145]

"The hill Doms" are largely artisans, and many of them by their industry and enterprise have become well-to-do and even men of substance. But they still find themselves looked down upon by the hill Brahman and Rajput.

The Dumans in Gurdaspur district constituted the maximum number of untouchables. Choudhry Ram Bhaj Dutt, himself belonging to Gurdaspur district, with the help of other Samaj leaders like Mahashya Raunak Ram and Mahashya Gokul Ram, purified these Dumnas after tremendous efforts.[146] Upto 1912, according to Ramchander Javed, Choudhry Ram Bhaj Dutt is supposed to have converted about one lakh Dumnas to the fold of Arya Samaj.[147] As in the case of Meghs, these Dumnas were renamed as 'Mahashya' and for the welfare of them a society named 'Mahashya Kaumi Sudhar Sabha' was established.[148]

145. *Census of India, 1921*, United Provinces Report, p. 56.
146. Narrating the difficulties which Ram Bhaj Dutt and his party had to face, he wrote two letters which were published in *The Tribune* on September 15, 1912 and October 2, 1912 and which are reproduced in the Appendix-I of the present work for the convenience of the readers.
147. Ramchander Javed, *Punjab ka Arya Sama*j (Jullundur: Arya Pratinidhi Sabha, Punjab, 1964), p. 26. *Arya Directory* gives the number of these converted Dumnas, perhaps erroneously, as about ten lakhs. See p. 193.
148. *Ibid.*

78   Shuddhi Movement in India

In 1913, yet another *shuddhi* campaign was started among the Vasisths of Jammu. It is reported that upto 1921, the year of the next Census, about 9,000 Vasisths were purified by the local Arya Samaj.[149]

It may however be pointed out that while the Arya Samaj was thus carrying on the purification of the low castes to keep them within Hinduism, it was not forgetting the purification of individuals from Christianity and Islam. It had been a redeeming feature of the first phase of its campaign in the last two decades of the nineteenth century.

Among others, Mr. J. Addison, I.C.S., Sub-Divisional Officer, Sirsa quotes one example of conversion of a born Muslim:[150]

But there is one case in which a Musalman by birth, named Karim Bakhsh, was admitted into the fold under interesting circumstances. He was the servant of B. Sant Ram, the manager of a theatrical company which came on tour to Sirsa. There happened to be a meeting of the Samaj and Sant Ram, who was an Arya, took his servant to the meeting, where he was admitted as a member. All the assembled people then ate sweetmeats distributed by him. This occurred on the 14th February 1910. They left Sirsa when the performances came to an end.

Similarly one Abdul Gafoor, also a born Muslim, who was a *julaha* (weaver by caste) of Hoshiarpur and who had joined Dev Samaj on February 16, 1900 was converted to Aryan fold on June 13, 1903 by Gujranwala Arya Samaj,[151] and was given

---

149. *Census of India, 1921*, Kashmir Report, pp. 59, 62.
150. *Census of India, 1911*, Punjab Report, p. 151.
151. *Arya Pratinidhi Sabha Punjab ka Sachiter Itihas*, published by Arya Pratinidhi Sabha, Punjab, Lahore, 1922 Vik., pp. 311-12.

the Hindu name Dharmpal.[152] Likewise some Europeans were also converted to Hinduism. A European Capt. I.C. Dicky of Scotland was converted on June 27, 1909 by the Arya Samaj, Ajmeri Gate, Delhi and was given a new name Dharm Dev.[153] On the same date another born Christian under the name of Mr. R.A. Sickie was admitted into the Arya Samaj in Delhi.[154] Yet another example of Miss L.C. Forster Thomas, an Australian lady who was converted to Arya Dharm and later on married to Raja Takkari, is available in the contemporary records.[155] However, this type of *shuddhi* never succeeded in winning masses of people to Hinduism.

The period from 1907 to 1911 is a landmark in the history of the *shuddhi* movement for the reason that by that time the Muslim League had come into existence and the Muslims were granted separate representation by the Act of 1909. These changes in the political climate of the country furnished a new dimension to the *shuddhi* movement. As early as 1907 it was felt that the *shuddhi* work should be followed in greater earnestness. Efforts should be made to fully integrate the new proselytes with the Arya society and special attention should be given to the low castes who were liable to join the ranks of Christians and Muslims if they were not purified by the Arya Samaj.[156]

Consequently an important step was taken to extend the work of *shuddhi* on a wider scale, hence the formation of Bharat Shuddhi Sabha or All India Shuddhi Sabha under the

152. For detail, see Qasim Ali Ahmadi (ed.), *Shuddhi ke Ashuddhi* (Delhi : Afzal-al-Matabai, 1909), pp. 3-10. Also see *Sanatan Dharm Pracharak*, April 1, 1912 in *SVNP, 1919*, Microfilm Reel No. 1, (NAI) p. 271.

153. Dharmpal, *Turk Islam* (Islam ka Parityaag) (Itava : Ved Parkash Yantralaya, n.d.), p. 3. Also see *Arya Pratinidhi Sabha Punjab Ka Sachiter Itihas*, p. 313.

154. *Home Deptt. Poll. Proceedings*, 1909, p. 10.

155. Qasim Ali Ahmadi, *op. cit.*, pp. 92-95. For more references, see *Census of India, 1911*, Jammu and Kashmir Report, p. 290.

156. *The Arya Patrika*, November 9, 1907, p. 7,

Presidentship of Choudhry Ram Bhaj Dutt.[157] Upto this time apparently the work of *shuddhi* had been carried on primarily in the Punjab proper, and at a few places outside, but now preparations were made and organization established to properly undertake the *shuddhi* work on all India level. Defining the purpose for the formation of this Sabha, Choudhry Ram Bhaj Dutt declared in his speech at Allahabad that:[158]

> Different Samajs and Sabhas have been doing the work of *shuddhi* on a large scale, but they have regarded it as one of merely secondary importance. This was why the Bharat *Shuddhi* Sabha was established to devote itself exclusively to this work, and the organization, therefore represented the various Hindu societies, and was in the enjoyment of the sympathy of the entire Hindu population.

The All India Shuddhi Sabha, though worked only in the Punjab at the initial stage, gained momentum, the testimony of which can be gauged from the following note of Choudhri Ram Bhaj Dutt:[159]

> The total number of persons purified or raised socially during the years 1901-10 in the Province of the Punjab is about sixty to seventy thousand as per details below: (1) The Rahtias, 3000 to 4000, (2) Ramdasias about 200, (3) The Ods about 2000 to 3000, (4) The Meghs about 30,000, (5) The Jats about 30,000, (6) Certain lower classes of Hindus have been raised in Kangra, Dalhousie, Hoshiarpur and Ambala Districts. Their number is unknown, (7) The number of those who have been reconverted from Islam and Christianity is not very large. It is going down year by year as conversion of the higher classes to these faiths has very much

---

157. *Ibid.*
158. *Hindustan,* January 6, 1911 in *SVNP, 1911,* p. 35.
159. *Census of India, 1911,* Punjab Report, p. 150.

decreased. To give a rough idea (and this is a pure guess work) the converts from Christianity must be about 2,000 and from Islam about double the number i.e. 4,000.

Referring to the social composition of the Arya Samaj on the basis of castes, a Census Report mentions:[160]

> The movement originated amongst the higher castes such as Brahman, Khatri and Baniya; and it is they who formed the bulk of the Aryas in 1901. A large proportion however of the new adherents of the Samaj are Meghs and other men of low caste, who are admitted as "clean", after going through a ceremony of purification known as *Shuddhi*. In certain districts of the Punjab, three-fifths of the Meghs and nearly half the Ods returned themselves as Aryas, while of the Khatris only 8 per cent, did so, of the Kayasthas 4, and of the Brahmans, Agarwals and Rajputs only 1 per cent. There is a special society which works under the auspices of the Samaj for raising the depressed classes in this way, and for converting Muhammadans and Christians to "Hinduism."

However, during the second decade of the twentieth century, the *shuddhi* movement suddenly reached a stage of animated suspension only to be revived after 1920. On the basis of internal evidence of the Arya Samaj we can logically presume that the efforts to purify the lower castes had led to internal dissensions among the two wings of the Arya Samaj movement i.e. the conservative and liberals—the former against and the latter for the purification of the low caste.[161]

The Arya's efforts on behalf of *shuddhi* created social difficulties as most of them retained binding relations with

---

160. *Census of India, 1911*, India Report, p. 124.
161. During this period the numerical strength of Christianity rose from 38 lacs in 1911 to 47 lacs in 1921. For reference, see Ganga Prasad Upadhayaya, *Ishai Mat ki Alochna*, Tract No. 15 (Prayag: Arya Samaj, Chowk, 1942), pp. 3-4.

their own caste brotherhood (*biradari*) while being members of the Arya Samaj. Undertaking of commensal relations with newly purified persons of a different caste or ritual status could endanger their standing in their own caste brotherhood. Therefore, many Aryas opposed extensive *shuddhi* efforts.[162] Even the militant Aryas who subscribed in theory to Swami Dayanand's belief that caste should not be considered a matter of status ascribed by birth but rather should be viewed as a status dependent upon a combination of qualities, actions and attitudes (*guna, karma* and *swabhava*), did not find it easy to behave consistently in accordance with that theory.[163]

A peep into the external factors for making the movement dormant during this period may also be referred to here. One, the growing revolutionary ferment due to the Peasant Agitation of 1907, assassination of Sir William Curzon Wyllie in England in 1909 by Madan Lal Dhingra, Delhi Conspiracy Case of 1912 in which attempt was made on the life of Lord Harding, the Ghadr Movement and the Lahore Conspiracy Case radicalized political atmosphere which also diverted the attention of the Arya Samajists from social work to freedom struggle. Two, the clouds of international crisis hovering on the European horizon and finally the start of the First World War, particularly the declaration of War against Turkey, strengthened the anti-imperialist forces while simultaneously dissolving the communal antipathy. Both external and internal factors largely contributed to in keeping social catalysts dormant, only to become reactive in the following decade.

162. James Reid Graham, *op. cit.*, p. i.
163. *Ibid.*

4

Development of Shuddhi Movement: The Second Phase (1920-1947)

After the First World War the political ferment in the Central Punjab due to the Rowlatt Acts and the Jallianwala Bagh massacre, then the Khilafat movement and finally the Non-cooperation movement kept the people involved deeply in the freedom struggle. But a drastic change in the attitude of the Arya Samajists was brought about by the Moplah rebellion in 1921-22.[1] The Moplahs of the Malabar Coast[2] after having been induced to join the Khilafat and non-violent Non-cooperation movement of the Congress, undertook to overthrow law and order in their region, and attacked not

---

1. Gail Minault, *The Khilafat Movement: Religious Symbolism and Political Mobilization in India* (Delhi: Oxford University Press, 1982), p. 167.
2. "The Moplahs were a band of fanatic Muslims, poor and ignorant about a million in number," writes R.C. Majumdar. He further describes them as the descendents of the Arabs who had come to settle on the Malabar Coast about eighth or ninth century A.D. and married mostly Indian women. *The History and Culture of the Indian People* (Bombay: Bhartiya Vidya Bhavan, 1978), Vol. XI, p. 360. Aso see *Census of India, 1901*, India Report, p. 385.

only government officials and public property but proceeded to the most savage attacks on the Hindus, destruction of their temples and forcible conversion to Islam.[3] Many Hindus were killed and others to avoid death allowed themselves to be converted.[4] Writing about the atrocities committed by the Moplahs on the Hindus, M.R. Jambunathan, an Arya Samajist, comments:[5]

> The terrible havoc wrought upon the poor Hindus took such a cruel and blood curding shape that people were forced to pass the whole night in jungles and they had to fill the mouths of the children with clothes that they may not cry out. Pregnant women were forced to give birth to their children in the forests, husbands were murdered and tortured before their wives, and rape and adultry was committed upon poor women.

The Moplah rebellion sent a shock wave throughout the country particularly among the Arya Samajists of Punjab who sharply reacted. For them the Non-cooperation movement became secondary as against saving their community from communal carnage. It consolidated the ranks of the Hindus.[6]

3. *Home Deptt. Poll.*, File No. 201 of 1923, p. 4. Also see H.N. Mitra (ed.), *The Annual Register*, 1922-23 (Calcutta: The Annual Register Office, 1923), p. 71. It reports that "even Mr. Montague, Secretary of State for India, agreed in the House of Commons on 25 October 1921 that there had been a considerable number of forcible conversions of Hindus to Muhammadanism."
4. *Ibid.*, File No. 241/XII of 1921, p. 7. The Hindus were charged of having assisted the local authorities in quelling the disturbances by many Muslim scholars. For reference, see Mushirul Hasan, *Nationalism and Communal Politics in India, 1916-1928* (New Delhi: Manohar Publication, 1979), p. 246.
5. M.R. Jambunathan, "The Malabar Reconstruction" in *The Vedic Magazine*, June 1922, p. 553. For the names of those Moplahs who were concerned in the forcible conversion of several Hindus and their families, see *Home Deptt. Poll.*, File No. 156/II of 1924, p. 4.
6. Bhai Parmanand, *Hindu Sangathan*, tr. from Hindi by Lal Chand Dhawan (Lahore: The Central Hindu Yuvak Sabha, 1936), p. 151. Also see Ganga Prasad Upadhyaya, *Arya Samaj* (Muttra: Dayanand's First Birth-Centenary Committee, Vik. 1981), p. 142.

Even this shock made the orthodox Hindus willing to accept the *shuddhi* policy and the methods of Arya Samaj, although a few years earlier it had accused the Arya Samajists of offending Hinduism by readmitting those who had left it.[7] Immediately the question arose whether or not such persons forcibly made Muslims against their will could be restored to Hinduism. While the Congress and the Khilafat political leaders who were committed to the slogan of 'Hindu-Muslim Unity' remained unperturbed over the startling effects of the news from South India, the Hindu and the Arya organizations mobilized support to provide material relief to the Hindus affected by the Rebellion and to seek suitable means to restore the forcible converts to their own religious community.[8]

In view of the whole situation Mahatma Hans Raj, an active member of the *shuddhi* campaign, and the then President of the Arya Pradeshik Pratinidhi Sabha, Punjab, took this matter into his hand. About the beginning of the Arya Samaj involvement, he writes:[9]

> It was Dewan Radha Krishan (an Arya Samajist) who first collected press cuttings from Bombay papers and sent them on to me with a request that I should do something to relieve the sufferings of the Hindus in Malabar.

He was not optimistic about the large-scale Arya efforts on their behalf, both because of the physical and cultural distance

---

7. Gene Robert Thursby, "Aspects of Hindu-Muslim Relations in British India: A Study of Arya Samaj Activities, Government of India Policies, and Communal Conflict in the period 1923-1928," Unpublished Ph. D. Dissertation, Duke University, 1972, p. 34.
8. Sukumar Sarkar, "The British Attitude towards the Moplah Uprising of 1921" in *Indian History Congress Proceedings*, 33rd Session, Muzaffarpur, 1972, p. 494.
9. Sri Ram Sharma, *Mahatma Hansraj: Maker of the Modern Punjab* (Jullundur: Arya Pradeshik Pratinidhi Sabha, Punjab, 1965), p. 114. (Hereafter quoted as *Mahatma Hansraj*).

between the Punjab and South India and also because the political atmosphere of the time did not seem conducive to the success of such a project. However, on September 21, 1921, during the anniversary celebration of the Simla Arya Samaj, he held an informal consultation on the matter at which several men from Madras were present to offer information and advice. Even though the South Indian consultants were not very hopeful about the Arya Samaj participation in reconversion activities in Malabar, Hans Raj decided to move forward with a two-fold programme of material aid and *shuddhi*.[10] On October 16, 1921 the Punjab Arya Pradeshik Pratinidhi Sabha met under his direction and resolved to help and to reclaim the forcibly converted Hindus of Malabar.[11] Thereupon, Lala Hans Raj issued an appeal for funds so that the work could proceed on a scale appropriate to the need. In part, his appeal stated:[12]

> ...Malabar is the home of untouchability and people there are steeped in several kinds of superstitions. It is possible that some caste-groups should offer opposition to the reclamation work. It is necessary, therefore, that some scholarly lovers of their religion should be there as soon as the material law is withdrawn, console the afflicated and wake the caste-groups to their duty so that they might become ready to reclaim them.

On November 1, 1921, Lala Hans Raj instructed another Arya Samajist Pandit Rishi Ram to go to Malabar. He was helped by Lala Khushal Chand who followed him.[13]

On reaching Malabar in the end of 1921, Pandit Rishi Ram began to publish and circulate pamphlets for the purpose of gaining popular support for the reclamation efforts.[14] But

10. *Ibid.*, p. 115.
11. *Ibid.*
12. Gene Robert Thursby, *op. cit.*, p. 35.
13. Sri Ram Sharma, *Mahatma Hansraj*, p. 117.
14. *Arya Mitra*, January 12, 1922, p. 38.

mere propaganda was not enough as the public was rather more tradition bound than it was in the Punjab particularly with regard to caste observances and the experience of purity and pollution. So, in addition, it was necessary to gain the support of traditional elite, such as the local arbiters of tradition, authoritative ritual specialists and ruling princes and great landowners of the area. Without their support, approval and participation, the *shuddhi* rites performed by the Arya Samaj were unlikely to be sufficient to make it legitimate for a caste to accept back forcible converts into full fellowship.[15] Therefore, Raja of Calicut was persuaded to call a large meeting of Namudri pundits to decide the future status of the forced converts, and a series of explanations for the specified offences was drawn up. As illustrations we may refer to the fact that for offences like cutting the tuft, repeating the *Kalima,* earboring of women and wearing Moplah jacket, the victim was to take *panchagavya* (five products of the cow: milk, ghee, curd, urine and dung) three days at any temple, to make whatever offerings they can and to repeat Narayan or Shiva at least 3,000 times every day. Circumcision and cohabitation as above, but for 12 days the prayers are to be repeated 12,000 times a day. Eating food cooked by Moplahs: wash sins off in holy Sethu; get certificate to that effect, and observe as in 1 and 2 for 41 days repeating sacred name 12,000 times per day.[16] After the procedure of reconversion was drawn up, the converted families were brought to Calicut and other safe places and readmitted to Hinduism with the result that the local gentlemen who were doubtful of re-admission took greater interest in the matter and advocated their re-admission in their respective circles of influence. Even after re-admission whenever any objection was raised by the orthodox people about giving equal treatment to the re-admitted persons, the Arya Samaj workers were sent to explain matters and to persuade the people to treat them as before the rebellion.[17] It is

15. Gene Robert Thursby, *op. cit.* p. 39.
16. James Reid Graham, "The Arya Samaj as a Reformation in Hinduism with special reference to Caste," Unpublished Ph. D. Dissertation, Yale University, 1942, p. 508.
17. *Ibid.*

interesting to note that in Malabar the Arya Samaj and the orthodoxy worked in close co-operation.[18] But for their co-operation, the reformers could have not successfully accomplished the work of purification of the forcibly converted people and their restoration of their caste privileges.[19] The bold effort of the Arya Samaj and consequent success in their efforts not only helped in the process of consolidation from within as co-operation of the orthodoxy removed to a large extent dissensions within the Hindu society but also provided an opportunity to the Arya movement to develop in South India. In the north it once again enhanced the prestige of the Arya Samaj and encourged to moblize its resources for social work particularly raising of funds for the *shuddhi* cause. By October 1922, the Arya Pradeshik Pratinidhi Sabha of the Punjab under Lala Hans Raj had collected a total of more than 70,000 rupees for the Malabar work. Before the momentum from this effort was lost, Swami Shraddhanand utilized it to begin *shuddhi* campaign in northern India and to make it a major effort which would drawn even broader support from the Hindu community.[20]

From the time of Rowlatt Satyagraha in 1919, Swami Shraddhanand was active in Indian National Congress, and during the Non-cooperation period he was drawn increasingly into concern for the status of Hindu untouchables.[21] In the Congress, the uplift of the untouchable was one of the cardinal purposes for which the Swaraj Fund, collected in the memory of B.G. Tilak who died in 1920, was to be used. But the Congress leaders, including Mahatma Gandhi, did not attach much importance to this problem as they were occupied with

18. R.K., Ghai, "Moplah Rebellion and the Arya Samaj" in *Punjab History Conference Proceedings*, 19th Session, Patiala, 1984, pp. 385-98.
19. N.B. Sen (ed.), *Punjab's Eminent Hindus* (Lahore: New Book Society, 1943), p. 113.
20. Gene Robert Thursby, *op. cit.*, p. 42.
21. K.N. Kapur, *Swami Shraddhanand* (Jullundur City: Arya Pratinidhi Sabha, 1979), p. 108.
22. *All India Congress Committee Proceedings*, File No. 10 of 1922, (NMML), p. 1. (Hereafter quoted as *AICC*).

other matters during Non-cooperation movement. Swami Shraddhanand, however, remained committed to the cause of the uplift of the untouchables. He became so impatient with the Congress attitude of indifference to the matter that in one of his letters to the General Secretary, All India Congress Committee, he warned that the question of removal of untouchability was closely linked with the Khadi movement and as such the success of the latter depends on the former. He writes:[22]

> I am of opinion that with a majority of six crores of our brethren set against us by the bureaucracy even the Khadi scheme cannot succeed completely. The members of the working committee, perhaps, did not know that on this side our depressed brethren are leaving the Khaddar and taking to buying cheap foreign cloth.

When the Non-cooperation programme was abruptly suspended by Mahatma Gandhi in early 1922, and the Congress was free from their political activities, Swami Shraddhanand attempted to gain great support within the organization for his own constructive programme—the uplift of the untouchables was its main feature.[23]

In response to his pressure on the Congress leaders for the constructive work, Swami Shraddhanand was nominated to a sub-committee consisting of four other members which was given the task of drawing up a programme of action for the amelioration of the depressed classes and the untouchables.[24] Finding the arrangements unsatisfactory and the amount of money[25] to be devoted to the work inadequate, he resigned from all the offices which he held in the Congress.[26] After his resignation from the Congress he was arrested in

23. K.N. Kapur, *op. cit.*, p. 110.
24. *AICC*, File No. 10 of 1922, p. 4. The other three members were Sarojini Naidu, Shri Ganga Ram Deshpande and Shri Indu Lal Yagnik. For reference, see K.N. Kanpur, *op. cit.*, p. 111.
25. K.N. Kapur, *op. cit.*, p. 113.
26. *AICC*, File No. 10 of 1922, pp. 15-29.

connection with Guru-ka-Bagh Morcha of the Akalies at Amritsor in September 10, 1922 and was imprisoned till December 22, 1922.[27] Within two months of his release from jail, his attention was drawn to the *shuddhi* work on behalf of a general category of people known as Malkanas. The Malkanas were scattered through a large number of villages in the Mathura, Agra, Etah and Mainpuri districts of the United Provinces of Agra and Oudh.[28] Though they had been under Muslim's religious and cultural influence for centuries yet they had retained many of the Hindu practices. But nearly all the Malkanas reported themselves as Muslims in the decennial Census of 1911. In reality, they considered themselves more Hindus than Muslims. Writing about the background of these Malkanas, the Census Commissioner reportes:[29]

> These are converted Hindus of various castes belonging to Agra and the adjoining districts, chiefly Muttra, Etah and Mainpuri. They are of Rajput, Jat and Bania descent. They are reluctant to describe themselves as Musalmans, and generally give their original caste name, and scarcely recognize the name Malkana. Their names are Hindu; they mostly worship in Hindu temples; they use the salutation Ram, Ram; they intermarry amongst themselves only. On the other hand, they sometimes frequent a mosque, practise circumcision and bury their dead; they will eat with Muhammadans if they are particular friends; they prefer to be addressed as Mian Thakur. They admit that they are neither Hindus nor Muhammadans, but a mixture of both. . . .

Since they were converted from among the Hindus and had retained many of the Hindu socio-religious practices, particularly the caste system, they received the attention of the early Hindu reformers. During the middle of the first decade of the

27. J.T.F. Jordens, *Swami Shraddhanand : His Life and Causes* (Delhi : Oxford University Press, 1981), pp. 127-29.
28. *The Vedic Magazine*, December 1922, p. 616.
29. *Census of India, 1911*, India Report, p. 118.

twentieth century a few feeble attempts were made to restore social relations between the Malkanas and the Hindus of like status and for that purpose the Rajput Shuddhi Sabha was established in 1909 for encouraging the establishment of commensal and marriage relations between the Malkanas and particularly the Hindu Rajput caste fellowship (*biradaries*).[30] As already noted, this Sabha remained into existence only for a year, but it did succeed in reconverting some of them to the fold of Hinduism.[31] During the second decade of the century the movement became inactive, apparently because it was unable to overcome the general reluctance of the Hindu Rajputs to establish effective and lasting networks of relationship with the purified Malkanas. It was not until 1922 after the Moplah rebellion that the influential Hindu Rajputs became sufficiently interested in the *shuddhi* of Malkanas.

After dissociating himself from the Congress, Swami Shraddhanand made final arrangements through the Sarvadeshik Sabha of the Arya Samaj for a great campaign for the uplift of depressed classes and the untouchables. The Sabha approved the establishment of an organization—the Dalitoddhar Mandal.[32] To achieve the purpose, Swami Shraddhanand was authorised by the Sabha to collect 1,00,000 rupees and to begin his work in early February 1923. In a public notice about the campaign he stated :[33]

30. *Home Deptt. Poll.*, File No. 198 of 1924, p. 24.
31. *Arya Directory*. (Delhi: Sarvdeshik Arya Pratinidhi Sabha, 1998 Vik.), p. 196.
32. Dalitoddhar Mandal means a society for the welfare of the downtrodden and untouchables. The Editor of the *Arya*, Lahore, June 1923 at pp 16-17 writes that though the lower castes were being *shuddh* (purify) by the Mandal but it had not got much success in the *Bhangi* (chuhras) of the Punjab especially in the district of Gurdaspur and Sialkot. Indra Vidyavachispati in his *Arya Samaj Itihas* at p. 249 writes that "for Dalitoddhar in the beginning the word *shuddhi* was used. But latter on it was realised that these two words had different meaning, the word Dalitoddhar came into use."
33. *The Leader*, February 7, 1923, p. 4.

Noticing even Congress powerless to absorb the so-called untouchables, I have made it the sole mission of my remaining life. I appeal to all Hindu Aryas, irrespective of religious or political differences who do not like their six crore (i.e. 60,000,000) brethren to be out away from their community, to help me with money and men.

Swami Shraddhanand's efforts for the uplift of untouchables were facilitated by the resolution of the Kshatriya Upkarni Mahasabha which met on August 30, 1922[34] deciding to reconvert all those Rajput Hindus in their original Rajput sub-castes who had been converted during the time of Aurangzeb.[35] This resolution was finally endorsed by this Sabha which met on December 31, 1922 under the Chairmanship of Sir Nahar Singh of Shahpura.[36] These resolutions when given wide publicity created a stir among the Muslims, particularly the Punjabi Muslims. They raised all type of means to stop this reconversion. A correspondent writing to the *Zamindar* avers that "the forcible conversion of Mussalmans to the Arya faith will prove most injurious to the interest of Hindu-Muslim unity.[37] "The Muslim *maulvis*," writes Bhai Parmanand, "continued to incite the *Malkanas* for a long time saying that the Arya Samajists were uplifting *chamars*, that they would convert them (Malkanas) also and make them accept food at the hands of those *chamars*."[38] Moreover, the Muslims sent their own missionaries to persuade the Malkanas

34. "On August 30, 1922, Kshatriya Upkarni Mahasabha decided at Kashi under the Presidentship of Raja Sir Rampal Singh to take back Hindu Rajputs who at one time or another turned Muslims." Swami Chidananda Sanayasi, *Shuddhi Vyavastha* (Delhi: Bhartiya Hindu Shuddhi Sabha, 1983 Vik.), p. 12.

35. Sri Ram Sharma, "Swami Dayanand and Shuddhi," Unpublished article in the possession of Professor Bhawani Lal Bharti, Head, Swami Dayanand Chair, Panjab University, Chandigarh, p. 3. (Hereafter quoted as *Swami Dayanand and Shuddhi*). Also see *Arya Directory*, p. 196.

36. Sri Ram Sharma, *Mahatma Hansraj*, p. 203.

37. *Zamindar*, March 7, 1923 in *Punjab Press Abstract*, *1923*, p. 145 (NAI).

38. Bhai Parmanand, *op. cit.*, pp. 184-85.

not to abandon their religion. These missionaries even preached to the Hindu Rajputs to keep the Malkanas out.[39] But in both these attempts, they had to stage a retreat, as the Malkanas themselves "did not respond to their efforts to convert them into conforming Musalmans."[40] Commenting upon the work done by the Muslims in this regard, the *Muslim Outlook* of Lahore writes :[41]

> The dilatoriness displayed by Muslims in the matter of Rajput apostasy is most disgraceful. While Hindus, both orthodox and hetrodox, are straining every nerve to bring the Rajputs into their fold, the Mussalmans are still occupied with concerting measures only....Threats of eviction of Malkanas who are in the clutches of Hindu *banias* and of violence of the Massalman preachers who try to approach other co-religionists are being freely resorted to and to add insult to injury, now lies have begun to be telegraphed to the effect that it is the Mussalmans who are threatening violence.

To evolve a strategy and organization to counter the challenge of Muslim missionaries, about 85 Hindu representatives of all shades and beliefs held a meeting at Agra on February 13, 1923.[42] Since Swami Shraddhanand was so well associated with that case, he was included among those invited to participate in the deliberations and discuss the prospects for *shuddhi*.[43] As a result of these deliberations in which Swami Shraddhanand took active part, an organization with the name 'Bharatiya Hindu Shuddhi Sabha' was founded with its head-

---

39. Sri Ram Sharma, *Mahatma Hansraj*, p. 204.

40. *Ibid.*

41. *Muslim Outlook*, March 11, 1923 in *Punjab Press Abstract, 1923*, p. 145.

42. Swami Chidananda Saraswati, "Shuddhi ka Naya Daur" in *Shraddhanand*, November 1954, p. 6.

43. *Ibid.* Also see Gene Robert Thursby, *op. cit.*, p. 48.

quarters at Agra.[44] Swami Shraddhanand accepted its Presidentship while Lala Hans Raj was named its first Vice-President.[45] The new joint organization of the conservative Hindu and the Arya Samajists in itself suggests that the orthodoxy had reconciled in the matter of *shuddhi* with the Arya Samaj. But it certainly caused internal dissensions among the Aryas as some of them believed that change was rather superfluous. Those who were being reclaimed, in their opinion, were simply being removed from one form of false religion and placed in another without any change of heart or conviction. For them orthodox Hinduism, with its emphasis upon image worship, caste destinctions by birth, and other superstitions seemed as remote as Islam from religious truth, and they found unwarranted the efforts of the Suddhi Sabha to reclaim people from the one to the other. As a result there were Aryas who refused to cooperate with the Sabha-they either withheld their support altogether or sought to encourage institution of an Arya-Vedic mode of purification.[46] The collaborative efforts of the orthodox Hindus and the puritanic Arya Samajists invited the reaction as some of the Hindus believed that *shuddhi* was untraditional and improper. There were still others who were uncomfortably acting in concert with the Aryas and, only a month after the establishment of the Bharatiya Hindu Shuddhi Sabha, they, the orthodox Aryas, began their own parallel organization—*The Punah-Samskar Samiti*.[47] At this juncture when the Hindus could ill-afford any division reached a compromise and the internal wrangling was avoided from growing into an open schism only when these two organizations divided the territories

44. *Bharatiya Hindu Shuddhi Sabha ka Sankshipt Itihas tatha Vivran (1923 to 1950)* (New Delhi: Bharatiya Hindu Shuddhi Sabha, n.d.), p. 1. Also see Sri Ram Sharma, *Swami Dayanand and Shuddhi*, p. 3.
45. Bharatiya Hindu Shuddhi Sabha: *Pratham Varshik Report* (Agra: Shanti Press, 1980 Vik.), pp. 1-2, and 4. Also see N.B. Sen, *op. cit.*, p. 113.
46. Gene Robert Thursby, *op. cit.*, p. 53.
47. According to Swami Dayanand, President, *Punah-Samskar Samiti*, it is a society for reclamation of the besighted Malkanas. For reference, see his article "The Psychology of Hindu-Muslim Unity" in *The Vedic Magazine*, July 1923, p. 715.

their respective work of *shuddhi*.[48] It may also be pointed out that the *shuddhi* work of Swami Shraddhanand was considerably eased by a resolution of the Hindu Mahasabha, a national political organization of the Hindus, held at Banaras on August 19, 1923.[49] By this resolution the Executive Committee was directed to "appoint a sub-committee of men learned in Hindu Shastras to consider with due regard to the needs of the present time, how and to what exten the idea (of *shuddhi*) could be translated into action...."[50] The question of untouchability was also referred to the sub-committee for framing of the rules and regulations "to secure for the members of the so-called untouchable classes, access to public meetings, drinking wells, temples and public schools."[51]

The sub-committee pondered on the question of *shuddhi* and untouchability and formulated its recommendations which were passed in the special session of Hindu Mahasabha held at Allahabad on February 5, 1924.[52] Contrary to the spirit and letter of the original resolution which recommended that efforts should be made for educating the untouchables, giving them access to public schools, to temples and to public wells, reservation was expressed "that it was against the scriptures and the tradition to give the untouchables 'yajyapavit', to teach them Vedas and to interdine with them, and the Mahasabha hoped that workers in the interest of unity would give up these items and social reform."[53] In the matter of *shuddhi* also a similar

---

48. Bharatiya Hindu Shuddhi Sabha: *Pratham Varshik Report*, pp. 2-3. The *Calcutta Samachar* of November 24, 1923 at p. 4 writes that *Punah Samskar Samiti* and Shuddhi Sabhas, two different institutions, were busy in reconverting the Malkana Rajputs.
49. *Amrita Bazar Patrika*, August 21, 1923, p. 4. Also see *The Leader*, August 24, 1923, p. 5 and *The Calcutta Samachar*, August 23, 1923, p. 3.
50. *The Calcutta Samachar*, August 25, 1923, p. 6.
51. *The Leader*, November 12, 1923, p. 5.
52. *Ibid.*, February 8, 1924, p. 5.
53. *Ibid.* For more references, see Satish Kumar Sharma, "Shuddhi— A Case Study of Role of a Religious Movement in the Status Improvement of Untouchables" in *Indian Journal of Social Research*, Vol. XXIV, No. 1, April 1983, pp. 70-77.

kind of reservation was expressed. It advised that "any non-Hindu was welcome to enter the fold of Hinduism, though he could not be taken into any caste."[54] But the passing of the resolutions for the eradication of untouchability and *shuddhi* greatly strengthened Swami Shraddhanand's hand, "who notwithstanding the fact that there has not always been much love lost between the orthodox Hindus and the Arya Samaj owing to religious differences, utilized the opportunity to his advantage."[55] The Hindu Mahasabha was not the only body which sanctioned the *shuddhi* programme of the Samaj at that time, but there were many other organizations such as Vidvat Parishad of Kashi, the Bharat Dharma Mahamandal, the Bengal Brahman Sabha, Maharashtra Hindu Dharm Parishad,[56] Bharat Sevashram Sangh, Vishwa Hindu Parished and the Masurashram, Bombay[57] which endorsed it. The U.P. Social Conference held on August 24, 1923 passed the following resolution :[58]

> This conference accords its whole-hearted support to the Shuddhi Movement now in progress in different parts of the country.

After getting the support of these Sabhas and Mandals, Swami Shraddhanand initiated his campaign by "converting *chamars* to the Arya Samaj and urged that the Hindus should allow them the use of all wells and places of worship without any let or hindrance."[59]

54. *Ibid.*
55. *Home Deptt. Poll.*, File No. 6/IX of 1924, p. 17.
56. J.F. Seunarine, *Reconversion to Hinduism through Suddhi* (Madras: The Christian Literature Society, 1977), p. 37.
57. Brahmachari Vishwanathji, *The Shuddhi Movement : Its Objectives and Difficulties*, A speech delivered at the All-India Hindu Religious Conference, Kumbha Mela, Ailahabad on January 16, 1977, p. 10.
58. *The Leader*, August 27, 1923, p. 5.
59. *Home Deptt. Poll.*, File No. 6/IX of 1924, p. 17. Also see File No. 206 of 1926, para 7.

The Bharatiya Hindu Shuddhi Sabha soon started a campaign of reclaiming the Malkana Rajputs, Jats, and Gujar Mussalmans of Meerut, Agra, Mathura, Mainpuri, Etah, Etawah, in the then United Provinces and Karnal, Ambala, Rohtak and Hissar in the then Punjab.[60] Resourceful as he was, Swami Shraddhanand collected funds and mobilized people, and as a result many Malkanas, Moole Gujars and Jats were reconverted to Hinduism.[61] According to the available government records, "Swami Shraddhanand and his lieutenants threw themselves into the struggle with great zeal to bring back the non-Muslims in Agra to the fold of Hindu religion...that as many as 300 converts had been obtained from one village alone."[62] *The Calcutta Samachar* reports that from February 26, 1923 to March 13, 1923 about 4500 Malkanas were reconverted by the Bharatiya Hindu Shuddhi Sabha and Rajput Kshatriya Mahasabha in 13 different villages.[63] The same paper reports that uptil March 30, 1923, about 7,000 Malkanas had been purified.[64] The press, particularly of the Punjab played a leading role in boosting the morale of those who were employed in the *shuddhi* work. For instance, the Editor of *Shanti* of Rawalpindi appealed the Hindus "to help the Bharat Hindu Shuddhi Sabha with men and money in the work of bringing Muhammadan Rajputs into the Hindu fold."[65]

These large scale efforts of converting Muslims caused immediate reaction of the Muslim organizations, like the Ahmadiyas of Qadian. Many local Muslim caste Sabhas and large organizations dedicated to the cause of Islamic religious

60. *Ibid.*
61. Swami Shraddhanand, "Shuddhi Hindu Sangathan ki Jaan Hai" in *Shraddhanand*, February 1951, p. 6.
62. *Home Deptt. Poll.*, File No. 6/IX of 1924, p. 17.
63. For full detail of the villages' list, see *The Calcutta Samachar*, March 22, 1923; p. 4.
64. *Ibid.*, March 30, 1923, p. 3.
65. *Shanti*, March 4, 1923 in *Punjab Press Abstracts*, p. 145.

and political life in India such as the Jam'iyat-ul-'ulema-i-Hind and the Central Khilafat Committee also joined the campaign of conversion to counter the Hindu effort in this sphere. The Punjab press, particularly the Muslim papers took the side of the Muslims. The *Zamindar* of Lahore appealed to the Muslims that "all possible efforts should be made to save the Muslim Rajputs of the United Provinces from abjuring Islam."[66] Referring to the proselytizing activities of the Arya Samaj among the Malkana Rajputs in the Agra district, the *Siyasat* of Lahore writes :[67]

> The Hindus should abstain from bringing themselves into conflict with the Mussalmans, who feel most exasperated over interference with their religion. If they do not abandon their present high-handed policy, it will not be possible for the Mussalmans to participate in any (political) movement, the defence of their religion becoming of the foremost importance for them.

The same paper published a letter of one Muhammad Abdullah of Peshawar, who charged the Hindu members of the Congress for taking great interest in this *shuddhi* work. He writes :[68]

> Will the Mussalman remain neglectful even now ? How long will they continue a prey to (Hindu) diplomacy and when will they come to their senses ? They should remember that if the Hindus can undertake this work today India will become worse than to hell and *dar-ul-harab* to them tomorrow and they will be subjected to the sort of treatment which was meted out to their co-religionists in Spain.

The Muslim press even tried, of course in vain, to instigate the Sikh sentiments to serve their purpose. The

---

66. Zamidar March 6, 1923 in *Ibid.*
67. *Siyasat*, March 24, 1923 in *Ibid.*, p. 172.
68. *Ibid.*

Loyal Gazette of Lahore asked the Sikhs "to consider if they immune from the influence that have brought about the reconversion of Malkana Rajputs. They should save their community from the danger by giving up caste restrictions and *chhut* and ceasing to call themselves Aroras, Khatris, etc."[69] But the Sikhs did not immediately respond to the instigation as is evident from the following statement of Lal Singh Akali, the Secretary, Punjab Khalsa Sabha, Samundari, Lyallpur who says :[70]

> The Muslims are agitated over the *shuddhi* of Malkanas and were threatening the Hindus; but the Sikhs would not tolerate any persecution of the Hindus.

However, less than a month after the establishment of the Bharatiya Hindu Shuddhi Sabha, the President of the Jam'iyat-ul-'ulema issued an appeal for workers "who have good morals and preaching experience" and for funds to combat the effects of Swami Shraddhanand's efforts, which he anticipated would cause a half million followers of the Prophet to be "beguiled into becoming renegades."[71] Other Muslim organizations and institutions, schools in particular, cooperated by encouraging volunteers from their own ranks to join the several "deputations" sent out under the aegis of the Jam'iyat. On March 10, 1923 a deputation of fifteen members was sent to Malkana villages to preach and propagate. The appeal for workers clearly stated that they would have to live in villages and engage themselves in preaching Islam and in educating ignorant Muslims. "If needed," in addition, "they shall also have to debate with Aryas."[72]

---

69. *Loyal Gazette*, March 25, 1923 in *Ibid*.
70. Swami Chidananda Sanyasi, *op. cit.*, p. 2. Similar views were expressed by Inder Singh, a leader of the Namdhari movement of the Sikhs. For reference, see *Home Deptt. Poll.*, File No. 198 of 1924, p. 17.
71. *The Leader*, March 12, 1923, p. 7.
72. *Ibid.*, March 24, 1923, p. 10.

Caught in the middle of a pincers of opposing communal interest over the reclamation question, particularly of the Malkana Rajputs, the leaders of the Indian National Congress sought to relieve the intensity of the counter pressures which they apprehended would lead to an open communal confrontation harming the national freedom struggle.[73] The mobilization of men and money for a project which was openly religious and which was certain to provoke inter-religious antagonism among the Hindus and Muslims alike was more perilous for the programme of the Congress. So in April 1923, the Congress Committee "decided that Mr. C.R. Dass, Pandit Moti Lal Nehru, Mrs. Sarojini Naidu and Maulana Abul Kalam Azad should join Swami Shraddhanand in making a tour in the area concerned in order to find out whether the Malkanas were really willing to enter the Hindu fold of their own accord."[74] Although the Committee unanimously conceded "the right of the Hindus to welcome back the Malkanas into their fold" but "they called upon Swami Shraddhanand... to dissociate himself from the movement"[75] presumably to save the Congress from embarrassment. *The Leader* observed that the Committee's report was a document designed for the purpose of drawing a balance between competing claims in the interest of communal harmony.[76]

The Non-cooperation movement had kept the masses involved in the struggle against the government giving little opportunity to the fissiparous to raise their head. But once the movement was withdrawn, these forces got let loose. In the case of the *shuddhi* movement the malicious propaganda of the Hindus and Muslims against each other impelled the Congress, particularly Mahatma Gandhi, to make a big effort

---

73. R.E. Miller, *Mappila Muslims of Kerala: A Study in Islamic Trends* (Bombay: 1976), pp. 124-47.
74. Sri Ram Sharma, *Mahatma Hansraj*, p. 206.
75. *Ibid.*
76. *The Leader*, April 8, 1923, p. 5.

to check it from causing a great communal divide.[77] To pacify them for national unity, Mahatma Gandhi appealed both the parties to desist from rivalry. He said,"if the Malkanas wanted to return to the Hindu fold, they had a perfect right to do so whenever they liked. But no propaganda can be allowed which reviles other religions. For that would be negation of toleration."[78] But contrary to the Congress effort, the conservative elite of both the communities aligned with their respective community interests. In the Muslim camp there was a general belief "that the Maharaja of Kashmere as well as some of the Rajput Hindu Princes in Rajputana have been lending their support in this conversion movement," while on the other hand the Hindus, as is evident from the government records, took a serious "objection to an old *firman* extant in Bhopal whereby apostasy from Islam is a penal offence."[79] Mutual distrust and fear led to a yawning gap between the two communities which frustrated the efforts of the Congress to bridge it.

While the Congress under the leadership of Mahatma Gandhi was making frantic efforts in persuading both the communities to desist from malicious propaganda,[80] the organizational efforts on behalf of *shuddhi* rapidly reached high water mark during the summer. Upto July 1923 "reclamation work has been done in 147 villages and more than thirty thousand Malkanas had been brought back to the Hindu fold."[81] Lala Hans Raj who played a leading role in the reclamation work, went from village to village during the hot

---

77. M.K. Gandhi, *Communal Unity* (Ahmadabad: Navjivan Publishing House, 1949), pp. 56-57.
78. *Young India*, May 29, 1924, pp. 180-81.
79. *Home Deptt. Poll.*, File No. 6/IX of 1924, p. 17.
80. *Harijan*, April 4, 1934, p. 4.
81. Sri Ram Sharma, *Mahatma Hansraj*, p. 219. R.C. Majumdar mentions the number of the converted Malkanas as four and half lakhs. *Op. cit.*, p. 420.

months but had to leave the scene by the middle of July 1923 because of his health.[82] Swami Shraddhanand also announced in September 1923 that the state of his health no longer permitted him "to continue the important work of *shuddhi* with the zeal with which I have been doing it hitherto."[83] He staged an exit from the scene but he never withdrew from this work as in March 1926 he performed a *shuddhi* of a Muslim lady, Asghari Begum and her two children in Delhi.[84] But it can also not be denied that during this period he devoted himself more to the uplift of the untouchables especially in South India than to the *shuddhi* and *sangathan* movements.[85] The exit of these two great leaders, who were first among the champions of the cause of *shuddhi*, was bound to adversely affect the *shuddhi* movement. Nonetheless, the organizational work, which was being carried on under the auspices of Bhartiya Hindu Shuddhi Sabha, achieved a great success in the field. It is reported that the Shuddhi Sabha had purified, since its inception in 1923 to March 1931 about 1,83,342 persons.[86] There are numerous references to reconversions which took place at various places in India during 1929-30 which indicate the *shuddhi* movement in the cases of individuals[87] and small groups continued even after 1930s.

82. *Ibid*.
83. *Bande Mataram*, September 22, 1923, in *Selections from the Vernacular Newspapers published in the Punjab, 1923*, p. 512. (Hereafter quoted as *SVNP*).
84. *The Leader*, October 2, 1926, p. 5.
85. J.T.F. Jordens, *Swami Shraddhanand: His Life and Causes* (New Delhi: Oxford University Press, 1981), pp. 130-67.
86. *Arya Directory*, p. 198.
87. The most significant example is that of Hiralal Gandhi (Abdulla Gandhi) son of Mahatma Gandhi who had been converted to Islam and was reconverted by the Bombay Arya Samaj. *Modern Review*, Vol. LX, December 1936, p. 725. Also see Lakhan Singh, *Shuddhi ek purai karya* (Aligarh: Bhartiya Vedic Siddhant Parishad, 2030 Vik.), p. 9. Also see Appendix-II.

According to an official paper of the Bhartiya Hindu Shuddhi Sabha, Delhi about 42,150 persons were purified from 1931 to 1947 by this Sabha alone.[88] *Arya* of Lahore mentions that at Sialkot 500 Dooms, 1300 *chamars*, etc. were purified during the year 1926.[89] The same paper reports that about 12,000 persons were purified during the year 1925.[90] According to the Census Reports about 62,844 converts from Muslims, Christians and tribal religions were added to Hinduism during the year 1927-28.[91] Moreover, under the supervision of Swami Vinayak Maharaj Masurkar, the founder of Masurashram at Bombay about 10,000 Gaon Christians were reconverted on February 26, 1928 "within the territory of Goa itself under the very nose of the Portuguese Government and Christian Church."[92] *Dharam Vir* of Sukkur mentions that 61 Khojas were converted to Hinduism by the Hindu Sabha, Bombay in December 1928.[93] The activities of the Sabha continued upto the early 1930s, when this Sabha was further divided into two—Bhartiya Hindu Shuddhi Sabha and Akhil Bhartiya Shraddhanand Shuddhi Sabha—the latter being established on April 29, 1934.[94] After it the *shuddhi* became almost redundant for it appeared only in stray cases. At least, socially its relevance began to dwindle as all the communities became highly conscious, and the movement began to gradually melt into the Hindu communal consciousness.[95] However, as claimed by the Bhartiya Hindu Shuddhi Sabha

88. *Shuddhi Samachar*, March 1, 1985, p. 2.
89. *Arya*, June 1926, pp. 16-67.
90. *Ibid*.
91. *Census of India, 1931*, India Report, p. 387.
92. "Masurashram (A Socio-Cultural Institution working in different fields from last 65 years)", a pamphlet issued by Masurashram, Goregaon (East), Bombay.
93. *Dharam Vir*, December 15, 1928, p. 5.
94. *Arya Directory*, p. 199. This Sabha claimed to have converted 6,553 persons from the date of its inception to 1940. For reference, see *Ibid.*, p. 202.
95. R.K. Ghai, "Shuddhi Movement: Its Explanation" in *Punjab History Conference Proceedings*, 17th Session, March 12-14, 1982, p. 251.

and from the figures given below, if the figures are accepted as valid, that the *shuddhi* campaign continued even after 1934:[96]

Details of shuddhis from 1934 to 1947

Year	Shuddhis performed
1934-35	9,719
1935-36	2,194
1936-37	2,165
1937-38	2,004
1938	1,000
1939	1,734
1940	1,977
1941	2,000
1942	1,000
1943	4,435
1944	2,046
1945	2,000
1946	2,827
1947	3,347

The Arya Samajists under Swami Shraddhanand and Lala Hans Raj, no doubt, obtained great success in the field of *shuddhi*, but it was obvious that this success would not leave the Muhammadans unmoved to violent reaction of the Muslims. Writing on it Bhai Parmanand observed:[97]

96. Reproduced from *Shuddhi Samachar*, March 1, 1985, p. 2. Also see *Bharatiya Hindu Shuddhi Sabha Delhi ka Sankshipt itihas tatha vivran*, pp. 1-2.
97. Bhai Parmanand, *op. cit.*, p., 184. For similar views, see *The Tribune*, March 29, 1923, p. 4.

As soon as Hindus began a campaign for the uplift of the depressed and to welcome back into their fold their strayed brethren, the Muslims lost their temper. In spite of the fact that they claim, and very proudly, too, that Islam preaches equality of men, when Hindus began to accord equal rights to their untouchables in matters of social intercourse and interdining, the Muslims at various places became ready to break their heads and commit riots. They could not tolerate the raising of the status of *chamars* and others by Hindus. This was the root-cause of the riots at Meerut and other places.

The Muslims gradually realised the wider political significance of a nominally religious movement as it had begun to woo away the masses.[98] In order to understand the larger context of the *shuddhi* movement and its contribution to Hindu-Muslim conflict, we must examine briefly its broader programme of Hindu consolidation i.e. the *sangathan*.

The *sangathan*, meaning unification, integration, or consolidation was closely related to the Hindu Sabha movement which got its start in the early years of the twentieth century as something of a Hindu counterpart to the Muslim League.[99] Tracing its origin Lala Lajpat Rai writes:[100]

> The Sangathan movement also (or to call it by its proper name, the Hindu Sabha movement) represents an old idea. The object was present in the mind of the Arya Samaj. But the Samaj signally failed to realise it.... I remember that... a Hindu Sabha was formed at the house of Raja Harbans Singh of Shekupura in Lahore. That Sabha died in its infancy. Then the movement was revived towards the end of the last century at the house

---

98. *Home Deptt. Poll.*, File No. 206 of 1926, p. 18.
99. D.C. Gupta, *Indian National Movement and Constitutional Development* (Delhi: Vikas Publishing House, Pvt. Ltd., 1976), p. 50.
100. Lajpat Rai, "The Hindu-Muslim Problem" in *The Tribune*, December 13, 1924, p. 7.

of the late Lala Balmokand, Rais, Lahore. Even this organization, however, remained almost lifeless while the late R.B. Lal Chand put life into it. But somehow or other, the movement never took root. It has benefited individual members, but it has done no good to the Hindu community as a whole. It has two formidable rivals: on the political side the Indian National Congress, on the socio-religious side, the Arya Samaj.

However, the movement was strong in provinces where Muslims were an important factor in political life—Punjab, Bengal and the United Provinces. In the light of the special provisions for Muslims in the constitutional reforms granted by the British, Lala Lal Chand wrote a series of letters to the Editor of *Panjabee* in 1908-09, which were subsequently published in the book form entitled *Self-Abnegation in Politics* in which he urged the Hindus to consolidate themselves for their own interest. In one of his letters he states:[101]

> I also intended and I have evidently succeeded partly to instil into the Hindu mind what some people choose to call sectarianism; but which I regard as the very breath of life, viz., that a Hindu should not only believe but make it a part and parcel of his organism, of his life and of his conduct, that he is a Hindu first and an Indian after. Here I wish to reverse the dominant idea propounded by the Congress that we are Indian first and Hindus next, and that even if need should be.

In spite of Lal Chand's rejection of the fundamental principle and article of faith of Indian National Congress, the annual sessions of the All India Hindu Mahasabha were held at the same time and place as the annual sessions of the Congresss during most of the second decade of the century. But the events which occurred in Malabar and in Multan in 1921 and 1922 respectively,[102] which were recalled freshly in

---

101. R.B. Lal Chand, *Self-Abnegation in Politics* (Lahore: The Central Hindu Yuvak Sabha, 1938), p. 70.
102. *Census of India, 1931*, Punjab Report, p. 21.

the press time and again, provided the Hindu community a general rationale to consolidate themselves. "Events in Malabar and Multan have opened the eyes of the Hindus," stated the *Hindustan*, "who have begun to realize that they cannot live unless they organize themselves."[103] To the charges that *shuddhi* and *sangathan* were the main reasons why Hindu-Muslim unity had transformed into Hindu-Muslim enmity within the time space of two or three years Swami Shraddhanand squarely put the onus on the Muslims. He wrote:[104]

> The Muslim aggression on Hindus in Malabar and Multan are the main reasons for this enmity. It is true that *shuddhi* is a cause of Muslim dissatisfaction, but the Muslims are responsible for it. Muslims think that they are made to do the beating and Hindus are for beating. The incidents at Malabar and Multan hurt the Hindus very much. Muslim leaders of the civil disobedience movement like Maulana Hasrat Mohini and Maulana Azad Subhani declared that the Moplahs were not guilty of any aggression…. The present enmity is not due to Hindus. Its cause is the Muslims. Many of the Muslim religious leaders have said in their speeches that the snake and the mongoose can be friends, but there can be no unity between Hindu Kaffirs and Muslims.

When asked to indicate the way out from the impasse of Hindu-Muslim antipathy, Swami Shraddhanand finding no solution for harmony and unity stated that the only way out was "to remove this enmity is to organize ihe Hindus and to make them the strongest."[105] Reiterating him Bhai Parmanand suggested:[106]

103. Serious Hindu-Muslim riots took place at Multan in September 1922 in consequence of a dispute between the two communities arising out of the Muharram procession. Vijaya Chandra Joshi (ed.), *Lala Lajpat Rai: Writings and Speeches 1920-28* (Delhi: University Publishers, 1966), Vol. II, p. 479.
104. *Aj*, July 24, 1923, pp. 6-7.
105. *Ibid.*
106. Bhai Parmanand, *op. cit.*, pp. 190-91.

Hindu Sabhas should be set up at various places to organize the Hindus; the social evils prevalent among the Hindus, that is, those bad customs that tend to weaken them should be eradicated; interest in physical exercise should be created among them. Hindu young men should be trained to, and encouraged to adopt both the brain and brawn. The Hindus should accord equality to those of their brethren who happen to occupy a low position in society. And above all they should start the *shuddhi* campaign in right earnest in order to put a stop to the conversion of Hindus to other religions. These plans can succeed only by organizing the Hindus, that is, by means of Hindu Sangathan.

Another Hindu leader, Shanti Narain, formerly the Editor of the *Bande Mataram* observing the object of Hindu *sangathan* in one of his letter to the *Akash Vani* of Lahore wrote:[107]

The oppression and atrocities which Muhammadans have practised on the Hindus in Multan, Amritsar, Meerut, Panipat, Saharanpur and Agra make even the staunchest advocate of Hindu-Muslim unity pause and consider how far Mussalmans can be expected to promote the entente. There can be no doubt that union is essential for the attainment of Swaraj and political independence. But so long as Muhammadans believe that they can easily burn down and repress Hindus, it is absurd to look for unity between the two. It is necessary that Hindus should adopt measures for removing their weakness. This is the main object of the Hindu Sangathan.

And after the collapse of Non-cooperation movement, the Hindu reflections on the previous few years "resulted in the conclusion that Muslims had been applying continual pressure not only on the British but also on the Hindus for the satisfaction of their need."[108] In April 1923, an editorial in *The*

107. *Akash Vani*, September 9, 1923 in *SVNP*, 1923, p. 492.
108. Gene Robert Thursby, *op. cit.*, p. 72.

Leader of Allahabad succinctly stated the theme in milder form—perhaps Hindus are not literally a "dying race" as Swami Shraddhanand would have it, but indeed their basic rights were being compromised. It states:[109]

> Far-seeing Hindu leaders have for long fought against the communal spirit of the Mahomedans, but their efforts have been of no avail. The Mahomedans have, if anything, become more communal than ever before. Nothing is now left for the Hindus but to organize themselves certainly not with a view to encroach upon the legitimate rights of Mussalmans, but to protect their rights from being encroached upon by others. They must as a community inspire respect before they can have unity on reasonable and equal terms with the Muslims. Their first duty, in their own interest, in the interest of the country and also in that of Hindu-Muslim unity, is that they should organize, organize, organize.

Evidently the conservative Hindu opinion was in favour of establishing an organization for the unity and consolidation of the community "in order to maximize the Hindu potentialities of moral and ritual purity, physical strength, numerical increase and political power."[110] The above mentioned statement clearly indicates the Hindu perceptions of the situation. Holding Muslim aggression responsible for the rise of Hindu consciousness for consolidation, they did not deny the need for the Hindu-Muslim unity for attaining swaraj. But for political justice and unity, an honourable collaboration between them was possible, in their opinion, by organizing the Hindus. High incidence of communal riots during the 1920s and extensive references to the torture and killing of Hindus in the popular press made Hindus conscious of the need of giving training in martial arts to defend and protect themselves.[111] Therefore, it was proposed to set up a

109. *The Leader*, April 2, 1923, p. 3.
110. Gene Robert Thursby, *op. cit.*, p. 73.
111. *Muslim Outlook*, March 11, 1923 in *Punjab Press Abstract*, 1923, p. 145. Also see *Siyasat*, March 34, 1923 in *Ibid.*, p. 172 and *Hindustan*, April 12, 1923 in *Ibid.*, p. 213.

large number of *akharas* (practice centres) and hold competitions in physical exercises as part of *sangathan* programme.[112] Eliciting a similar kind of response from the Muslims who started many *akharas*, the communal hostility climaxed in 1924.[113]

The seventh annual meeting of the Hindu Mahasbha was held at Banaras on August 19, 1923 separately from the Indian National Congress for the first time.[114] It was presided over by Pandit Madan Mohan Malaviya, a brahman from Allahabad who was long active in the religious and political affairs of the Hindus and Indian National Congress. Although there was a general agreement on the issue of *sangathan* of the Hindus but a major controversy sparked off over the issue of *shuddhi*. Swami Shraddhanand tried to achieve passage of strongly positive resolution in favour of *shuddhi* and against untouchability by having the assembly so define the subject that it would not need to be referred to the orthodox for approval. A motion was introduced that *shuddhi* should not be considered a religious subject because it is not mentioned in the oldest and most authoritative religious texts for the simple reason that there were no converts among Aryan religion in the ancient period. Pandit Madan Mohan Malaviya endorsed the idea of Swami Shraddhanand for the admission of untoucables into the Mahasabha sessions. But his effort with regard to certain *chamars* produced strong

---

112. Writing to the *Bande Matram*, June 1, 1923, one Mohan Lal Bhatnagar suggested that "fencing should be taught in every Hindu school and college. A Hindu Defence Force could then be raised and the Hindus enabled to defend themselves. Hindu Sabhas be established at places where none exist at present. The students of Hindu girls schools also should be taught fencing, lathi playing and nethi (torch-whirling)." *Punjab Press Abstract, 1923*, p. 314.
113. *Home Deptt. Poll.*, File No. 2 of 1926, para 13. The *Vakil*, June 3, 1923 warned the Muhammadans to make a careful note of these preparations of the Hindus. *Punjab Press Abstract, 1923*, p. 314.
114. *Ibid.*, File No. 198 of 1924, p. 35.

opposition from the orthodox and necessitated an apology from him to the pandits of Banaras.[115]

However, the change in policy may be shown by summarising some of the decisions of the Hindu Mahasabha. Briefly these were (a) unity of races essential to attain swaraj, (b) the formation of a Samaj Sewak Dal to encourage physical culture amongst Hindus, (c) advancement of *sangathan* (unity) necessary for the progress of the community and the spread of Hindi essential to the former, (d) adoption of *swadeshi* cloth with the corresponding boycott of foreign cloth, (e) recognition of *shuddhi* extending to an agreement that all reclaimed, whatever caste, should be retaken into their former caste, and an appeal to all Hindus to extend a hearty welcome to Hindus returning from abroad and to all the depressed classes; this later clause was urged as a means of preventing the thinning of the Hindu community.[116]

For the religious propaganda and social *sangathan*, the formation of active branch sabhas was urged in the next meeting of the Hindu Mahasabha which was held in January 1924 on the occasion of the Kumbh Mela at Allahabad in which the Mahasabha affirmed its previous decisions regarding the depressed classes, but modified this by declaring that such were not entitled, under the Sanatan Dharm, the *Shastras* and from public propriety, to the sacred thread, the learning of the *Vedas* and inter-dining.[117] It further affirmed that non-Hindus might be admitted into Hinduism, but not into the existing castes.[118]

Swami Shraddhanand and Pandit Malaviya continued to cooperate within the Hindu Mahasabha in support of the

115. *Ibid.*, File No. 206 of 1926, p. 11.
116. *Ibid.*, p. 14.
117. *The Leader*, August 25, 1923, p. 6 and February 8, 1924, p. 5.
118. *Ibid.* Even the special session of Hindu Mahasabha which held at Prayag on February 2, 1924 could not take any clear cut decision in this regard. For reference, see *Dharam Vir*, February 23, 1924, p. 1 and *Sant Samachar*, February 12, 1924, p. 2.

programme for the uplift, organization and strengthening of the Hindu community until the middle of 1926, "when the Hindu Mahasabha decided to set up its own candidates in the elections and to participate in political activities."[119] Swami Shraddhanand resigned from it, for he was, as Thursby calls him, "an enthusiast rather than conscientious politician and nearly any organization seemed to thwart him and his goals."[120]

There was a mixed reaction to the *sangathan* movement among the Hindus and Muslims. The nationalist leaders, however, reacted to the formation of such an organization on unity lines. Defending the *shuddhi* and *sangathan* movements, Maulana Mohamad Ali remarked:[121]

> Every community is entitled to undertake such social reform as it needs and if the Sangathan is organized to remove untouchability and to provide for the speedy assimilation of the *Imtyaj* (distinction) and their complete absorption into Hindu society I must rejoice at it both as a Mussalman and as a Congressman.

On the question of physical cultural societies and gymnasium as part of *sangathan* programme, he remarked:[122]

> Another feature of the Sangathan movement is the increase of interest in physical culture. This is all to the good, and if flabbiness and cowardice can be removed from any section of the Indian people, there is cause only for joy. Here, too, however, there arises the question of the spirit, and I am sincerely glad that the frank discussions at Delhi last September gave an opportunity to Pandit Madan Mohan Malaviya to

---

119. Sankar Ghose, *Socialism, Democracy and Nationalism in India* (Calcutta: Allied Publishers, 1973), pp. 155-56.
120. Gene Report Thursby, *op. cit.*, p. 70.
121. *The Modern Review*, Vol. XXXV, February 1924, p. 240.
122. *Ibid.*

proclaim to the world that he himself favoured the creation of common 'akhadas' in which young men of all communities can take their share.

Whereas Muslim leaders of the Congress favoured the *sangathan* movement to appease the Hindus, the Hindu leaders criticised it for the simple reason, perhaps to appease the Muslims and for the sake of unity between these two communities which was necessary for the attainment of swaraj. Even Lala Lajpat Rai in one of his articles entitled "The Hindu-Muslim Problem" to *The Tribune*, almost disapprovingly stated:[123]

> The present movement is a reaction of the Hindu-Muslim situation. There is nothing in its aims and objects or its constitutions that need it anti-Muslim but to be frank, the fact that anti-Muslim is the only thing that keeps it alive.

The appeals of the nationalist leaders did not create any impact on the masses as both communities had become more communal towards each other and every festival thus became a possible occasion for collision and during the period from 1921 to 1924 such collisions were frequent and in many cases serious.[124] Moreover, success of the Arya Samaj in the *shuddhi* movement particularly in the case of Malkana Rajputs, caused serious deterioration in the relations between the Hindus and the Muslims.[125] These communities, according to R.C. Majumdar, had already been divided into two hostile camps.[126] It may also be asserted that the failure of the Khilafat movement disillusioned the Muslims so much that they staged a

123. *The Tribune*, December 13, 1924, p. 7.
124. *Report on the Working of the System of Government: United Provinces of Agra and Oudh (1921-28)* (Allahabad: Government of India, 1928), p. 7.
125. L.F. Rushbrook Williams, *India in 1923-24* (Calcutta: Government of India, Central Publication Branch, 1924), p. 258. Also see B.M. Sharma, *Swami Dayanand: His Life and Teachings* (Lucknow: The Upper India Publishing House, 1933), pp. 156-157.
126. R.C. Majumdar, *op. cit.*, pp. 151-52.

sudden retreat to communal politics, notwithstanding Gandhi's effort to the contrary.

In retaliation against the *shuddhi* and *sangathan* movements, the Muslims started definite communal movements called *tabligh* and *tanzim*.[127] In order to organize the Muslims, the Mussalmans of Aligarh under the leadership of Kunwar Abdul Wahab Khan, who was himself a Mussalman Rajput, formed a society known as 'Tabligh-ul-Islam' in April 1923,[128] and in July 1923, a 'Central Jamiat-i-Tabligh-ul-Islam' was formed.[129] This was a purely militant proselytizing effort on the part of the Muslims to counteract the *shuddhi* movement of the Arya Samaj.[130] The other movement known as *tanzim* which literally means organization, was started by Dr. Kitchlew, obviously to organize the Muslims against the *sangathan*.[131]

All these movements and counter-movements had great repercussions. Both tried their best to strengthen their communities for petty gains. The need for a common front against the British having pushed to the background, both the communities saw each others with distrust. The Muslims suspected "that the object of the removal of untouchability was not the absorption of the suppressed classes into the Hindu society, but merely to use them as auxiliaries on the

---

127. Imtiaz Ahmad, "Secularism and Communalism" in *Economic and Political Weekly*, Special Number, July 1969, p. 1142. Also see R. Sheikh Muhammad, "Hindu-Muslim Problem: Who is Responsible for the Present Condition", *The Muslim Outlook*, February 16, 1924 in *Home Deptt. Poll.*, File No. 198 of 1924, p. 24.
128. *Home Deptt. Poll.*, File No. 6/IX of 1924, p. 19.
129. *Ibid*. Also see Zafar Imam (ed.), *Muslims in India* (New Delhi: Orient Longman, 1975), p. 52.
130. *Ibid.*, p. 14. Also see Gail Minault, *op. cit.*, p. 193.
131. *Ibid.*, p. 13. According to the *Census of India, 1931*, India Report, p. 390, the *tanzim* movement "primarily directed to the reconversion of the *shuddhi* converts. . . ."

Hindu side."[132] Commenting upon the situation, Lala Lajpat Rai writes:[133]

> Shuddhi and Tabligh thus set up one against the other, created a situation the like of which was not known to Indian history. Riots, disturbances, murders, abduction of women and minors and other kinds of violence created an atmosphere of a warring camp in India. The Muslims hated the Hindus and *vice-versa*.

The *sangathan* movement was discredited by the Muslims on the basis that it was a narrowly political movement in the trappings of religious renewal.[134] In the same fashion, the *shuddhi* movement was also condemned by the Muslims. One U.P. paper *Rozana Akhbar* condemning the *shuddhi* movement writes that "the *shuddhi* movement has eclipsed the swaraj, the Khilafat and the non-cooperation movements."[135] The Hindus, on the other side, alleged the uncalled for interfence in their religious affairs by the Muslims. They felt that they were perfectly justified in converting or reconverting others to their own faith, a right which the Muslims and Christians had exercised all along and which alone accounted for their number in India. In defence Swami Shraddhanand retorted that the Muslims had created hue and cry against *shuddhi* and *sangathan* without any base and provocation.[136]

Throughout the 1920s, the questions of *shuddhi* and *sangathan* of the Hindus and *tanizm* and *tabligh* of the Muslims had been the main topic of discussion in the meetings of the

132. R.C. Majumdar, *op. cit.*, p. 425.
133. Lajpat Rai, *The Arya Samaj: An Account of Its Aims, Doctrine and Activities, with a Biographical Sketch of the Founder* (Lahore: Uttar Chand Kapur and Sons, 1932), p. 250.
134. Mian Sir Fazl-i-Husain, "Punjab Politics" in *The Panjab Past and Present*, Vol. V, Part I, April 1971, pp. 142-49.
135. *Note on the Press: United Provinces of Agra and Oudh*, No. 18 of 1923, p. 1.
136. Swami Shraddhanand, "Hindu-Muslim Unity—Shuddhi and Sangathan" in *The Calcutta Samachar*, August 16, 1923, p. 3.

Hindu Mahasabha and the Jamait-ul-Ulema respectively.[137] They defended their religious movements while they condemned those of the others.[138] The revival of mutual suspicion and distrust between these two communities resulted in very serious communal riots, which vitiated the political atmosphere of India from 1923 onwards. The two rival institutions, *shuddhi* movement of the Hindus and *tabligh* of the Muslims, were, writes Brij Mohan Sharma, "chiefly responsible for most of the communal riots in India, which have undoubtedly retarded the political progress of this unfortunate country, at a most critical period of its history."[139] The recriminations between Swami Shraddhanand and Khwaja Hassan Nizami, a well known *Pir* and an experienced pamphleteer, became so acute that the lives of both were threatened by the followers of each other. In April 1923 the situation became so tense in a group of villages in Agra that police action under section 144 C.P.C. was found necessary for maintaining peace.[140]

The Congressmen and Khilafatists were obviously at a disadvantage in such situation as their efforts were thwarted.[141] They adopted the posture of neutrality as they would not favour one against the other for losing the pretence of national movement.[142] The religious fervour swamped the politics of the country.[143] The posters and pamphlets issued by both the rival parties condemning each other added fuel to the existing

---

137. R.K. Ghai, "Tabligh and Shuddhi Movements in the Nineteen Twenties" in *The Panjab Past and Present*, Vol. XX, Part I, April 1986, pp. 217-25.

138. *The Indian Annual Register, 1923*, Supplement, p. 192.

139. B.M. Sharma, *Swami Dayanand* (Lucknow: The Upper India Publishing House, 1933), p. 156.

140. Chand Karan Sharda, *Shuddhi Chandrodya* (Ajmer: Vedic Yantraylaya, Vik. 1984), pp. 242-43.

141. *Home Deptt. Poll.*, File No. 6/IX of 1924, p. 18.

142. *Ibid.*, File No. 206 of 1926, p. 11.

143. *Ibid.*

communal fire.¹⁴⁴ The Hindu-Muslim relations continued to deteriorate in 1925 and 1926 causing serious riots in Delhi, Allahabad, and Calcutta and at many other places during the period and afterwards.¹⁴⁵ A serious riot took place in Calcutta in April 1926 over the question of music before mosque resulting in many casualties and injuries.¹⁴⁶ The Hindus reacted sharply against the Government's unsuccessful effort to control the hours of music before mosques. They offered *satyagraha* against these measures which showed that Hindu *sangathan* had assumed the role of religio-political movement. And the same idea was substantiated by the statements of Lala Har

144. Y.B. Mathur, *Muslim and Changing India* (New Delhi: Trimurti Publications, 1972), p. 1.

145. Gopal Krishan in an article "Communal Violence in India : A Study of Communal Disturbances in Delhi" gives vividly the enormity of the riots. He writes : "The frequency of riots increased during the 1920s and every province was affected. The Moplah rebellion of 1921 had strong communal aspects. There were riots in Malegaon (1921), Multan (1922), Lahore, Amritsar, Saharanpur (1923). The year 1924 saw some major outbreaks in Allahabad, Calcutta, Delhi, Gulburga, Jubbalpore, Kohat, Lucknow, Nagpur, Shahjahanpur.... From 1925 on a new cause, namely religious conversion, came to be added to the existing sources of conflict. Now militant organizations of Hindus, Shuddhi and Sangathan, launched by the Arya Samaj, and Tanjeem and Tabligh among the Muslims added to the scale of communal violence. The major riots of Calcutta, Bombay of 1926 and 1928 respectively, resulted in very large number of casualties and damage to property; in Calcutta, in a series of 3 riots 141 persons were killed and 1296 were injured; in Bombay in 1928 the death toll was 117 and the injured 791. The study of 1930s and the 1940s is, if anything, more depressing. The 1931 riots in Kanpur resulted in the killing of 294 persons and injuring of 2529. In the Bombay riot of 1932, 214 persons were killed and 2686 injured. If we take only the major riots between 1924 and 1940, the total number of persons killed was 1175 and the injured 7615. In the 1940, the major riots were part of the movement for participation and the scale of violence enormous. By then communal riots had become an instrument of politics." *Economic and Political Weekly*, Vol. XX, No. 2, January 12, 1985, p. 62.

146. R.C. Majumdar, *op. cit.*, p. 434.

Dayal in 1925 which were published in the *Pratap* of Lahore and subsequently were reprinted widely. In one of his letters he stated:[147]

> I declare that the future of the Hindu race, of Hindustan and of the Punjab, rests on these four pillars: (1) Hindu Sangathan, (2) Hindu Raj, (3) Shuddhi of Moslems, and (4) Conquest and Shuddhi of Afghanistan and the frontiers. So long as the Hindu nation does not accomplish these four things, the safety of our children and great-grand-children will be ever in danger, and the safety of the Hindu race will be impossible. The Hindu has but one history and its institutions are homogeneous.

The communal hatred became so acute in the year 1926 that Swami Shraddhanad, against whom the Muslims cherished bitter hatred due to his role in the *shuddhi* and *sangathan* movements,[148] was murdered on December 23, 1926 by Abdul Rasid of Bulandshehar.[149] It proved, perhaps, the last nail in the Hindu-Muslim unity and the temporary truce reached on April 4, 1919 between Swami Shraddhanand and the Muslims, when the former addressed a Muslim gathering in Jumma Masjid, Delhi[150] was shattered completely immediately after the collapse of Khilafat movement. And thus from the early 1920s onward till the participation of India in 1947, the Hindu-Muslim communal conflicts continued to exert a pervasive influence in the lives of the people of the Indian sub-continent.

147. Rajendra Prasad, *India Divided* (Bombay: Hind Kitabs, 1946), p. 19.
148. Pandit Ganga Ramji, "Swami Shraddhanand ka Hatyara Kaun" in *Arya Sewak*, December 1982, pp- 5-6. Also see J. Coatman, *India in 1926-27* (Calcutta: Government of India, Central Publications Branch, 1928), p. 13.
149. *Sant Samachar*, a weekly of Amritsar reports that Swami Shraddhanand was killed by Abdul Rasid due to his role in the *shuddhi* of Malkana Rajputs. It further reports that the assassin also wanted to kill Lala Lajpat Rai and Pandit Madan Mohan Malaviya. January 4, 1927, p. 4.
150. Swami Shraddhanand, *Inside the Congress* (New Delhi : Dayanand Sansthan, 1984), p. 69.

The phase from 1920 to 1947 is very significant for the fact that the character of the *shuddhi* movement underwent a radical change.[151] What was till then a social movement for gaining converts began to acquire political overtones as all the communities organized themselves into political parties. Their impact and relevance in national politics began to increase causing a fair degree of polarization. Having organized into solid communal parties working for retaining their followings, the commual politics after the withdrawal of the Non-cooperation movement began not only to undermine the freedom struggle but create serious wedge which surfaced itself in the form of communal riots, and demonstrations and battle of pamphlets accusing and abusing one another in most unbecoming and unethical manner. Acute communal consciousness among the masses itself began to stem the process of conversion. From 1930 onward the *shuddhi* movement in the new communal ferment, indicating that the communal divide had taken place, had thus become irrelevant as it is in some individual cases that the *shuddhi* was performed.

151. During this period the Hindu Mahasabha took active part for Hindu *sangathan*, removal of untouchability and *shuddhi* under the active command of Mr. V.D. Savarkar. *The Indian Annual Register*, July-December 1931, p. 255.

5

Social Dimensions of Shuddhi Movement

The social dimensions of the *shuddhi* movement are very complex primarily because this innovation was designed to dissolve hierarchy and rigidity of the caste system; these two features of the Hindu social structure were and still are fundamental realities of the Indian society for these not only direct a large number of social functions but also are integral parts of the psyche of the Hindus. Therefore, a large number of persons who were converted to Hinduism or were purified from the lower castes to join the higher castes on equal level, experienced difficulties and tensions for they were not readily acceptable for social intercourse or social relations. James Reid Graham, therefore, rightly remarks that *shuddhi* was a departure in the history of Hinduism and *ipso-facto* "consciously or unconsciously represents a significant modification of caste theory."[1] Therefore, any innovation of the kind of *shuddhi* movement was bound to cause multi-dimensional social problems.

1. James Reid Graham, "The Arya Samaj as a Reformation in Hinduism with special reference to Caste," Unpublished Ph.D. Dissertation, Yale University, 1942, p. 286.

The nature of the problem under study reveals that the *shuddhi* symbolized conversion of an individual or a group from one religion to another without the change in religious or moral or ethical world view, or in other words, without transition from theological to philosophical and finally to intellectual grasp of the new religion. It may, therefore, be accepted that the *shuddhi* is generally a denominational change ritualistically affected, at the most a strategy to counteract the proselytizing propaganda of the Christian missionaries. Moreover, since there was an absence of such a tradition, it is contended that the change was rather superficial affecting only the fringe of the Hindu society. With built in self-sustaining mechanism with purity-pollution and hierarchical features forming procrustean base, the Hindu society reveals limited adjustive and adaptive qualities.[2]

Nevertheless, the *shuddhi* movement reveals many complex social dimensions as it created, contrary to the magnitude of the movement sharp socio-political reactions from within the Hindu society as well as from without. From within the Hindu society, tensions emerged from the problem of integrating the purified with the caste structure which governed the net work of social relations particularly the inter-dining and inter-marriage. Commenting upon this aspect of the problem, Kenneth W. Jones writes:[3]

> For being a Hindu was not merely a matter of religious belief, but also of function, and the question of readmission to caste privileges presented Samajists with an immense obstacle to reconversion, let alone outright conversion of non-Hindus.

So rigid and stratified the Hindu society was that even the reformist Arya Samaj experienced schism within its ranks.

2. Richard Lannoy, *The Speaking Tree: A Study of Indian Culture and Society* (London: Oxford University Press, 1971), pp. 145-56.
3. Kenneth W. Jones, *Arya Dharm* : *Hindu Consciousness in 19th Century Punjab* (New Delhi : Manohar Book Service, 1976), p. 130. (Hereafter quoted as *Arya Dharm*).

Though under the influence of reformism, efforts were made to dissolve internal divisions yet, being a reaction to the Christian proselytization, it tended to consolidate the Hindu society against the external danger and in the process the Arya Samaj movement as a whole shed its liberalism and became a vanguard of conservatism. In this perspective an effort shall be made to study, one, the social problems relating to the purified individuals and groups, and two, the extent of reform or change the *shuddhi* movement brought about in the social relations of the Hindu society.

As has already been discussed, three types of people were involved in the conversion from the Hindu fold to other religions such as Islam and Christianity. One category of such persons consisted of those who inadvertently or otherwise infringed the established moral code of the Hindu society.[4] Second category of the converts comprising depressed classes was of those who were denied the basic social equality with those of the 'twice-born' in the Hindu society. They allowed themselves to be converted *en masse* to Islam and Christianity for it promised them equal status in the society.[5] Third category of the coverts consisted of Hindus who were or whose ancestors had adopted Islam or Christianity centuries ago for one reason or the other.[6]

4. For instance, one Chuni Lal Mahajan, a resident of Delhi due to some family dissentions "left Delhi and went to Kalanaur, district Rohtak. There he became a Muhammadan because the Muhammadans served him faithfully and had to eat and drink from their hands during his illness. . .," was excommunicated by the Hindu orthodoxy for any Hindu who took food or drank water from the hands of non-Hindus was considered contaminated and hence excommunicated from the *biradri* for ever. Again, "A Hindu of Dera Ghazi Khan District who had fallen in love with a Muhammadan woman and professsed Islam for six years. . ." was also excommunicated. For reference, see *Census of India 1911*, Punjab Report, p. 151.

5. Shyamala Bhatia, "Social Change and Politics in the Punjab 1898-1910," Unpublished Ph.D. Thesis, Delhi University, 1984, pp. 215-16.

6. *Census of India, 1921*, Punjab and Delhi Report, p. 181.

A study of the instances of *shuddhis* described in the two preceding chapters reveals a number of interesting facts. In the early phase the Arya Samaj sought to purify people in close cooperation with the orthodoxy. They felt no qualms about the performance of traditional Brahminical rituals which were contrary to the basic tenets of the Arya Samaj. In the latter phase, these records reveal only a superficial process of purifications. There is no indication that any of the people concerned had any clear idea of what was involved in their purification. Although several of the cases recorded seem to indicate possible moral lapses, there is no hint of any moral change being demanded or achieved before the person was purified. In such circumstances, James Reid Graham raises a pertinent question: "One may well ask from what the person was supposed to be purified and in what way his purification was supposed to take place?"[7]

Complex as the Hindu society was, the response and reaction of the Hindus varied from person to person and from group to group, revealing their emotional, psychological and rational, and sometime a mixed character. In most cases the acceptance of food from the hands of the reconverts at the time of purification irritated many orthodox castemen and at times those who took sweets etc. from them were excommunicated by their orthodox caste brotherhood.[8] *The Arya Patrika* reports that fifteen "Arya Samajists of Moradabad were outcasted by the members of the orthodox community on the offences of drinking Ganges water from Christians who had become Hindus again."[9] Similarly in Lahore after the purification ceremony of the Rahtias, the Aryas were boycotted socially by the local residents. They were not allowed to take water from the wells. The *Arya Directory* reports that Lala Somnath whose mother died during this period of social boycott had to face this kind of opposition.[10] In Hoshiarpur when militant

7. James Reid Graham, *op. cit.*, pp. 459-60.
8. *The Arya Patrika*, December 31, 1889, p. 4.
9. *Ibid.*
10. *Arya Directory*, p. 191.

Aryas purified members of the Kabirpanthi sect who were sweepers by caste, the lowest of social groups, with the most demeaning of professions, publicly inter-dined with them, the local orthodox society led a movement to outcaste all the Aryas.[11] The opposition of the Sanathan Dharam Sabha of Hoshiarpur against the Aryas and their Chamar adherents continued as late as 1909 when they succeeded in excommunicating the local Aryas, at least for a while.

Significantly in many cases another difficulty of equal gravity encountered by the reformers was that some members of the Arya Samaj itself were not ready to welcome the purified ones. About the intransigent attitude of some Arya Samajists *The Arya Patrika* reports:[12]

> The Arya Samaj converts Mohammadans and Christians but most of the Arya Samajists are not willing to mix socially. This is really shutting the door of the Arya Samaj practically if not [in] theory…members of the Samaj are afraid the Hindu Biradri will expel them.

Testifying it, Lajpat Rai observes that most of the Arya Samajists displayed reluctance in having any kind of social intercourse with Alakhdhari who was converted by Swami Dayanand himself, and was uptil his death a member of the Arya Samaj, Dehra Dun. He further adds: "the prejudice was so strong then…that even the Arya *Sanyasis* and missionaries would not take food touched by him."[13] Some Samajists even went so far as to propose that Muslim converts be organized into separate groups, thus eliminating the necessity of adjusting converts into the existing caste structure.[14] Contrary to the original spirit of reforms of Arya Samaj, such suggestions were offered as compromises for avoiding an open schism in the

---

11. Kenneth W. Jones, *Arya Dharm*, p. 308.
12. *The Arya Patrika*, April 17, 1897, p. 6.
13. Lajpat Rai, *The Arya Samaj: An Account of its Aims, Doctrine and Activities, with a Biographical Sketch of the Founder* (Lahore: Uttar Chand Kapur & Sons, 1932), p. 251.
14. James Reid Graham, *op. cit.*, p. 463.

Hindu society. It was primarily due to the fact that the Arya Samaj did not reject completely the caste customs and did not break with their orthodox caste brotherhood.

So pervasive was the influence of the orthodoxy that in the beginning the Arya Samaj adopted Brahminical ritualistic methods to avoid conflict with the orthodoxy.[15] But after having attained confidences, the Arya Samaj evolved its own system[16] thus making it in accordance with the spirit of the Ten Principles of Arya Samaj.[17] But the adoption of the new method did not solve the problem of inner social cohesion of the Arya Samaj. The *shuddhi* movement not only divided the Arya Samaj into two groups but the "reluctance of many Aryas to enter into daily social relations with the newly purified"[18] was more serious. The social programme of the *shuddhi* movement had many immediate social implications for those who engaged themselves in this work and also for those who were purified. We have mentioned earlier in the beginning that there was a reaction from within the Hindu society against those who carried on the work of *shuddhi* and consequently some Arya Samajists were excommunicated to deter them from the *shuddhi* policy. But there has been no determined and organized effort on the part of orthodoxy to stop the *shuddhi* work. Even when the Samaj dispensed with the orthodox expiatory ceremonies in 1893, the latter did not protest to the idea of purification of lower castes or the elevation of the purified ones to caste privileges. It was feared that Hinduism might dwindle in numbers, losing importance both politically and socially due to the mass conversions to other religions. Nonetheless, there was no enthusiasm on the part of orthodoxy to admit

15. The Brahminical ritualistic methods being *praschit*, eating of cow dung, paying of a visit to the Ganges and feeding the Brahmans.
16. Namely the ceremony of tonsure, or cutting of hairs, the offering of the *Hom*, or fire-sacrifice, investment with the sacred thread and the learning of the sacred *Gaytri Mantra*.
17. For full detail of Ten Principles of the Arya Samaj, see Appendix III.
18. Kenneth W. Jones, *op. cit.*, p. 133.

them to Hindu society and its privileges on the basis of equality. It was perhaps under the circumstances that the orthodoxy assumed the attitude of toleration. As Census Commissioner reports:[19]

> The Hindus (orthodox) as a rule assume the attitude of toleration and let the purified or reclaimed people slip into their fold without any protest. The educated Hindu does it and professes that he does so. The Hindus of the old school, illiterate and conservative at time and in places have opposed the movement bitterly and put the Arya Samajists to great trouble, but in the majority of cases, they have yielded in the end. It would be a sheer act of ingratitude if I were not to acknowledge that much of our success is due to the help and co-operation of the enlightened Hindu public both literate and illiterate.

The orthodoxy on many occasions particularly in Malabar where it was very tradition bound and intransigent agreed to cooperate with the Samaj if the latter accepted types of expiation approved by them.

In spite of the lukewarm attitude of the orthodoxy the *shuddhi* movement could not achieve much success. It was primarily due to the rigid caste structure which ritualistically had segmented Indian society into autonomous sub-groups. Even within the Arya Samaj the caste ties were so strong that no amount of reformism could eliminate caste feelings among the Arya Samajists. Though Swami Dayanand had conceived the theory of class by merit instead of by birth yet, as Tara Chand notes, it did not make much headway. He writes:[20]

> The Arya Samaj condemned the classification of the Hindus on the basis of birth, yet few Arya Samajists had the courage to marry outside their caste.

19. *Census of India, 1911*, Punjab Report, p. 150.
20. Tara Chand, *History of the Freedom Movement in India* (Delhi : Government of India, 1967), Vol. II, p. 428.

Social Dimensions of Shuddhi Movement   127

The rise of *Jat Pat Todak Mandal* (organization of destruction of caste) in Lahore in the year 1922,[21] with the help of Arya Bhratri Sabha[22], testifies to this fact. Its objects and programmes[23] further testify that even the Arya Samajists had not broken its ties with their caste customs in spite of their long cooperation for about three decades in the field of *shuddhi* campaign.

One of the very significant dimensions of conversion to Hinduism, particularly of the low caste groups, is that these groups after conversion began to acquire the characteristics of caste or in other words there began to develop autonomous sub-groups in which the members of the Arya Samaj finding unfavourable reaction of the Arya Samajists themselves played a significant role. Therefore, the Arya Samaj created religious specialists from among the ranks of the converted low caste to minister to the religious needs of the coverts.[24] Mahashya Kaumi Sudhar Sabha was established to organize all the purified Dumnas who were given the name 'Mahashya' after their purification.[25] Likewise Megh Uddhar Sabha was established to look after the religious as well as other social needs of the newly purified Meghs of Sialkot.[26] James M. Sebring, who conducted a fieldwork in 1963-64 in Almora

21. *Jat Pat Todak Mandal, General Review, 1939,* pp. 1-2. Also see *Arya*, January 1926, pp. 18-19.
22. This Sabha came into existence in the year 1895 to protest and modify the caste-customs among the Arya Samajists on the basis of Swami Dayanand's teachings. James Reid Graham, *op. cit.*, pp. 1, 481.
23. For the objects and programmes of *Jat Pat Todak Mandal* see Appendix IV.
24. James M. Sebring, "The Formation of New Castes : A Probable Case from North India" in *American Anthropologist*, Vol. 74, Number 3, June 1972, pp. 587-88.
25. Ramchander Javed, *Punjab ka Arya Samaj* (Jullundur : Arya Pratinidhi Sabha Punjab, 1964), p. 26.
26. Lala Ganga Ram and Lala Charu Dass, *The Uplift Movement at Sialkot : A Brief Report of the Working of the Arya Megh Uddhar Sabha* (Aryan Mission for the Uplift of the Megh Untouchables) *Sialkot, Punjab* (Calcutta : A. C. Sarkar, 1915), p. 48.

District, U.P., found that the conversions carried out by the Samaj in 1930 created a new class of Brahmans among the Shilpkar artisan, who occupied a low position in the social hierarchy.[27] He also points out that after the purification of these artisan Shilpkars "Arya Samaj personnel chose men from among the Artisan Shilpkars and instructed them in the rudiments of performing life-cycle rities for their fellow caste members—rites which elsewhere are performed for Sanskritizing castes by authentic, although indigent and usually low status, Brahmins."[28] Thus a new class of artisan Shilpkar "Brahmans" was created and persons "on the basis of their reputation for piety and goodness, being men who had made a habit of privately observing as many practices of Hinduism" were chosen to perform the religious rites for other artisan Shilpkars.[29] They abandoned their traditional occupation, which was mainly carpentry, and became like the high caste Brahmans, performers of rituals connected with birth, naming, sacred thread investiture, marriage and death.[30]

Such a development is very interesting for, as Sebring suggests, the conversions of the artisan caste led to the strengthening of the inter-caste boundaries and stability rather than shaking of the caste system.[31] Moreover, the emergence of new caste groups and existence of castes within the Arya Samaj itself further closed its door in having commensal and matrimonial relations with the purified castes. Proliferation of castes was not only inconsistent with the progressive role which the Arya Samaj intended to play in the Hindu society but was conditional to the success of the *shuddhi* movement for the spirit of *shuddhi* demanded integration of the untouchables with, at least, the Arya society.[32] Accepting that the *shuddhi* movement had helped in mitigating some of the harshness of

27. James M. Sebring, *op. cit.*, pp. 588-89.
28. *Ibid.*, p. 589.
29. *Ibid.*
30. *Ibid.*
31. *Ibid.*, p. 598.
32. James Reid Graham, *op. cit.*, pp. 519-20.

the untouchability, James Reid Graham observes:[33]

> Having to choose between orthodox connections and close relationships with converts, the Samaj as a whole has chosen the former. Thus one may treat with reserve some enthusiastic claims made by Arya Samajists to the effect that all caste differences are disregarded within the ranks of Samajists.

Some of the Arya Samaj leaders such as Lala Munshi Ram (later on Swami Shraddhanand), Pandit Lekh Ram, Mahatma Hansraj, Choudhry Ram Bhaj Datt and Lala Lajpat Rai were acutely conscious of the growing contradiction within the Arya Samaj. They took up the cause in all seriousness and by their eloquent plight of the low-caste Hindus. In this regard we may draw upon the writings of Lala Lajpat Rai who represented the socially radical group of the Arya Samaj and expressed his views in unequivocal terms. In his opinion the development of social upliftment of the lower classes had two dimensions: one, the *shuddhi* movement had raised "the status of castes not entitled to wear the sacred thread"; two, it had raised "the untouchables to the rank of the touchables, and educating them to higher social ideals, with a view to eventually raising them to social equality with other Hindus."[34] Like a protagonist of the depressed classes, Lajpat Rai pleaded to the Hindus from three points of view, namely humanism, Hinduism and nationalism. As a liberal humanist he said:[35]

> In my opinion...no greater wrong can be done to a human being endowed with intellect than to put him into circumstances which make him believe that he is eternally doomed to a life of ignorance, servitude, and misery, and that in him any sort of ambition for his betterment is a sin.

33. *Ibid.*, p. 520.
34. Lajpat Rai, *op. cit.*, pp. 257-58. Also see *Census of India, 1911*, Punjab Report, p. 151.
35. *Ibid.*, p. 259.

He further added:[36]

> No slavery is more harmful than that of mind, and no sin is greatar than to keep human beings in perpetual bondage. It is bad enough to enslave people, but to create and perpetuate circumstances which prevent them from breaking their chains and becoming free, is infamous.

Stressing on the same question as a Hindu he warned his co-religionists not to ignore them in the larger interest of Hinduism itself for:[37]

> The depressed classes or the vast bulk of them are Hindus; they worship Hindu gods, observe Hindu custom, and follow the Hindu law. A great many of them worship the cow and obey their Brahman priests. They have no desire to go out of Hinduism unless it be impossible for them otherwise to better their position religiously, socially, and economically. Nay, they cling to Hinduism in spite of the knowledge that by giving it up and adopting other faiths they have an immediate prospect of rising both socially and economically. There are agencies prepared to receive them with open arms if only they give up their ancestral faith, of which they know little, and whose priests care so litle for them.

As a nationalist he said:[38]

> It is to be remembered that national decline has its origin in the oppression of others, and if we Indians desire to achieve national self-respect and dignity, we should open our arms to our unfortunate brothers and sisters of the depressed classes and help to build up in them the vital spirit of human dignity. So long as we have these large classes of the untouchables in this country we make no

36. Ibid.
37. Ibid., pp. 261-62.
38. Ibid., p. 258.

real progress in our national affairs, for this requires a high moral standard; and this is unthinkable where the weaker classes are unfairly treated. No man may build his greatness on his brother's weakness; man shall stand or fall by his own strength.

It may be accepted that a section of the Arya Samaj and their leaders committed to the uplift of the low caste Hindus did a substantial work to assimilate these depressed and untouchable classes and raise them to a respectable position in the social scale.[39] But *shuddhi* itself being a radical movement to the extent that it was opposed to the Hindu tradition it was not expected to achieve instant success against the pervasive rigid caste structure. Converting people of other religions and admitting them to the privileges of the *Dwijas*, administering the *Gayatri* to them, investing them with the sacred thread, conferring on them the privilege of performing *Hom*, and starting inter-dining and in a few cases even inter-marriage with them were some of the steps which were quite radical if viewed in the perspective of those times. The success of these steps required a total change in the consciousness of the Hindus which was not possible if these efforts were backed by a programme of economic change.

With the dawn of the twentieth century, the *shuddhi* movement underwent transformation as it became an agency for the mass purification of the low caste groups.[40] The initial successes of the Samaj in the purification of the Rahtias in 1900 led the militant Samajists to a much more massive campaign among other groups who were low in the social scale of Hinduism. In fact, such groups began flocking to the banner of the Arya Samaj for the elevation of their social status. Because of the success achieved by the Arya Samaj in purifying the Rahtias, Ods, Dumnas and Meghs and also because of opposition of the conservative Hindus, the *shuddhi* enthusiasts organized local Sabhas to retain them within the fold of

39. *The Tribune*, January 6, 1911, p. 5.
40. James Reid Graham, *op. cit.*, p. 488.

Hinduism as in the case of Dumnas and Meghs.[41] These new institutions were created in the image of caste groups of the Hindus with the network of autonomous social relationship.

The effects of *shuddhi* on the socio-religious life of the converts depended upon their previous social status.[42] The purified ones if they came in groups or sub-groups retained their group identity within the realm of the touchables, instead of being without it among the untouchables. Explaining the situation, the *Census Report of 1911* divides them into two categories—those who do not pollute by touch and those who do. The problem of integrating the latter was acutely felt as there was hardly a chance of ever developing commensal relationship with them for they followed "unclean professions."[43] But "others who did not actually pursue an unclean occupation sank to the same level by associating with the untouchables. It is the latter class which is being gradually retained to a higher status."[44] Through the persuasion of the Arya Samaj these reclaimed ones were allowed the use of the village wells, and were not treated quite as contemptuously as before. In the case of individual converts who had been born Hindus, they were simply received back into their old castes, thus giving them all privileges they formerly enjoyed.[45] "But if the purified ones were individual converts from Christianity or Islam, orthodoxy was quite reluctant to admit them to caste *biradaris*, and it was often a matter of great difficulty for them to find a suitable social standing."[46]

41. *Home Deptt. Poll. Proceedings*, 1908, pp. 111-18. Also see Ramchander Javed, *op. cit.*, pp. 6-8.
42. J.T.F. Jordens, "Reconversion to Hinduism, the Shuddhi of the Arya Samaj" in G.A. Oddie (ed.), *Religion in South Asia : Religious Conversion and Revival Movements in South Asia in Medieval and Modern Times* (New Delhi : Manohar Book Service, 1977), p. 154.
43. *Census of India, 1911*, Punjab Report, p. 151.
44. *Ibid.*
45. J.T.F. Jordens, *op. cit.*, p. 154.
46. James Reid Graham, *op. cit.*, p. 518. Also see *Sant Samachar*, February 12, 1924, p. 2.

The purified low castes as well as those reclaimed from Islam and Christianity were permitted to attend the Arya Samaj meetings. But this association was more symbolic than real and substantial as they were not, in overwhelming majority of the cases, absorbed into the social structure because of the pressure of *biradari* and resistance of the orthodoxy.[47] So much so that many members of the Arya Samaj who were busy with the *shuddhi* work refrained from having any social intercourse and marriage with the converts[48] out of the fear of being excommunicated from their own *biradaris*.

Although with the passage of time and with the changing political climate of the country, the hostility of the orthodox Hindus towards the *shuddhi* workers and protagonists transformed into a kind of resignation[49] and a few converts were integrated with social structure of the caste Hindus,[50] yet it must be stated that the effect of *shuddhi* of the untouchables was singularly marginal. Promises of the use of wells, admission in schools and employment on equal terms with the caste Hindus made at the time of the purification ceremonies were conveniently forgotten by those who made them.[51] The

47. Even the Hindu Mahasabha which adopted *shuddhi* and upliftment of the untouchables in its programme ruled out in the matters of inter-dining and inter-marriage. *The Leader*, February 8, 1924, p. 4. Also see *Indian Quarterly Register*, 1925, Vol. I, p.p 377-82.

48. "The Arya Samajists eat with the Bhagats, as their Megh converts are called; and they take daughters from Bhagats for their sons, but do not give their daughters to converts." James Reid Graham, *op. cit.*, p. 518.

49. Kenneth W. Jones, "The Arya Samaj in the Punjab : A Study of Social Reform and Religious Revivalism, 1877-1902." Unpublished Ph.D. Thesis, University of California, Berkeley, 1966, p. 263. (Hereafter quoted as *The Arya Samaj in the Punjab*).

50. James Reid Graham, *op. cit.*, p. 518.

51. A letter from Shraddhanand Sanyasi to General Secretary, All India Congress Committee, June 3, 1922 in *All India Congress Committee Files*, File No. 10 of 1922, p. 1 (NML).

purified lower caste groups got disillusioned[52] as they remained where they were and "had not gained very much in reality."[53] The following statement of Ram Bhaj Dutt in this context is self-explanatory :[54]

> As the Arya Samaj has been unable to make proper arrangement for the education and material and social advancement of those who came under its protection it is useless to go on adding to the number of raw proselytes. Although we admit the charge brought against the Samaj, we fail to see in it a valid reason for stopping the work of Shuddhi. If we cannot make them ideal Aryas, there is no reason why we should not raise them to our level... It is our duty to raise them and provide them with all means in our power for their mental, moral and religious training and advancement....The Moslems will not respond, and the outcastes will; the latter will become Christians or Mohammadans if not Arya Samajists... The time is ripe for the Arya Samaj to take up the work of Shuddhi in right earnest. People all over India look to the Arya Samaj for this work.

Similarly Satish Kumar Sharma basing his study mostly on the field work, also mentions a statement of an old man belonging to the Mahashya community about the social change which the *shuddhi* process brought about :[55]

> .... The whole society has advanced and progressed but we are at the same old place. The only change has been our movement from our traditional Dumna name to Mahashya. But we are still the same old Dumnas in actual. The social segregation and our placements on the fringe of the society on low lying areas has brought us only dirty water of caste Hindus during rains.

52. Satish Kumar Sharma, *Social Movements aud Social Change : A Study of Arya Samaj and Untouchables in Punjab* (Delhi : B.R. Publishing Corporation, 1985), p. 87.
53. J.T.F. Jordens, *op. cit.*, p. 156.
54. *The Arya Patrika*, November 9, 1907, p. 7.
55. Satish Kumar Sharma, *op. cit., p.* 94.

The Arya Samaj, confesses Lajpat Rai, was "only on the fringe of the area to be conquered, and many a battle will have to be fought before the victory is achieved."[56] So the Arya Samajists had to carry a resolute struggle to secure a better social status for the depressed and untouchable classes. Many organizations had to be started for the removal of untouchability, for the dissimination of education among untouchables and for their general, social, moral and economic uplift. Among the various measures adopted by the Samaj for the social upliftment of the untouchables was the foundation of Dayanand Dalitoddhar Mandal, Punjab in February 1925 on the occasion of Dayanand Birth Centenary. This Mandal reclaimed, as Ganga Prasad Upadhyaya writes, 93,283 persons upto 1938.[57]

Another organization of the Arya Samaj for its social work was the All India Dayanand Salvation Mission which was founded at Hoshiarpur in the latter part of 1933 by the late Mahatma Devi Chand with the following objects :[58]

(i) to rescue Hindu girls and widows from the clutches of the ruffians and save them from molestation by bad characters:

(ii) to establish rescue homes, children homes at important centres; and

(iii) to convert non-Hindus to Hinduism.

From the date of its establishment to 1938, about 8,684 persons had been converted and 448 girls and women rescued.[59] Dayanand Dalitoddhar Sabha, different from the aforesaid Mandal of similar name came into being on May 11, 1930 at

56. Lajpat Rai, *op. cit.*, p. 269.
57. Ganga Prasad Upadhaya, *The Origin, Scope and Mission of the Arya Samaj* (Allahabad : Arya Samaj, Chowk, 1940), p. 126.
58. *All-India Dayanand Salvation Mission*, 5th Annual Report, 1938 (Hoshiarpur : Ram Dass, n.d.), p. 2.
59. *Ibid.* According to its 50th *Annual Report 1983-84*, about 3,38,338 persons have been purified by this Mandal so far.

Lahore under the Presidentship of Lala Roshan Lal. It arranged *pathshalas* (schools) for the children of the untouchables.[60] The Akhil Bhartiya Shraddhnand Dalitoddhar Sabha established in 1932 at Delhi worked for the welfare of the untouchables.[61] These organizations were established to ameliorate the social condition of the down-trodden and goad them to eschew the idea of leaving their religion. The work done by the various Shuddhi Sabhas, Mandals and Missions aroused a new hope and consciousness among the low-caste Hindus to improve their social status. In addition to these works, they also engaged themselves in other social and philanthropic activities such as opening of dispensaries and schools in the remote villages especially in the areas where the *shuddhi* work had been in progress, organizing community dinners frequently in which the participants took food prepared by Bhangis, *chamars*, and other low caste classes.[62] Such acts for promoting integration among various social segments not only gave the Samaj a good field for preaching but also boosted its prestige and elevated the status of the untouchables. Thus besides its religious, social and education programme, female education, widow remarriage,[63] famine relief, inter-dining and inter-marriage,[64] measures to ameliorate the

60. *Arya Directory*, pp. 45, 193.
61. *Ibid.*, p. 194.
62. Satish Kumar Sharma, *op. cit.*, p. 71.
63. "A notable widow 'marriage' took place at Gujranwala a few days ago. An Arora lady put an end to the miseries of widowhood by availing herself of the custom of 'Chadar Daina.' Our correspondent does not report whether the Lucky No. 2 is an Arora or belongs to some other castes." *The Tribune*, February 7, 1894, p. 7.
64. The *Arya Patrika* reports that "The marriage of Shrimati Hemant Kumar, the second daughter of our revered brother Lala Munshi Ram, with Mr. Sukhdev constitutes a land-mark in the history of social reform in the Punjab. Lala Munshi Ram is Khatri by birth and Mr. Sukhdev an Arora. There could be no alliance between the two according to the prevailing customs. But arbitrary customs and conventionalities are no barrier to those who, with a firm and implicit faith in the Divine Providence, are determined to follow the dictates of their own conscience." *SVNP, 1901*, p. 732. For more references, see *Shamim-i-Hind*, November 9, 1901 in *Ibid*, p. 718 and *Public Gazette*, November 24, 1901 in *Ibid.*, p. 748.

social and economic condition of the low castes were also included in the *shuddhi* programme.

To improve the economic condition of the depressed classes, the Sialkot Arya Samaj opened as early as June 1903 a Central Industrial School to give technical education to the Megh boys.[65] This school was located in the Arya Samaj Mandir and mainly "an efficient manual training in weaving, tailoring, carpentry, smithy and drawing[66] was given to the Meghs who were by tradition a weaving community.[67]

Apart from the D.A.V. institutions established in almost all the major cities of Punjab and some of other north Indian towns, there were many Gurukuls which were also opened to impart Sanskrit and Vedic knowledge; first Gurukul being established in 1902 at Kangri, Hardwar with the help of Lala Munshi Ram.[68] In the D.A.V. institutions and the Gurukuls, education was imparted to all especially to the purified untouchables irrespective of their caste and creed. Ramchandra and Ishar Datt, two Megh boys were admitted to the Gurukul Kangri along with the sons of well-to-do high caste Hindus.[69] The effects of this education system were manifold. It created a naw elite class among the depressed classes with new opportunities to secure government jobs, but they could not get good government jobs because of the competition with the high caste men who were more educated due to their economic resources. Most of them therefore continued to live in extreme poverty and hence commanded no respect in the society at large.[70] The vast majority of these ex-untouchables

65. Lala Ganga Ram and Lala Charu Dass, *op. cit.*, p. 21.
66. *Ibid.*, p. 30.
67. *Ibid.*, p. 3.
68. Lajpat Rai, *op. cit.*, pp. 220-21.
69. Lala Ganga Ram and Lala Charu Dass, *op. cit.*, p. 42.
70. Satish Kumar Sharma, "Shuddhi—A Case Study of Role of a Religious Movement in the Status Improvement of Untouchables" in *Indian Journal of Social Research*, Vol.XXIV, No. 1, April 1983, p. 74. (Hereafter quoted as *Shuddhi—A Case Study*).

remained in the villages, pursuing their traditional occupations, and in total economic dependence upon the dominant castes. But this had not always been the case. The Arya institutions such as schools, colleges, orphanages and others have rendered some help to educate and care for members of these groups.[71] In some instances the Samaj has been able to even get land for the new converts.[72] But on the whole socially and economically the *shuddhi* achieved only a marginal success because of the fact that the educational and economic measures undertaken by the Arya Samaj for the uplift of the downtrodden were not launched on a vast scale commensurate with the number of the converts. Lack of resources was one great cause. Moreover, the primary intention was to boost up numbers and not to ameliorate their condition. The majority of the Aryas, leaving aside the radicals, did not take much interest in improving their economic status. It was also due to the inherent clash of class interest as almost all the Arya Samajists belonged to the petty middle class, deeply interested in securing jobs. They, therefore, were not ready to promote the low class converts in those fields as it could threaten their own interest. But the primary reasons seem to be the exclusion of the low caste converts from inter-marriage and inter-dining on account of rigidity of caste structure and conservatism of the Hindu society. But, as Ganga Prasad Upadhyaya writes:[73]

> In the last fifty years we have solved the problems of *roti* but not *beti* (have solved the problem of inter-dining, but not class inter-marriage). Some Rajputs were willing to give away their daughters to neo-Hindu Rajputs but not to accept theirs. Their argument is that if they took their daughters their own families would be mixed or polluted or their purity finished.

In concluding the discussion on the social dimentions of *shuddhi*, one may say that on the whole it did not result in the

---

71. James Reid Graham, *op. cit.*, p. 520.
72. Lala Ganga Ram and Lala Charu Dass, *op. cit.*, p. 30.
73. Quoted in *Arya Mitra*, August 7, 1947. Also see *Bharatiya Hindu Shuddhi Sabha Delhi ki Varshik Report (January 1, 1948 to December 31, 1948)* (Delhi: Imperial Book Depot, n.d.), p. 22.

breakdown of caste division.[74] Where individuals were purified they had great difficulty in finding a social group to which to belong, and when they were admitted to one it was necessarily one of old orthodox groups. There was here no hint of a caste society based on qualities, as proposed by Swami Dayanand, nor was there much evidence of any relaxation of food and marriage restrictions to Samajists.[75] When groups from the lower strata of society were purified, they retained their old caste or social grouping. The *shuddhi* movement helped them to advance up their caste scale where they found themselves within the pale of respectability and touchability. Whether they received the rights and privileges of social intercourse with the higher castes to any appreciable extent is doubtful, but still the movement was able to remove some of the harshness of untouchability. Thus, although the *shuddhi* movement did not work for the total removal of the caste system, its contribution in lessening the evils of untouchability cannot be overlooked.[76]

As regards the effects of *shuddhi* on untouchables in the field of their socio-economic betterment, nothing tangible could be achieved, notwithstanding the efforts of the Mahashya Kaumi Sudhar Sabha, Arya Megh Uddhar Sabha and Swami Shraddhanand Dalitoddhar Sabha, which worked, though independently, for the uplift of the depressed classes socially. Tracts of land were acquired to settle the converts; primary and central schools were established; better housing facilities were provided; wells were dug up; and hospitals were established.[77] But on the whole, these measures did not prove adequate. Socially, the converts continued to be treated by the high caste men as before. They were not allowed to mix freely with the caste men except in the gathering of the Arya Samaj. There also they were not allowed to perform the *Hom*

---

74. Sri Santram, B.A. attributes the failure of *shuddhi* to *varanvavastha*. *Hamara Samaj* (Bombay : Nalanda Prakashan, 1949), p. 190.
75. James Reid Graham, *op. cit.*, p. 521.
76. *Ibid.*
77. J.T.F. Jordens, *Reconversion to Hinduism*, p. 156.

ceremony freely. Economically also, they could not secure any benefit even after the purification. The *chamars*, who left their traditional caste-based occupation of skinning and tanning of leather under the pressure of the Samaj members had to face the resentment of their own caste-men who opined that by leaving leather work, they had lost their professional autonomy and had become dependent upon the high castes for their economic activities.[78] The ex-untouchables continued to work in factories as workers and labourers. Moreover, the high land-owning castes did not want to lose control of the *chamars* and sweepers who had been working in their fields from the time immemorial.[79] Thus, by and large, the economic position of the untouchables remained the same with a few exceptions, where they switched over to a new occupation and earned money which was considered necessary for a good social status in the society.[80]

78. Satish Kumar Sharma, *Shuddhi—A Case Study*, pp. 74-76.
79. *Ibid*.
80. Sri Ram Sharma, *Mahatma Hansraj : Maker of the Modern Punjab* (Jullundur : Arya Pradeshik Pratinidhi Sabha, 1965), p. 75.

6

Political Dimensions of Shuddhi Movement

As is clear from the discussion in the preceding chapters that the *shuddhi* movement was essentially a social movement for the consolidation and regeneration of Hindu society but it was "rediscovered for very pressing practical political purposes,"[1] or it was started to lay the foundation of Hindu nationalism.[2] But Lajpat Rai appears to be nearer the truth when he says that the *shuddhi* was started by the Arya Samaj "as a purely religious propaganda, with political motives at the back of the minds of only some of its members."[3] Since Lajpat Rai was a contemporary and was connected with the affairs of the Arya Samaj, his contention may be accepted to the extent that the movement which was primarily socio-religious began to acquire political overtones since the days

1. J.F. Seunarine, *Reconversion to Hinduism Through Shuddhi* (Madras: The Christian Literature Society, 1977), p. 54.
2. Ramesh Chandra Majumdar, *History of the Freedom Movement in India* (Calcutta : Mukhopadhyay, 1962), Vol. I, p. 298.
3. Lajpat Rai, *The Arya Samaj : An Account of its Aims, Doctrine and Activities, with a Biographical Sketch of the Founder* (Lahore : Uttar Chand Kapur & Sons, 1932), p. 250.

of its inception.[4] It can be logically argued that to meet the challenge of Christianity, Swami Dayanand Saraswati started the *shuddhi* movement basically as a defensive social strategy to protect the Hindu society from the onslaught of proselytization. The dimension and dynamism of this strategy underwent gradual transformation in the face of rapidly growing political consciouness along with communalism as one of the parallel currents particularly in the Punjab. Rooted in Hindu communalism and confronted with the similar urge of the other communities, the defensive strategy of *shuddhi* assumed aggressive and offensive social overtones in the defence of the general interests of Hinduism, apparently embracing political interests.

The establishment of *shuddhi* followed by its successful campaign to bring back converts into its fold brought it into direct conflict with the Christians and Muslim missionaries,[5] which inaugurated a malicious propaganda against each other's religion, leading to the murder of Pandit Lekh Ram on March 6, 1897 which perhaps proved the last nail in the Hindu-Muslim unity in Punjab.[6] Commenting upon the situation which prevailed after the death of Pandit Lekh Ram to whom the radical section of the Samaj considered a martyr, Kenneth W. Jones writes:[7]

> The legacy of Pandit Lekh Ram left a permanent anti-Muslim bias in the Arya Samaj, a bias that was to find added justification in the coming years. The Arya-Muslim clashes of the eighteen eighties and eighteen nineties were seen, in retrospect, as forerunners of the Hindu-Muslim struggles of the twentieth century.

4. Michael Adwards, *A History of India from the Earliest Times to the Present Day* (London : Thomas and Hudson, 1961), p. 319.
5. *Ibid.*, p. 249.
6. Norman G. Barrier, "The Arya Samaj and Congress Politics in the Punjab, 1894-1908" in *Journal of Asian Studies*, Vol. 26, 1966-67, p. 368.
7. Kenneth W. Jones, "Communalism in the Punjab : The Arya Samaj Contribution" in *Ibid.*, Vol. 28, 1968-69, p. 52. (Hereafter quoted as *Communalism in the Punjab*).

The association of the Arya Samajists with the Indian National Congress, the Land Alienation Act of 1901, the partition of Bengal in 1905 and finally the establishment of All India Muslim League in 1906, a few of the outside factors and the policy of mass conversion by the *shuddhi* leaders led to increasing the gap between the Hindus and Muslims. Moreover, these events injected communalism in the Indian body politic. But the formation of the Muslim League was a great success of the British policy of 'divide and rule.' An Arya link with the Congress especially at a time when communal tension was building up inculcated as early as 1893 a feeling in the minds of the Muslims that the Hindu leaders were planning to establish in the country their own government and authority.[8] So they established a Muslim political organization known as All India Muslim League, parallel to the Congress, the object of which was, as *The Tribune* reports:[9]

> to develop a political instinct among the Indian Mussulmans, inculcating the true spirit of loyalty to the British Government to enable them to grasp accurately their political situation and to review with calm, deliberate and studied vigilance the different phases which our political life may present at various times, thus safeguarding the public interests of the Mahomedan community.

In reaction to the establishment of the All India Muslim League many Arya Samajists abandoned the Congress politics, which was, though dominated by the Hindus, and explicitly led the Hindus into a communal politics and joined the movement of social rejuvenation of the Hindus by making effective use of *shuddhi prachar*, education, and social uplift of the

---

8. In 1893, a Muslim newspaper wrote : "There is another party in Congress whose sole object in joining the movement is oppressing the *yavanas*. They are all Hindu revivalists... their object is nothing more or less than to establish a purely Hindu government." M.M. Ahluwalia, *Freedom Struggle in India, 1858-1909* (Delhi : Ranjit Printers and Publishers, 1965), p. 366.
9. *The Tribune*, April 24, 1906, p. 5.

society which they considered to be the only effective methods for the survival of the Hindus.[10] The formation of the Muslim League, which put pressures on the government for special grants and additional seats in the legislative councils[11] and declining of numerical strength of the Hindus due to the Christian conversions and more so due to redefinition of the term 'Hindu' by the Census reports created an apprehension in the minds of Punjabi Hindus who believed that "the time has come to organise and protect themselves."[12] In this connection, Lala Lal Chand, a staunch Arya Samajist of Punjab, wrote a series of letters to the well-known newspaper *Panjabee* in which he highlighted the necessity of an organization for the proper consolidation of Hindus[13] and which perhaps laid the foundation of the Hindu Mahasabha movement at the later stage.[14] Consequently, a Punjab Hindu Sabha was founded in the Punjab in January 1907[15] with a view to "watching and safeguarding the interests of the entire Hindu community in all respects."[16]

At the time of the announcement of the proposed Morley-Minto Reforms of 1909, the Punjab Hindu Sabha[17] submitted a long memorial to Lord Minto, the then Governor-General, drawing his attention to the "differential treatment in the distribution of government patronage" and the "disadvantageous position" in which the Hindus would be placed in

10. Kenneth W. Jones, *Arya Dharm* : *Hindu Consciousness in 19th Century Punjab* (New Delhi : Manohar Book Service, 1976), p. 280. (Hereafter quoted as *Arya Dharm*).
11. Norman G. Barrier, *op. cit.*, p. 379.
12. *Ibid.*, p. 378.
13. R.B. Lal Chand, *Self-Abnegation in Politics* (Delhi : The Central Hindu Yuvak Sabha, 1938), p. 6.
14. Indra Prakash, *A Review of the History and Work of the Hindu Mahasabha* (Delhi : Hindu Mahasabha, 1952), pp. 9-11.
15. K.K. Sharma, *Life and Times of Lala Lajpat Rai* (Ambala Cantt. : Indian Book Agency, 1975), p. 210.
16. Parshotam Mehra, *A Dictionary of Modern Indian History—1707-1947* (Delhi : Oxford University Press, 1985), p. 304.
17. R.B. Lal Chand, *op. cit.*, p. 6.

the matter of representation in the legislative council[18] due to the proposed constitutional reforms. So from the date of its establishment, the Punjab Hindu Sabha worked as the spokesman for Punjabi Hindus.[19] Thus the place of secular Congress was taken over by the "communal organizations determined to protect Hinduism at any cost."[20] Deriving strength from the Arya Samaj and the *shuddhi* movement, the Hindu Sabhas had "powerful, if sinister, overtones on the national plane."[21] Consequently, the Punjabi Hindus resorted to the increased use of *shuddhi* regardless of the possible opposition either from the Hindu orthodoxy or the non-Hindu leaders. Though they had already achieved much success in converting the Rahtias, Ods, Dumnas, and the Meghs in the first decade of the twentieth century yet the *shuddhi* movement remained largely a provincial phenomena.[22]

The Morley-Minto reforms which promised communal electorate to the Muslims and equated numbers with strength, infused a new spirit to the movement. In spite of the fact, that the *shuddhi* movement was a conservative social reaction to the challenge of Christianity, but in the wake of growing demand for representation on communal basis, it assumed political dimension as from the first decade of the twentieth century all the leading communities viz., Hindus, Muslims and Christians tried their best to increase their number in order to gain weightage in the legislative councils and local bodies.[23]

18. Parshotam Mehra, *op. cit.*, p. 304.
19. Norman G. Barrier, *op. cit.*, p. 379.
20. *Ibid.*
21. Parshotam Mehra, *op. cit.*, 305.
22. J.T.F. Jordens, "Reconversion to Hinduism, the Shuddhi of Arya Samaj" in G.A. Oddie (ed.), *Religion in South Asia : Religious Conversion and Revival Movements in South Asia in Medieval and Modern Times* (New Delhi : Manohar Book Service, New Delhi, 1977), p. 157.
23. Ganga Prasad Upadhyaya, *Swami Dayanand's Contribution to Hindu Solidarity* (Allahabad : Arya Samaj, Chowk, 1939), p. 117. Also see Khushwant Singh, *A History of the Sikhs* (Delhi : Oxford University Press, 1979), Vol. II, p. 217.

Although the *shuddhi* movement had achieved considerable success in converting the depressed sections of society yet this work had become necessary as well as significant in the light of 'Gait Circular' of 1910[24] which suggested that outcaste groups which could not really be considered Hindus be listed separately in the special table in the coming Census. Nevertheless, it was proposed that they should be retained as Hindus in the general tables.[25] This deliberate attempt of the British government to separate all Hindu outcastes from their community was widely resented by the Hindus who thought that if the outcastes were returned separately from the Hindus, the percentage of the Hindus would be dropped which, it was apprehended, would prove harmful to their political interest "including the proportioning of political representation..."[26] so they laid stress on the continuation of *shuddhi* and the existing reconversion and social uplift movements for the survival of their community. In this connection, the views of Ganga Prasad Upadhyaya are worth mentioning who appealed to his co-religionists that:[27]

> You rob a person as well as murder him, nationally as well as spiritually when you say to him "Vedic light is not meant for the outcastes." This is his individual spiritual loss so far as to deprive him of spiritual progress. But it is the loss of the whole nation too because the nation has been deprived of the services of an individual which might have been valuable to any extent. And who can deny this enormous national loss in these days when numerical strength is being taken into account in ascertaining its political rights, and when religious, social and economic rights of a people cannot be safeguarded except by having political rights.

24. 'Gait Circular' is a note from the Commissioner of the Census, E.A. Gait issued to his provincial Superintendent which was published in *The Tribune*, Novembar 12, 1910, p. 5.
25. *Ibid*.
26. Kenneth W. Jones, *Arya Dharm*, p. 306.
27. Ganga Prasad Upadhyaya, *op. cit.*, p. 12.

Whereas the *shuddhi* work of the Samaj was interrupted by the outbreak of First World War in 1914, but it brought the Muslim League closer to the Congress, though temporarily.[28] The Lucknow Pact of 1916, which accepted both separate electorates and weightage to the Muslims and subsequent incorporation of this scheme in the Montague-Chelmsford Reforms of 1919 brought them nearer.[29] The end of the First World War and the dismemberment of the Turkish Empire, caused widespread consternation among the Indian Muslims. And Mahatma Gandhi seized the opportunity of championing the cause of the Muslims over the Khilafat question in order to win their confidence and enlist their support for the freedom movement.[30] So there was apparent unity between the Hindus and the Muslims during the period 1919-1922.[31]

The *shuddhi* movement, which had been a provincial phenomenon so far, suddenly erupted on to the scene of national politics in early 1920s. As Congress politics went into a decline, separate communal consolidation became the main concern of both Hindus and Muslims.[32] The aftermath

28. Uma Kaura, *Muslims and Indian Nationalism* (New Delhi : Manohar Book Service, 1977), p. 19.
29. Ishwari Prasad and S. K. Subedar, *Hindu-Muslim Problems* (Allahabad : Chugh Publications, 1974), p. 61.
30. *Ibid.*, p. 66.
31. "The Hindu-Muslim unity brought about by Gandhi in 1920-21 was artificial in character and did not produce any real change of heart. It was based on the common hostility and hatred entertained, for quite different reasons, by the Indian nationalists and the khilafatists towards the British, and was sustained by the militant programme of Non-cooperation and Civil Disobedience. The suspension of the Civil Disobedience and Non-cooperation programme chilled the enthusiasm of the khilafatists, and when Kamal Pasha showed no concern for the holy places of Islam, and finally abolished the Caliphate, the khilafat movement died a natural death. The need for a common front against the British having thus disappeared, the Muslim politics again resumed its communal character," writes R.C. Majumdar (ed.), *History and Culture of the Indian People* (Bombay : Bhartiya Vidya Bhavan, 1965), Vol. XI, p. 424.
32. John C.B. Webster (ed.), *Popular Religion in the Punjab Today* (Delhi : I.S.P.C.K., 1974), p. 51.

of Moplah rebellion had serious repercussions on the Hindu society. The question of purification of those forcibly converted Hindus during the rebellion "dramatically placed the Arya Samaj and its work on the national stage, and it conclusively convinced the orthodox of the importance of *shuddhi*."[33] From this day, the orthodoxy started viewing the Arya Samaj as the saviour of the Hindu society.

Encouraged and backed up by the popular support of the Hindus, the Arya Samaj took up again the reconversion work of the Malkana Rajputs.[34] The case of the reconversion of the Malkana Rajputs is significant because soon after the withdrawal of the Non-cooperation movement the social forces which till then had presented the semblance of unity began to disintegrate on the communal lines, and the issue of reconversion of the Malkanas proved a catalyst assisting the process of polarization on communal lines. The Hindus organized institutions like *sangathan* and *shuddhi*[35] whereas Muslims in response to the virulent propaganda and reconversion work evolved *tanzim* and *tabligh*.[36] The result of these movements and counter movements was the organization of both the communities into rival religious camps as a direct result of which was increased communal bitterness breaking forth into increased communal rioting.

Although Hindu Sabhas had already been established on the provincial level to look after the interests of the Hindus, they remained almost lifeless for "it had two formidable rivals:

33. J.T.F. Jordens, *Reconversion to Hinduism*, p. 158.
34. *Census of India, 1911*, India Report, p. 118. The Malkana Rajputs were scattered most in the western part of the United Provinces. As has already been discussed, they retained many Hindu practices though they tended in the Census to declare themselves Muslims. Between 1909 and 1911 very serious efforts were made to reconvert the Malkanas and other Rajputs of the United Provinces and Rajputanas into the fold of the Arya Samaj. For more detail, see the preceding chapters.
35. *Home Deptt. Poll.*, File No. 6/IX of 1924, p. 14.
36. *Ibid.*, p. 17.

on the political side the Indian National Congress, on the socio-religious side, the Arya Samaj."[37] The All India Hindu Mahasabha which took its birth in 1915[38] also proved ineffective because of its pro-British outlook.[39] However, the Hindu-Muslim riots particularly at Malabar and Multan and the *tabligh* and *tanzim* movements rekindled the Hindu Mahasabha spirit. Although several attempt had been made by the Congress to induce the Hindu Mahasabha to interest itself in the anti-untouchability movement, nothing concrete could be done till 1923. The ninth session of the Hindu Mahasabha which held on August 19, 1923[40] at Banaras under the Presidentship of Pandit Madan Mohan Malaviya was very important event in the history of *shuddhi* movement. In this meeting both Swami Shraddhanand and Pandit Madan Mohan Malaviya, the former representing the radical group and the latter orthodox group, collaborated in the matters such as removal of untouchability and *shuddhi*.[41] Their efforts to have a resolution adopted to this effect had to be dropped because of orthodox opposition[42] but the country was stirred by the appeal of Pandit Malaviya who spoke as one representing orthodox Hinduism and took up the case enthusiastically.[43]

Besides affecting communal divide and consolidating a part of the Hindu society into a political organization for the protection and attainment of rights for the community it

37. Vijaya Chandra Joshi (ed.), *Lala Lajpat Rai: Writings and Speeches 1920-28* (Delhi : University Publishers, 1966), Vol. II, p. 208.
38. K.K. Sharma, *op. cit.*, p. 211.
39. J.T.F. Jordens, *Swami Shraddhanand : His Life and Causes* (Delhi : Oxford University Press, 1981), p. 135.
40. *Amrita Bazar Patrika*, August 21, 1923 in *Home Deptt. Poll.*, File No. 198 of 1924, p. 35.
41. *Ibid.*
42. Gene Robert Thursby, "Aspects of Hindu-Muslim Relations in British India : A Study of Arya Samaj Activities, Government of India Policies, and Communal Conflict in the period 1923-28," Unpublished Ph.D. Dissertation, Duke University, 1972, p. 70.
43. S. Natarajan, *A Century of Social Reform in India* (Bombay : Asia Publishing House, 1962), p. 153.

represented through political action, the *shuddhi* and *sangathan* movements of the Hindu and *tabligh* and *tanzim* of the Muslims, thus, helped in reviving the old communal spirit which resulted in very serious riots between these communities over petty issues.[44] The opposition of the Muslims to *shuddhi* movement can be well gauged from the following statement of Chaudhri Fateh Muhammad Sial, Head of the Ahmadiya sect in Western United Provinces, who asserted :[45]

> the shuddhi movement is a collective political attack by Hindus on Mussalmans. In making this attack all the baser sentiments have been excited and an effort has been made to apostatize village Rajputs by portraying before them the so-called oppressions of Muhammadan rulers. It is quite wrong to compare the shuddhi movement with the Islamic religious propaganda. In order to overpower the small Rajput community the whole country was set in motion, an uproar was caused through the press and by means of lectures, and lies were indulged in to such an extent as to eclipse even European propagandists. The result was that ill-feeling between Hindus and Mussalmans went on increasing until they became ready to cut each other's throats. Hindus in general and Arya Samajist leaders in particular are responsible for the present quarrels which have inflicted humiliation in the whole country.

The Muslims' suspicion with regard to the *shuddhi* and *sangathan* was resented by the Hindus who "felt themselves perfectly justified in converting or reconverting others to their own faith, a right which the Muslims and Christians had exercised all along and which alone accounted for their number in India."[46] These views were shared by the nationalist leaders like Rajendra Prasad who writes :[47]

44. Gene Robert Thursby, *op. cit.*, p. 73.
45. *Al Fazl*, October 30, 1922 in *Punjab Press Abstract, 1923*, p. 597.
46. R.C. Majumdar, *op. cit.*, p. 426.
47. Rajendra Prasad, *India Divided* (Bombay : Hind Kitabs, 1946), p. 123.

Political Dimensions of Shuddhi Movement

The Shuddhi movement of Swami Shraddhanand has come in for a great deal of criticism both from the nationalists and Mussalmans. Whatever one may have to say about its opportuneness at that particular movement, it is difficult to understand how Christians and Mussalmans can object to it on merits. They are constantly engaged in their proselytising mission and converting Hindus to their own faiths. If the Hindus on their side also start converting non-Hindus to their faith, it is no business of non-Hindus, specially if they are themselves engaged in the work of conversion, to object. The Hindus must have the same right of propagating their faith as others have. But men are not always guided by logic or by a sense of justice and fairness.

Although almost all the prominent leaders of these organizations such as Swami Shraddhanand, Pandit Madan Mohan Malaviya, Dr. Saifuddin Kitchlew and Mohammad Ali and also of the Congress were prone to the idea of Hindu-Muslim unity for the attainment of swaraj,[48] their efforts were thwarted by the war of pamphlets between Khwaja Hasan Nizami and Swami Shraddhanand both condemning and defending respectively their point of view in respect of *shuddhi* and *sangathan* movements.[49]

As regards the Sikhs, from limited cooperation with the Hindus,[50] they began to move towards communal mobilization

---

48. Ram Gopal, *Indian Muslims : A Political History (1858-1947)* (Bombay : Asia Publishing House, 1964), p. 161.
49. *Home Deptt. Poll.*, File No. 6/IX of 1924, p. 18. Also see J.T.F. Jordens, *Swami Shraddhanand*, pp. 140-41.
50. The instances of the cooperation between the Sikhs and Hindus in Punjab and their differences have been detailed out in the chapter III of the thesis. The differences mainly emerged between the two communities on the issues of the comments on the Sikh Gurus in the *Satyarth Prakash*, pork-test and the conversion of Rahtia Sikhs. However, the two communities remained socially well-knit which is evident from the statement of Prakash Tandon :

(Contd.)

seeking special weightage in representation to counter the Muslims' prescriptive majority in Punjab particularly after 1909. Since no degree of conversion could have given a position of political reckoning, the Sikhs attempted at communal mobilization to which the Hindus were not hostile as both the communities formed regional minorities in Punjab.[51] However, the Hindu-Sikh relationship in Punjab operated at two distinct levels, namely, at social level the Sikhs gradually consolidated the community in terms of evolving independent identity, whereas at political level they cooperated with the Hindus to counter Muslim majority in the Punjab.[52]

Nevertheless it cannot be denied that *shuddhi* movement did contribute in the already strained relations between the Hindus and Muslims. Even the staunch Arya Samajists did agree to this point. Lala Lajpat Rai writes that :[53]

Shuddhi was not the direct cause of these riots. But the wound inflicted on Muslim sentiment by the *Shuddhi* was

---

We Hindus and the Sikhs had the same castes and customs, and they were always members of our brotherhood—*biradaris*. In the villages we lived together and celebrate the same festivals. . . After all, we and the Sikhs stemmed from the same stock; most Hindus had Sikh relations, and inter-marriage was common. In our own family my elder brother married a girl who was a Sikh on her father's side, but a Hindu on her mother's.

It clearly indicates that there was no hostility between the two communities during the struggle for freedom. For detailed reference, see Prakash Tandon, *Punjabi Century : 1875-1947* (London : Chatto & Windus, 1961), p. 263.

51. Baldev Raj Nayar, *Minority Politics in the Punjab* (Princeton, N.J. : Princeton University Press, 1966), pp. 150-55. Also see Mohinder Singh, *The Akali Movement* (Delhi : The Macmillan Co. of India Ltd., 1978), pp. 137-50 and K.L. Tuteja, *Sikh Politics (1920-40)* (Kurukshetra : Vishal Publications, 1984), pp. 174-207.

52. For detail, see R.K. Ghai, "The Sikhs and the Arya Samaj : A Study of Mutual Response and Reaction" in *Punjab History Conference Proceedings*, 20th Session, March 1986, pp. 340-48.

53. Donald Eugene Smith, *India as a Secular State* (Princeton : Princeton University Press, 1963), p. 458.

undoubtedly one of the basic causes which produced the atmosphere which led to these riots and other exhibitions of violence. The motives were partially political, partially economic and partially religious.

Moreover, the *shuddhi* and *sangathan* movements not only served a setback to the freedom struggle but projected communal issues on the national scene pushing other social, economic and political issues into the background. Since the numerical strength of communities had an "important political implication in view of the system of separate electorates", V.D. Savarkar, a leader of the Hindu Mahasabha observed :[54]

> Political power in democracies hinges more and more on the population strength of a community which in the case of the Hindus must depend in the main on the proportion in which the Hindus succeed in stopping the dreadful conversion activities of alien faiths and in accelerating the reclamation of the alienated members back to the Hindu fold. In a country like India where a religious unit tends inevitably to grow into a cultural and national unity, the *shuddhi* movement ceases to be merely theological or dogmatic, but assumes the wider significance of a political and national movement. If the Muslims increase in population, the centre of political power is bound to be shifted in their favour.

For the Hindus *shuddhi* was "the lynch-pin" which linked the reformist zeal of the Arya Samaj with the Hindus' efforts for consolidation with a view to "engineering a new birth of Hindu consciousness and self-respect."[55] As an organization the *shuddhi*, on the one hand countered the threat of the Muslim and Christian proselytizing zeal for conversion, and on the other sustained the communal politics of Northern India as it had prepared the Hindus psychologically to face the

54. V.D. Savarkar, "The Hindu Mahasabha" in *The Indian Year Book 1942-43* (Bombay : The Times of India Press), p. 826.

55. J.F. Seunarine, *op. cit.*, p. 26.

challenge of Muslims which led to political violence and hardening of attitude of different communities.

During 1920s with the establishment of *shuddhi and sangathan* and *tanzim and tabligh*, the communal division between the Muslims and Hindus had come to stay and competed with each other for constitutional concessions and political power. As it had become a part of the national scene, the communal political organizations with their aggression politics protected the interest of their respective communities. In that process the *shuddhi* had laid the foundation by making the Hindus conscious of their communal identity and the need to maintain it against the growing Muslim communalism. After having performed the catalystic action, the *shuddhi* retreated to the background so that communal political party i.e. the Hindu Mahasabha more solidly organized and with greater resources than the *shuddhi* organization, could, as it did, take up the responsibility of protecting the interest of the conservative Hindus which even the Gandhian mass politics could not thwart. It, as Barrier believes, contributed, by promoting communal politics, to the partition of India.[56]

---

56. Norman G. Barrier, *op. cit.*, p. 379.

7

Conclusions

Although traditionally *shuddhi*, as a ritualistic means to purify individual qualifying him both to perform religious rites and participate in social relationship did not remain relevant in the medieval and the late-medieval period of Indian history[1] yet the word acquired a different connotation in the context of social milieu of the nineteenth century. It became an agency to convert people from the religions and purify the lower castes to ascribe them a higher status in society to counter the threat of Christianity and also Islam. In a way it was a defensive strategy of the reactive nature as the Hindu caste society, rigidly organized on purity and pollution concept, did not allow entry into the Hindu social structure except on the basis of birth. The dimension and dynamism of the strategy underwent gradual transformation in the face of rapidly growing political consciousness which was developing on communal lines, particularly in Punjab wherein the Hindus were a minority. Without high priesthood, the growing petty

---

1. To avoid confusion it must be mentioned that the cultural assimilation of the Greeks, Hunas, the Sakas, Kusans and host of other tribes, both indigenous and foreign who adopted Brahminical rituals and customs, were never converted by any *shuddhi* rituals. Hence, it cannot be termed as conversion.

bourgeoisie enthusiastically responded to *shuddhi* as an instrument to counteract Christian and Muslim efforts to proselytize the Hindus. Rooted in Hindu communal consciousness and confronted with the similar urge of the other communities the defensive strategy of the *shuddhi* assumed aggreessive and offensive overtones. Since the movement had no roots in the Hindu socio-religious traditions, it could not successfully operate for the lack of general social acceptability of the converted or the purified. Moreover, as is evident, the *shuddhi*, by its very nature and function, was a strategy with a limited purpose i.e. to stem the tide of conversions of the Hindus to other religions. It, therefore, could not establish its relevance in the Hindu society as a permanent feature because the movement gradually melted into the Hindu communal consciousness. As all the communities became highly conscious of their communal identity, the *shuddhi* movement of the Hindus like those of the other communities reached a bottleneck caused by their competitive spirit, particularly after 1930 during which we find mostly the cases of conversion of individuals or extremely small groups.

In the context of nineteenth century social history, the *shuddhi* movement signifies as a religious ritual for the conversion of people outside the Hindu caste. By virtue of this fact it was essentially a social movement as this innovation was designed to dissolve the hierarchy and rigidity of the caste system, the basic and the most distinct feature of the Hindu social structure. Spearheaded by the Indian middle classes with a view to maintaining their hegemony in a highly stratified Hindu society and to consolidate it for countering the political preponderance of the Muslim in Punjab, the significance of the *shuddhi* movement lies in the fact that it was adopted as an institution to transform Hinduism into a conversion religion. It was an acute realisation of the educated middle classes [which lacked class cohesion due to the absence of industry] of the magnitude of adverse consequences on the Hindu society of not mobilizing the Hindus on the basis of religion. The increasing awareness and liberal outlook which they had imbibed due to their contact with the Western culture helped the *shuddhi* movement to develop as an institution to affect reform of the Hindu society from within and to counter challenge the proselytizing efforts of other conversion religions. As regards the first, it may be pointed out that the *shuddhi* movement achieved a limited success. The psyche of the Hindu and the well-knit organization of the caste—rigid and hierarchical—inhibited social change to a great extent. Though Swami Dayanand, the founder, redefined the caste system on the basis of *gun*, *karam* and *svabhav* to dilute its rigidity yet there was built-in resistance from some of the members of Arya Samaj and certain groups of the Hindu society to modify caste structure and its customs. To meet its challenge the Arya Bhratri Sabha was organized as early as in 1895. But the majority of the Samaj members declined to break with their caste *biradaris* for the fear of excommunication. Although the militant groups of the Samaj slated a programme of social regeneration by initiating schemes such as educating the girls, raising the marriage age and in arranging the remarriage of widows, organizing community dinners, and propagating against social evils like the caste system, the reformatory movements had only influenced the fringe of Hindu urban society. The social relations of masses in villages and towns were still governed by the traditional religious customs and social practices. Even at a later stage the reformation movement could not cut across the caste barrier as it tended to grow on caste lines by the formation of caste Sabhas.

The formation of caste Sabhas within the Hindu community is an evidence of the fact that the caste group and not religion structured the fabric of social relationship of the Hindu community. This tendency deeply influenced the course and character of the *shuddhi* movement. By the turn of the present century the *shuddhi* switched over to the conversion of Rahtias, Meghs, Dumnas and Ods, the groups considered as untouchable. Because of the strong sense of purity and pollution, the Hindu caste *biradaries* refused to integrate and absorb them in their caste groups. Consequently, these groups of the lower caste desirous of elevating their status formed new caste having their own network of relationships within the Hindu caste structure. Though this satisfied the Hindu orthodoxy yet it signifies only a formal change.

Because of the emergence of new caste groups, the Hindu orthodox closed all doors of having any kind of social relations with the purified except during the Samaj functions. All appeals in this respect made by the radical groups of the Arya Samajist could not make any dent in the attitude of the Hindus. Even the Hindu Mahasabha, in spite of its consensus on *shuddhi* and uplift of the untouchables, had to bow before the orthodoxy on the question of inter-marriage and inter-dining.

Even the socio-religious reformation movement got divided into small streams influencing the delta-like caste *biradaries* including those which were formed by the lower caste groups. Many mandals and sabhas were organized for the social uplift of the untouchables and due to their programme of *shuddhi*, they were able to reconvert the lower castes and stem conversion of depressed classes to other religions. But for all practical purposes these efforts did not yield concrete results in terms of social change. As the majority of Arya Samajists and the Sanatanis were still opposed to giving the untouchables a status equal to that of the high caste Hindus, Swami Shraddhanand turned towards Congress politics to help ameliorate the condition of the depressed classes. But when for political reasons he found the Congress ineffective, he put his pressures on the Hindu Mahasabha which also could not oblige him due to the pressures of the orthodox members of the Sabha.

The reformatory programme of the Arya Samaj as among the Sikhs, had created a kind of duality in their social conduct. In the social gatherings of the Samaj, its members tended to project themselves as radicals while at homes and *biradari* meetings they behaved like most of the traditionalists and conservatives fearing the wrath of the caste *biradari*, a powerful social organization in the absence of class-based social cohesion. Therefore, the progress of *shuddhi* movement was seriously impeded by the intransignce of the Hindu society as well as the hegemonic interest of the middle classes. However, it cannot be denied that the *shuddhi* movement despite these social constraints succeeded in loosening the caste chains which had immobilized the Hindu society for centuries and as such allowed some social mobility more in order to meet the exigencies of the situation than to affect a social change.

As regards the political overtones of the *shuddhi* movement, they may be traced to the changing collective psyche of Hindus. The rise of the extremist ideas in the first decade of the twentieth century and the establishment of Muslim League in 1906, Minto-Morley Reforms of 1909 which promised communal electorate to the Muslims, and the 'Gait Circular' of 1910, in the changing socio-political milieu, were viewed as anti-Hindu measures of the government which alarmed the Hindus of Punjab. Leaders, like Lala Lal Chand who advocated the idea of Hindu consolidation on communal basis[2] because, as Kenneth W. Jones points out, "Communal unity, loyalty and patriotism offered hope for the future."[3] Thus the consolidation of people along the communal lines became the foremost aim of the religious reform movements of which *shuddhi* was a part.

The establishment of Punjab Hindu Sabha in 1907 on purely communal lines and the intensive *shuddhi* work by the Rajput Shuddhi Sabha brought the Arya Samaj movement into direct conflict with the Muslims of India. The establishment of Bhartiya Hindu Shuddhi Sabha in 1923 for the purification of Malkana Rajputs of United Provinces which put the *shuddhi* movement on all India basis and the subsequent organizations of Muslims like *tabligh* and *tanzim* as against *shuddhi* and *sangathan* led to disastrous socio-political consequence. The war of pamphlets and riots tore apart the social

2. R.B. Lal Chand, *Self-Abnegation in Politics* (Lahore : The Central Hindu Yuvak Sabha, 1938), p. 100.
3. Kenneth W. Jones, *Arya Dharm* : *Hindu Consciousness in 19th-Century Punjab* (New Delhi: Manohar Book Service, 1976), p. 287.

fabric and inaugurated an era of communal distrust and violence.

The Moplah rebellion of 1921 led even the orthodox section of the Hindus to give their sanction and tacit support to the *shuddhi* work for purely political reasons. The establishment of *Punah Samskar Samiti* by the orthodoxy only a month after the establishment of Bhartiya Hindu Shuddhi Sabha in 1923 are some of the acts indicative of this trend. The changing political climate of the country made all the communities conscious of consolidating their number and increasing their strength numerically by securing converts from other religions.

Unique in nature and character and incompatible with the Hindu tradition, the *shuddhi* was the product of historical situation comprising of the strands of reformism, revivalism and nationalism. It was adopted as an instrument of defence and consolidation of Hinduism against the proselytizing efforts of Christianity and Islam. A double-edged weapon, it, on the one hand, aimed at organizing the Hindu community by dissolving caste rigidity and hierarchy from within and on the other defending it from external danger by adopting the same strategy with which the proselytizing religions threatened it. Achieving limited success in diffusing caste distinctions, it certainly helped in creating communal consciousness amongst the Hindus which ultimately got submerged in communal politics, sharpening the communal contours of body-politic of the country. For Hindus it temporarily served in stemming the tide of conversion to other religions; but being a national majority the Hindu communalism acquired the garb of petty bourgeois nationalism which, in the absence of well-defined class formation, did not differ in its intrinsic spirit and nature from communal politics.

APPENDICES

Appendix I

Letters of Ram Bhaj Datt Chaudhri*, President, All India Bharat Shuddhi Sabha, Gurdaspur regarding the opposition which the purified Dumnas had to face from the orthodox Hindus and Muslims alike

Letter No. 1

Raising of the Depressed Class in the Gurdaspur District

I. Dina Nagar

Dissuaded and disheartened by the opposition only thirteen Doomnas came forward to be purified and raised out of the hundreds who had come to the anniversary of the Dina Nagar Arya Samaj. The major portion of them had remained in their villages. This was the information received when I went to see the Nagar-kirtan procession start. Twenty here and thirty there, ten in one place and fifteen in another, the Doomnas were standing and talking in great confusion. Even Lala Bakhshih Ram, the life and soul of the local body, could not persuade them to come together; 9 P.M. was the hour announced for my address. Till about 10 P.M. I waited for them in the Samaj Mandir but none turned up, so I repaired

*Reproduced from *The Tribune*, September 15, 1912, p. 2 and October 2, 1912, p. 2.

to the place where they had put up. I had to wake up many who were already asleep. A serious conference took place after I had addressed them for over an hour. Their doubts were set at rest, they felt convinced of the falseness of the rumour that they would be taxed ten rupees per head for purification.

But Doolo of Bahadar Lahri, an influential of theirs, was not fully satisfied yet. He stood up and said: "Sir, a Rajput ruler of one district married a young Rajput princess. While bringing her home her palanquin was ordered to be put on the ground and the retainers were asked to retire. The Raja asked his bride, "what would you do if I were to die." "I will die a sati with you on the same pyre," was the reply. On this Raja unseathed his sword and beheaded the Rani. Seven times he married young daughters of recognised Rajput families, and each time he beheaded his new wife in similar fashion. For the eighth time he married the sister of the ruling prince of Jammu. The same question was repeated, but the answer was different on this occasion. The proud princess of Jammu answered "I will examine your dead body when it is brought home by the soldiers from the battle-field. If I find all the cuts and injuries on your face and breast and none on your back I will burn myself alive as your sati wife, but if I find the mark of a cut or of a short on your back I will spit on the body and cry no more." The Prince appreciated the reply and took her home. He began, however, to burn every day, a citadel of Jammu made of papers. The young Rani could not bear the repeated insult to her people. She sent word to her brother to come with arms and put an end to the insult daily offered to the great Jammu Raj. A terrible fight took place between her brother and her husband. Both fell in the battle-field. True to her word she examined the body of her noble lord and singing his praises the Rani immolated herself on the same pyre with her husband."

Doolo continued, "Take us the Doomnas to be the eighth Rani. We will die to a man to carry out your religious instructions; we will suffer calmly the persecution on the orthodox but we will not waver from the path of truth and righteousness, if only you agree to stand by us,' and not show your back at the time of trial."

I was struck by the appeal of this so-called untouchable man. There was no time to consult my colleagues and I was pressed to give my own personal assurance which I gave after some deliberation. The moment I did so they all agreed to undergo the ceremony giving expression to their feeling in touching words. I wish their words could reach the ears of the millions of the indifferent and hard hearted Hindus so that they might stretch a helping hand to their fellow beings.

Nine hundred and six Doomnas were purified the next day after my appeal on their behalf to the thousands of Hindus present. The audience reminded me of the audience that I had to address at Sialkot some twelve years ago on the occasion of the first *Shuddhi* ceremony of the Meghs. Here, too, the Hindus came with a mind as much biased against the ceremony as they had done in Sialkot but here as there they soon became sympathetic. As in Sialkot so in Dina Nagar they resolved unanimously, on my putting the matter to the vote, to receive the purified ones with open arms into their fold. At Sialkot, too the Meghs were frightened and sent back to their villages the same way as the Doomnas here. In Sialkot Lala Ganga Ram was the moving spirit so as Lala Bakhshish Ram in Dina Nagar. I hope the latter will prove as persistent in the efforts as the former.

II. Sujanpur

The 6th August was the date fixed for the purification of their brethren at Sujanpur. The news of a serious opposition reached me at Lahore on the morning of 4th August. The Hindus of Sujanpur had resolved to excommunicate those who would render the least assistance. Nobody would lend the use of a house or a baithak for putting up the Arya preachers and singers whose services and cooperation I had secured. The deputation has formed on behalf of and at the expense of the All India Bharat Shuddhi Sabha, Swamis Dharmanand and Permanand, Pundits Dev Datt and Prag Datt, Guranditta Sant Ram Bhajnaik constituted the deputation besides myself. My wife was also very kindly accompanied me in my mission to the hot and malarial villages of Gurdaspur.

Late at night we reached at Sujanpur. A little after midnight I took down the names of the leaders of the various Hindu castes and communities. The next morning I went from shop to shop and house to house and to the delight of us all we soon rallied them on the...truth; but I was told that Lala...had yet to be won over. I went to him, held a conference with him for over an hour and get his promise of support. He is known to be man of his word and so he proved to be. I called on a leader of the Mahomedans also and went to the only Parsi gentleman in the station. Both helped me. Mr. Jehangir gave me every possible help, granted leave to those of his subordinates whose services I required and sent me carpets, matting and chairs & c., for the people.

In the evening of the 5th I delivered a speech calling on the Mahomedans to render assistance. Sheikh Gulam Nabi, the recognised leader of the Mahomedans of the town, stood up in the meeting and promised help. Though later in the evening Maulvis preached against us, much Mahomedan opposition was conciliated.

The next day was the day of purificiation, but up to midday none of the Doomnas appeared.

However, there was a large gathering by 3 o'clock in the afternoon and I was addressing a crowd of six to seven thousand people. About four hundred Hindu ladies were present. The next two days were spent in performing the ceremony of purification. On the 7th I requested the Hindu leaders to allow the purified men to draw water from their wells. They granted me prayers. Chaudhri Jalal Din, the energetic and popular Sub-Inspector of Police, came to the place of meeting. In a body we rose and went accompanied by hundreds of the purified persons to the heart of the Hindu quarter known as Mohilla Qanungoan. There was a large crowd. The large open square round the well was filled with men. One of the leaders of the purified men was called to come up and draw water. With the permission of the Hindus present he did so. The gathering dispersed after a public prayer and thanksgiving to the king Emperor, the Government, the Police and the Bradri of Sujanpur.

Education

It has been made obligatory on the purified families to send their children of a school going age to the public schools under Government control. For in my humble opinion the very object of taking these people into the fold of our society is lost if separate schools are established for them.

Letter No. 2

Murara

Sir,—From Sujanpur we proceeded to Murara. At Pathankot I was warned of the impossibilities of the roads. Riding through submerged rice fields, tracing our way somehow up to the banks of Nawani Khal we had to come to a halt. The Khal was swollen with flood, there was neither boat nor bridge. We swam across. On the other side of the bank an old Mahomedan gentleman cheered us and spoke despairingly of the cowardice displayed by certain so called Arya Samajists of Bahrampur in going to Hardwar to do *prayaschit* for joining in the *shuddhi* of the depressed at Dinanagar. He assured me he would manage the Mahomedans of Murara and that they would not oppose us in our good work. The Hindu opposition however was great. The rumours of their holding evil intentions towards us was so thick that the same old kindly Mahomedan came up to me just before sunset at a time when they were becoming too troublesome to me in the course of my speech and said in whisper: "For God's sake don't stop here for the night. They will kill you. I have come here with the mere object of escorting you back to my village Bharatpur where you will find yourself absolutely safe."

I was very grateful to this old gentleman of a different faith who sympathised with our cause and felt so much concerned for our personal safety. I made him understand that there was nothing to fear: it was God's cause and under the protection of a benign Government. So he need not fear about our safety; we were doubly protected—by God and by Government. Another old Hindu Sadhu had started on a journey from his village Galri Bawian to stop me from going to Murara. He went to Gurdaspur, followed me to Dinanagar but retraced his steps hearing that I had already left as he was too old to swim across the Nawani. He went back but waited on the other side of the water to meet us and help us at Dorangala, when the deputation went there three weeks later.

Our worthy host Chaudhri Fateh Chand and Lala Labhu Ram did all they could do for us. The other Hindu leaders were obdurate till Chaudhri Rahim Bakhsh, a leading Zamindar and *sufedposh* of Murara, got up in the meeting just after I had finished thanking the old Mahomedan for his kind offer of protection and said:

> Punditji for two hours you have been beating your head in vain against this wall of Hindu obstinacy. Your work is God's work but they understand not. Do place in my hand some half a dozen of your *doomnas* and allow me to make them embrace Islam. Then see who dares refuse him drawing water from the well.

The words went deep into Chaudhri Suchet Singh's heart (a leading Rajput Zamindar of Adalatgarh) who till then was thoroughly opposed to the uplifting of the depressed classes. Next day he brought all the depressed in his village to undergo the ceremony of purification. Owing to the impossibility of the stream all round only two hundred and three persons could come to join the ceremony. After the water...little too late the next day and when our party had already left Murara for another place, a large number of the poor people came there for *Shuddhi* encouraged by those who had joined our first meeting.

Nainakote

Nainakote was the next place we visited. It is a small but important Hindu town in Shakargarh Tehsil. To reach there we had to cross the Trimma Junction of the Ravi and Ugh in high waters. A great battle had been fought here between the English and the Sikhs. The women fold of our host refused to cook for us. Lala Ramditta Mal and Chaudhri Jaggat Ram were left alone by all those who in easy times call themselves reformers. At three I found myself addressing and debating before a huge gathering with hundreds of women on the top of the surrounding houses. In the meeting the opposition was led by the Sikh Jats. After 4 hours' hard struggle the votes were called for; there was none either for or against. A voice came from a prominent man, "purify them. All are for, but none dare say so."

Still next day out of the several hundred present only 48 Doomnas came forward for the *Shuddhi*. I soon found out the cause. The unfortunate people had been told that a certain bridge had fallen and human heads were required to lay the foundations of that bridge. That is why we were enticing them to lay their heads bare before us. Every head thus saved was doomed to be severed from its shoulders was the rumour which with different modifications had been set afloat all over the district. At Kathlour one man told me, "Punditji you are our *Maibap*, tell me plainly and I am ready to give my head for the sake of Dharama, but for God's sake don't take it by deception." I explained to them the absurdity of the rumour with the result that four hundred men got themselves shaved and got purified next day.

I had hardly finished exposing the absurdity of the rumour when a Brahmin came with a number of followers to hold Shashtrarth with us. In spite of my best efforts to avoid a Shashtrath which results only in party feeling, we were forced into it. The Pundit, however, soon found his position untenable and unceremoniously left the meeting, one of his friends hurling a stone at us. The Police were up and alert and were making several arrests, but on my special request they left the matter drop. The Pundit had come from some adjoining village and he was not aware of the Conference I had held with the leading Hindus of the town in the morning. Another meeting of the Biradri was called by me again; but this time not to ask their permission to draw water from the Hindu wells but to secure friendly feelings between the two factions of the Hindu Biradri whose mutual enmity and discord had resulted in several criminal and civil cases pending at the time in Gurdaspur Courts. After the parties had given vent to their feelings and had had their say I proposed an opening of the heart, certain terms which were accepted by all and a settlement arrived at. The Brahmin leaders, who had kept aloof from the Shuddhi Conference of the first day, had all come to this meeting and approved and confirmed the resolution of the previous meeting that the purified ones be allowed to draw water from joint Hindu Mahomedan wells and that their untouchableness be removed.

Here we went a step beyond the one we took at Sujanpur. The purified ones were not only allowed to draw water from the wells but they were given the duty of drawing and distributing water to thousands of Hindus and Mahomedans gathered there to see the ceremony. The success of the Shuddhi work here was due to the fearlessness of Lala Ramditta Mal and Chaudhri Jaggat Ram and Pandit Ralla Ram and to the good sense of the Hindu Biradri and their leaders Lala Chhajju Ram and Lala Shankar Das.

It would be ungrateful to me if I were not to publicly thank Sayed Nawab Shah, the Imam of the Town, for his promising help in response to my appeal in the next day's meeting. That this gentleman was sincere to the backbone was made clear to me when I heard him addressing a small audience of about 20 Musalmans who were against allowing the raised ones to draw water from the joint Hindu-Mahomedan wells. He said, "Are you Musalmans who neither keep *Roza* nor say your *Namaz*, why worship the tombs and do so many acts of infidelity!" You are Kafirs if you oppose those who have undertaken to give up many and worship one God."

Masrur

The bitterest opposition that we met with was at Masrur, a village owned by Brahmins. Our host, one of the Brahmin Zamindars soon found it impossible to keep us in his house being threatened with excommunication. There were open threats that both the purifiers and the purified would be belaboured with lathis during the performance of the ceremony, if it was done inside the village boundaries. So it was suggested by one of us that it would be wiser to have the purification outside the village limits. But the Doomnas objected to it on the ground that if they were to leave their village for good after the purification it would be best to have the ceremony outside, but if they were to live in their own houses even after the purification it should take place within the village.

While the ceremony was going on, a bumptious Zamindar on horse back came and asked in a threatening voice "who is responsible for this act." The poor depressed got frightened but on the man being confronted by me with the words "I am responsible and not these men," he wheeled his horse round with curses and abuses for the Doomnas and left. Two hundred and twelve persons were purified.

At my finding fault with these people for not attending the meeting with clean clothes and for not putting on *Dhoties* instead of loin cloth and on my enjoining them to always keep their bodies, dresses and houses clean, they requested me to inspect their houses before I left the village. I went round and saw that they were exceptionally clean and well kept. At the second house its owner brought out a clean shirt and

Dhoti and said, "Sir, we have these things, but we are not allowed to put them on except on the sly. The Chaudhries of our village object to our looking as clean as they themselves. If we wear a *Dhoti* reaching below our knees and look like them they would beat us to death." I was struck dumb with the revelation in the man's words. Here we are Hindus of the upper classes who cannot bear the Hindus of the lower classes even look as clean and human as ourselves.

Appendix II

Some Cases of Reconversion of Individuals and Small Groups During the Year 1929-30

1. On June 21, 1929, 42 Beildars were purified by Balia branch of Bhartiya Hindu Shuddhi Sabha. The *Shuddhi Samskar* was done on the Sanatan Dharam pattern by giving them *janeu* and performing *Katha* and *Havan*. After the purification ceremony, the people of all castes participated in the feast where they accepted food from the newly purified.

2. On June 23, 1929, Arya Samaj, Sagar (Central Provinces) reconverted a person who had become a Christian a year ago. After his purification he was named as Panna Lal.

3. On October 1, 1929, 3 men, one woman and one child were purified by the Calcutta branch of the Shuddhi Sabha.

4. One Sriram Keshab, a 32 years old Padri, who was converted by Swadeshi Alliance Mission, was purified by Surat branch of the Shuddhi Sabha. He left his wife and children behind.

5. On October 21, 1929, a born Muslim lady whose name was Rummo was purified by Ettah Arya Samaj. A new name, Ram Pyari was given to her.

6. On October 21, 1929, one Dost Muhammad was purified by the Baranganiya Arya Samaj (Muzaffarnagar). He was given a new name Ganesh.

7. On December 19, 1929, a Christian family of 7 members was purified by Shuddhi Sabha, Katra (Prayag). They all were given new names: Mr. Prem Singh Arya (Mr. John William), Shrimati Sundri Devi (Mrs. Sunder) and the children were renamed as Hira Singh, Hari Singh, Partap Singh and Premwati. The whole audience accepted water from them.

8. On January 19, 1930, two women were purified in Alawalpur village by Farrukhabad branch of the Shuddhi Sabha.

9. On February 28, 1930, one Sewa Ram who was converted to Islam six months ago was purified by Bareli branch of the Shuddhi Sabha. All acccepted prasad from him after the purification ceremony.

10. On March 2, 1930, one Bhairon Parsad who was converted to Islam and was given a new name Ashif Ali was reconverted by the Arya Samaj, Shahjahanpur.

11. On March 20, 1930, Srimati Nandi Devi Christian (Nurse) with her son and daughter was purified by Mugal Sarai branch and she distributed food to all present.

12. On March 25, 1930, one Musmaat Nawab Jan, daughter of Allah Kabir Vaishya whose age was 17 was purified on her request by Shuddhi Sabha, Ambala. She was given a new name Kaushalya Devi. All present accepted sweets from her hand.

13. On March 31, 1930, a family of 9 persons was purified by Shuddhi Sabha, Mathura.

14. One Wazir Khan of Nawab Ganj (Kanpur) was purified and renamed as Wazir Chand on June 15, 1930.

15. One person was purified on July 20, 1930 by a Sanatanist Brahmin in Baksar (Bengal).

16. On July 23, 1930, 41 persons were purified at Madupur (Bihar). These people were Kahar of Maccuha caste.

17. On September 25, 1930, one Maulvi Hafiz Ali was purified at Chitroli, District Baitool, Madhya Pradesh. He was renamed as Gyian Chand.

18. On October 19, 1930, one Deen Mohammad, a neo-Muslim was purified in the Arya Samaj Mandir, Darbhanga (Bihar). He was renamed Anant Lal. After *shuddhi* sweets were distributed by him.

For references, see *Shuddhi Samachar*, August 1929, pp. 371, 374; December 1929, pp. 534-37; February 15, 1930, pp. 80-81, 84; April 15, 1930, pp. 168-69; June 15, 1930, p. 274; August 15, 1930, pp. 362, 365; October 10, 1930, p. 451; and November 11, 1930, p. 491.

Appendix III

Ten Principles of the Arya Samaj

1. God is the primary cause of all true knowledge, and of everything known by its means.
2. God is All-truth, All-knowledge, All-beautitude, Incorporeal, Almighty, Just, Merciful, Unbegotten, Infinite, Unchangeable, without a beginning, Incomparable, the support and the Lord of all, All-pervading, Omniscient, Imperishable, Immortal, Exempt from fear, Eternal, Holy and the Cause of the Universe. To Him alone worship is due.
3. The Vedas are the Books of true knowledge, and it is the paramount duty of every Arya to read or hear them read, to teach and preach them to others.
4. An Arya should always be ready to accept truth and renounce untruth when discovered.
5. All actions ought to be done conformably to virtue, i.e. after a thorough consideration of right and wrong.
6. The primary object of the Samaj is to do good to the world by improving the physical, spiritual and social condition of mankind.
7. All ought to be treated with love, justice and due regard to their merits.

8. Ignorance ought to be dispelled and knowledge diffused.

9. No one ought to be contented with his own good alone; but every one ought to regard his prosperity as included in that of others.

10. In matters which affect the general social well-being of our race he ought to discard all differences and not allow his individuality to interfere, but in strictly personal matters every one may act with freedom.

Appendix IV

Objects and Programmes of Jat Pat Todak Mandal*

(i) Educating and organizing public opinion against the caste system and hammering down the caste mentality by propaganda from press and platform.

(ii) Establishing an Inter-caste Marriage Department in order to encourage and help in arranging inter-caste marriages amonst all sections of the Hindu society inside or outside the various Provinces of India.

(iii) Encouraging and arranging inter-caste dinners and adopting such other means of social intercourse as would be conducive to the removal of untouchability.

(iv) Inculcating among the Hindus the dignity of labour by persuading them to adopt any honest profession.

(v) Creating a common platform for the Hindus, irrespective of race, caste, creed, language, or domicile.

(vi) Starting propaganda Papers or Journals and publishing such literature as would be necessary for the propagation of the Aims and Objects of the Mandal.

*Reproduced from *Jat Pat Todak Mandal, General Review*, 1939, pp. 1-2.

(vii) Creating and organizing public opinion amongst the Hindus against the returning of caste in educatinal, legal and other government documents including the Census.

(viii) Opening branches of the Mandal and establishing Centres of Activity in the various Provinces of India and abroad.

(ix) Undertaking all such other things as are incidental and conducive to the objects of the Mandal.

Bibliography

A. PRIMARY SOURCES

1. Reports and Proceedings of the Arya Samaj

Annual Reports of the Arya Pratinidhi Sabha, Punjab.

Bhartiya Hindu Shuddhi Sabha. *Pratham Varshik Report,* Agra: Shanti Press, 1980 Vik.

Bhartiya Hindu Shuddhi Sabha. *Dvitiya Varshik Report.* Agra: Shanti Press, 1981 Vik.

Bhartiya Hindu Shuddhi Sabha. *Tritya Varshik Report.* Lucknow: Shukla Printing Press, 1982 Vik.

Bhartiya Hindu Shuddhi Sabha. *Chaturth Varshik Vivran.* Delhi: Arjun Press, n.d.

Bhartiya Hindu Shuddhi Sabha. *Pancham Varshik Vivran.* Delhi: Swami Chidanand, n.d.

2. Reports and Files of the Government and other Organizations

All India Congress Committee Files.
Annual Reports on the Popular Education in the Punjab.
Census of India, Baroda Reports (1881 to 1931).
Census of India, Bihar and Orissa Reports (1881 to 1931).
Census of India, Gwalior Reports (1881 to 1931).
Census of India, India Reports (1881 to 1941).
Census of India, Jammu and Kashmir Reports (1881 to 1931).

Census of India, Punjab Reports (1881 to 1941).
Census of India, United Provinces of Oudh and Agra Reports (1881 to 1931).
Home Department Political Files (From 1909 to 1931).
Imperial Gazetteers of India (From 1881 to 1908).
Punjab Government, *Gazetteer of Dera Ismail Khan District (1883-84).*
Punjab Government, *Gazeetter of Ludhiana District, (1888-89).*
Punjab Government, *Gazeetter of Sialkot District (1883-84).*

3. Newspapers and Periodicals of the Arya Samaj

Arya
Arya Gazette
Arya Magazine
Arya Samachar
Regeneration of Arya Varta
Sat Dharm Pracharak
Shraddha
Shraddhanand
Shuddhi Samachar
The Arya Directory
The Arya Patrika
The Vedic Magazine and Gurukul Samachar

4. Contemporary Publications of the Arya Samaj

(a) English

Bhan, Suraj, *Dayanand, His Life and Work*, Allahabad: India Press, 1934.
Chamupati, Pundit, *The Ten Principles of the Arya Samaj*, Madras: Arya Samaj, 1919.
Chand, Diwan, *The Arya Samaj: What it is and What it Stands For*, Lahore: Arya Pradeshik Pratinidhi Sabha, 1942.

———, *The Arya Samaj: Its Teachings and An Estimate of it*, Lahore: Arya Pratinidhi Sabha, n.d.

Chand, Gokal, *The Luther of India*, Lahore: Youngmen's Arya Samaj Tract Society, 1912.

Chand, R.B. Lal, *Self-Abnegation in Politics*, Lahore: The Central Hindu Yuvak Sabha, 1938.

Chatterjee, B.R., *Ideal Aryan Life*, Lahore: Arya Pratinidhi Sabha, n.d.

———, *Life of Sreeman Dayanand Saraswati*, Lahore: Arya Pratinidhi Sabha, n.d.

Datta, Guru, *Wisdom of the Rishi or Works of Pt. Gurudatta Vidyarthi, M.A.*, Delhi: Sarvadeshik Pustakalaya, n.d.

Deva, Rama, *The Arya Samaj*, Gurukul Kangri: Saddharma Pracharak Press, 1911.

General Review of Jat Pat Todak Mandal, Lahore: Jat Pa Todak Mandal, 1938.

Ghurye, G.S., *Soical Tensions in India*, Bombay: Popular Prakashan, 1968.

———, *Caste and Race in India*, Bombay: Popular Prakashan, 1969.

Golaknath, Henry, *Golak, The Hero*, Bombay: The Times of India Press, 1932.

Greenfield, M. Rose, *Five Years in Ludhiana*, Edinburgh: Religious Tract and Book Society, 1886.

Mul Raj, *Arya Samaj and Dogmas*, Ajmer: Propakarni Sabha, n.d.

Nigam, Zorawar Singh, *The Vedic Religion and Its Expounder Swami Dayananda*, Allahabad: n. pub. 1914.

Parmanand, Bhai, *Hindu Sungathan*, Lahore: The Central Hindu Yuvak Sabha, 1936.

Prakash, Vishwa, *Life and Teachings of Swami Dayanand*, Allahabad: Kala Press, 1935.

Prasad, Durga, *An English Translation of the Satyarth Prakash*, New Delhi: Jan Gyan Prakashan, 1970.

Rai, Lala Lajpat, *The Life of Pandit Gurudatta Vidarthi*, Lahore, Virjanand Press, n.d.

———, *The Depressed Classes*, Lahore: Ishwar Chandra Arya Tract Society, n.d.

———, *The Arya Samaj: An Account of Its Aims, Doctrines and Activities with A Biographical Sketch of the Founder*, Lahore: Uttar Chand Kapur and Sons, 1932.

Ram, Ganga and Dass, Charu, *The Uplift Movement at Sailkot, Punjab: A Brief Report of the Working of the Arya Megh Uddhar Sabha* (Aryan Mission for the Uplift of the Megh Untouchables), *Sialkot, Punjab*, Calcutta: A.C. Sarkar, 1915.

Ram, Lala Ralla, *The Arya Samaj—What is it?* Lahore: Arya Pratinidhi Sabha, n.d.

Ram, Munshi, *The Arya Samaj and Politics, a Lecture of the Lahore Arya Samaj*, Lahore: Printing Works, 1920.

Ram, Munshi and Deva, Rama, *The Arya Samaj and its Detractors: A Vindication*, Kangri, Hardwar: Satya Dharm Pracharak Press, 1910.

Ram, Shri Sant, *Caste Must go, A Word about the Jat Pat Todak Mandal*, Lahore: Jat Pat Todak Mandal, 1938.

Sarab, Dayal, *Dayanand, the Secr*, Ambala Cantt: Arya Samaj, Kacha Bazar, n.d.

Sarda, Har Bilas, *Works of Maharishi Dayanand and the Paropkarni Sabha*, Ajmer: Vedic Yantralaya, 1942.

———, *The Life of Dayananda Saraswati*, Ajmer: Vedic Yantralaya, 1964.

——— (ed.), *Dayanand Commemoration Volume*, Ajmer: Vedic Yantralaya, 1933.

Seth, Madan Mohan, *The Arya Samaj, A Political Body, Being An Open Letter to Viscount Morley of Blackburn, His Majesty's Secretary of State for India*, Gurukul Kangri: Saddharma Pracharak Press, n.d.)

Sharma, Vishnu Lal, *Handbook of the Arya Samaj*, Allahabad: Arya Pratinidhi Sabha, 1912.

Shraddhanand, Swami, *Hindu Sangathan, Saviour of the Dying Race*, Delhi: Swami Shraddhanand, 1926.

Singh, Gurumukh, *My attempted Excommunication from the Sikh Temples and the Khalsa Community at Faridkot in 1897*, Lahore: Civil and Military Gazette Press, 1898.

Upadhyaya, Ganga Prasad, *Arya Samaj: A World Movement*, Allahabad: Arya Samaj, Chowk, 1913.

―――, *Shuddhi*, Allahabad: Arya Samaj, Chowk, 1930.

―――, *The Arya Samaj and Christianity*, Allahabad: Arya Samaj, Chowk, 1931.

―――, *The Arya Samaj and Islam*, Allahabad: Arya Samaj, Chowk, 1933.

―――, *Swami Dayanand's Contribution to Hindu Solidarity*, Allahabad: Arya Samaj, Chowk, 1939.

―――, *The Origin, Scope and Mission of the Arya Samaj*, Allahabad: Arya Samaj, Chowk, 1940.

(b) Hindi

Bhagwandatta (ed.), *Rishi Dayanand Saraswati ke Patra Aur Vigyapan*, Amritsar: Ram Lal Kapur Trust, 1955.

Bhartiya, Bhawani Lal, *Arya Samaj Ateet ki Uplabdhian Tatha Bhavisha ke Prashin*, Jullundur: Arya Pratinidhi Sabha, Punjab, 1978.

Choudhry, J.P., *Shuddhi Prasnouttari*, Kashi: Choudhry and Sons, 1929.

―――, *Shuddhi Sanatan Hai*, Banas City: Choudhry & Sons, 1930.

Darshananand, Swami, *Varna Vyavastha*, Lahore: Wazir Chand Sharma, n.d.

Javed, Ramchandra, *Arya Samaj ke Maha Purush*, Jullundur: University Publishers, n.d.

Jhalu, Dayal, *Shuddhi Se Nak Man Dam*, Lucknow: Talukdar Press, 1920.

Kanal, P.V., *Bhagwan Dev Atma*, Lahore: Dev Samaj Book Depot, 1942.

Mimansak, Yudhishter, *Rishi Dayanand ke Granthon ka Itihas*, Ajmer: Vijay Press, 1941.

Mukhopadhyaya, Devendra Nath, *Maharishi Dayanand ke Jiwan Charita*, Hi. tr. by Ghasi Ram, Calcutta: n. pub., 1896.

Narain Singh, Bawa, *Sikh Hindu Hain*, Amritsar: n. pub., 1899.

Pathak, Bansidhar, *Binno Devi* (Shuddhi ki Devi), Barelli: Shayamlal Satyadeva, 1928.

Pathak, R.P., *Arya Kaun Hai*, New Delhi: Sarvadeshik Arya Pratinidhi Sabha, n.d.

Pursharthy, Om Parkash, *Bharat Me Bhiunkar Ishai Sheduntur*, Delhi: Sarvdeshik Press, n.d.

Rai, Lajpat, *Svargiya Lala Lajpatrayji ki Atmakatha*, Ed. by Bhimsen Vidyalankar, Lahore: Navug Granthmala, 1932.

Santram, Sri, *Hamara Samaj*, Bombay: Nalanda Prakashan, 1949.

Sannyasi, Chidanand, *Shuddhi Samskar-Padhti*, Delhi: Bhartiya Hindu Shuddhi Sabha, 1983 Vik.

———, *Shuddhi Vyavastha*, Delhi: Bhartiya Hindu Shuddhi Sabha, 1983 Vik.

Sharda, Kanwar Chand Karem, *Shuddhi*, Ajmer: n. pub. n.d.

Sharma, Ram Chandra and Gupta, Tota Ram, *Dharma Itihas Rahassya*, Barelli: Vedic Pustakalaya, November 1929.

Shastri, Shriman Mehta Ramchandraji, *Pataton ki Shuddhi Sanathan Hai*, Lahore: Arya Pradeshik Pratinidhi Sabha, 1908.

Shraddhanand, Swami, *Dharmvir Pandit Lekh Ram Jivan-Charitra*, Jullnndur: Arya Pradeshik Pratinidhi Sabha, n.d.

Thakar Das, Bawa, *Sikh Hindu Hain*, Hoshiyarpur: n. pub. 1899.

Upadhayaya, Ganga Prasad, *Ishai Mat ki Alochna*, Allahabad: Arya Samaj, Chowk, 1942.

Vidyalankar, Bhimsena, *Arya Pratinidhi Sabha Punjab ka Sachitar Itihas*, Lahore: Arya Pratinidhi Sabha, Punjab, 1935.

Vidyalankar, Janmajya, *Shuddhi Aur Sangathan*, Delhi: n. pub. 1930.

(c) **Punjabi**

Azad, Prithvi Singh, *Arya Samaj ka Dig Darshan*, Jullundur: Arya Pratinidhi Sabha, Punjab, n.d.

Das, Jagan Nath, *Dayanand Math Darpan*, Tr. by Mohan Singh, Amritsar: Wazir Hind Press, n.d.

Dev Rattan, Munshi, *Dayanand Chariter*, Amritsar: Punjab Commercial Press, n.d.

Singh, Dit, *Dambh Vidaran Arthath Sadhu Dayanandji de sun 1875 issvi de Satyarth Parkash par vichar*, Lahore: Baldev Singh, 1902.

(e) **Urdu**

Dharmpal, *Turk Islam*, Itava: Ved Parkash Yantralaya.
Mehta, Radha Krishan, *Tarikh-i-Arya Samaj*, Lahore: n. pub. 1903.

5. **Private Papers**

Indra Vidyavachaspati.
Har Bilas Sarda.
Madan Mohan Malaviya.
Prithi Singh Azad.
Swami Shraddhanand.
V.D. Savarkar.

6. **Unpublished Manuscripts**

Sahni, Ruchi Ram, "Self-Revelations of an Octogenarian." (In the possession of V.C. Joshi, formerly of Nehru Memorial Museum and Library, New Delhi).

Sharma, Sri Ram, "Swami Dayanand and Shuddhi." (In the possession of Professor Bhawani Lal Bharti, Head, Swami Dayanand Chair, Panjab University, Chandigarh).

B. CONTEMPORARY NEWSPAPERS AND PERIODICALS

Amrita Bazar Patrika
Harijan
Kirpan Bahadur
Sant Samachar
Shuddhi Pattar: Khalsa Dharam Parkashak
The Khalsa Akhbar
The Khalsa Samachar
The Leader
The Panjabee
The Times of India
The Tribune
Veer Sudhar Pattar
Selections from the Varnacular Newspapers published in the Punjab.
Selections from the Varnacular Newspapers published in the United Provinces.
Punjab Press Abstracts.
Selections from the Records of the North-Western Province (Annual Reports published by the Government in Allahabad).

C. CHRISTIAN CONTEMPORARY LITERATURE

Board of Foreign Mission: North India Reports
Lahore Diocesan Records
Minutes of the Punjab Mission
Punjab Mission Reports
Reports of Lodiana Mission
Society for the propagation of the Gospel Mission: Rawalpindi and Murree.

D. SECONDARY SOURCES

Books

(a) English

Agarwal, Nirsinghdas, *The Hindu Muslim Question*. Calcutta: Agarwal, 1951.

Aggarwal, P.C., *Caste, Religion and Power: An Indian Study*, Delhi: Sri Ram Centre for Industrial Relations, 1971.

Ahluwalia, M.M., *Freedom Struggle in India 1858-1909*. Delhi: Ranjit Printers and Publishers, 1965.

———, *The Kukas, the Freedom Fighter of the Punjab*, Bombay: Allied Publishers, 1965.

Allchin, B. and Allchin, F.R.. *Birth of Indian Civilization India and Pakistan Before 500 B.C.*, Harmondsworth: Penguin Books, 1968.

Anderson, Charles H., *The Political Economy of Social Class*, New Jersey: Princeton Hall, 1974.

Andrews, C.F., *The Renaissance in India: Its Missionary Aspect*. London: Baptist Mission Society, 1912.

———, *Sadhu Sunder Singh: A Personal Memoir*, London: Hodder and Stoughton, 1938.

Archer, John Clark, *The Sikhs*, Princeton: Princeton University Press, 1946.

Bahadur, Lal, *The Muslim League, Its History, Activities and Achievements*, Agra: Agra Book Store, 1954.

Baig, M.R.S., *The Muslim Dilemma in India*, Delhi: Vikas Publishing House, Pvt. Ltd., 1974.

Bajwa, Fauja Singh, *Kuka Movement*, Delhi: Motilal Banarsi Das, 1965.

——— (ed.), *History of the Punjab*, Vol. III, Patiala: Punjabi University, 1972.

Banerjea, Surendra Nath, *A Nation in the Making*, Bombay: Oxford University Press, 1963.

Banerjee, A.C., *Two Nations: The Philosophy of Muslim Nationalism*, New Delhi: Concept Publishing Company, 1981.

Banerjee, Brojendra Nath, *Religions Conversions in India*, New Delhi: Harnam Publications, 1982.

Barid, Robert D. (ed.), *Religion in Modern India*, Delhi: Manohar Book Service, 1981.

Bose, Nemai Sadhan, *Indian Awakening and Bengal*, Calcutta: FKL Mukhopadhyay, 1976.

Brass, Paul R., *Language, Religion and Politics in North India*, Delhi: Vikas Publishing House, Pvt. Ltd., 1967.

Chabra, G.S., *The Advanced History of the Panjab*, Vol. II, Ludhiana: Parkash Brothers, 1962.

Chand, Tara, *Influence of Islam on Indian Culture*, Allahabad: Indian Press, 1963.

———, *History of the Freedom Movement in Innia*, Vols. II and III, Delhi: Government of India, 1974.

Chandraji, Kahan, *Is not Christianity a False and Fabulous Religion* ? Lahore : Wazir Chand Sharma, 1974.

Chirol, Valentine, *The Indian Unrest*. New Delhi : Light and Life Publishers, Indian Edition, 1979.

Clark, Sir Robert, *A Brief Account of Thirty Years of Missionary Work of the Church Missionary Society in the Punjab and Sindh, 1852-1882*, Lahore : n. pub. 1883.

Cole, W. Owen and Sambhi, Piara Singh, *The Sikhs : Their Religious Beliefs and Practices*, London : Routedge & Kegan Paul, 1978.

Creagh, O'Moore, *Indian Studies*, London : Hutchison & Co., n.d.

Crook, William, *The Popular Religion and Folklore of Northern India*, New Deldi : S. Chand & Co. Pvt Ltd. n.d.

Cunningham, Joseph D., *A History of the Sikhs from the Origins of the National to the Battles of the Sutlej*. Delhi : S. Chand & Co., 1966.

Datta, Kali Kinkar, *A Social History of Modern India*, Delhi : The Macmillan & Co. of India, 1975.

Datta Surendra Kumar, *The Desire af India*, London : Church Missionary Society, 1908.

Davis, Emmett, *Press and Politics in British Western Punjab, 1836-1947*, Delhi : Academic Publications, 1983.

Desai, A.R., *Social Background of Indian Nationalism*, Bombay: Popular Prakashan, 1981-82.

Dumont, Louis & Pocock, D. (ed.), *Contribution to Indian Sociology*, Vol. VII, Paris : The Hague, 1969.

Farquhar, J.N., *Modern Religious Movements in India*, Delhi : Munshiram Manoharlal, Indian Edition, 1967.

———, *The Crown of Hinduism*, London : Oxford University Press, 1915.

French, Hal W, and Sharma, Arvind, *Religious Ferment in Modern India*, New Delhi : Heritage Publishers, 1981.

Gandhi, M. K., *Communal Unity*, Ahmedabad : Navjivan Publshing House, 1949.

———, *Hindu Dharma*, Allahabad : n. pub. 1950.

———, *The Way to Communal Harmony*, Ahmedabad : Navjivan Publishing House, 1949.

Garg, Ganga Ram, *World Perspectives on Swami Dayananda Saraswati*, New Delhi: Concept Publishing Company, 1984.

Ghose, Aurbindo, *Dayanand: The Man and His Work*, New Delhi: Sarvdeshak Arya Pratinidhi Sabha, 1974.

Ghose, Sankar, *Socialism, Democracy and Nationalism in India*, Bombay: Allied Publishers, 1973.

Griffiths, Sir Percival, *Modern India*, London: Ernest Benn, 1962.

Gupta, D.C., *Indian National Movement and Constitutional Development*, New Delhi: Vikas Publishing House, 1976.

Gupta, Narendra Nath, *Reflections and Reminiscences*, Bombayi Hind Kitabs, 1947.

Gupta, S.L., *Pandit Madan Mohan Malaviya: A Socio-Political Study*, Allahabad: Chugh Publications, 1978.

Gulshan Rai, Prof., *Hindu Problem in the Punjab*, Lahore: Tribune Press, 1934.

Gustafson, W. Eric and Jones, Kenneth W., *Sources on Punjab History*, Delhi: Manohar Book Service, 1975.

Hasan, Mushirul, *Nationalism and Communal Politics in India 1916-1928*, New Delhi: Manohar Publication, 1979.

Heismath, Charles H., *Indian Nationalism and Hindu Social Reform*, Princeton, N.J.: Princeton University Press, 1964.

Husain, S. Abid, *The Destiny of Indian Muslims*, Bombay: Asia Publishing House, 1985.

Hutton, J.H., *Caste in India: Its Nature, Function and Origins*, London: Oxford University Press, 1963.

Ibbetson, Sir Denzil, *Panjab Castes*, Lahore: Government Printing Press, Punjab, 1916.

Jambunathan, M.R. (ed.), *Swami Shraddhanand*, Bombay: Bhartiya Vidya Bhavan, 1961.

Jones, Kenneth W. *Arya Dharm: Hindu Consciousness in 19th-Century Punjab*, Delhi: Manohar Book Service, 1976.

Jordens, J.T.F., *Swami Dayanand Saraswati: His Life and Ideas*, Delhi: Oxford University Press, 1979.

―――, *Swami Shraddhananda: His Life and Causes*, New Delhi: Oxford University Press, 1981.

Joshi, L.M., *Studies in the Buddhistic Culture of India (During the 7th and 8th Centuries A.D.)*, Delhi: Motilal Banarsidass, 1967.

―――― (ed.), *History of Punjab*, Vol. I, Patiala: Punjabi University, 1977.

Joshi, P.C. (ed.), *Rebellion 1857: A Symposium*, New Delhi: People's Publishing House, 1957.

Joshi, V.C. (ed.), *Lala Lajpat Rai: Writings and Specches*, Vol. II, 1920-28, Delhi: University Publishers, 1966.

———, (ed.), *Rammohan Roy and the Process of Modernization in India*, Delhi: Vikas Publishing House, 1975.

Kahol, Om Prakasha, *Hindu and the Punjabi State*, Ambala Cantt: Hindu Prachara Sabha, 1955.

Kailas, N.N., *Lajpat Rai: His Relevance for the Our Times*, New Delhi: Servants of the People Society, 1966.

Kamble, J.R., *Rise and Awakening of Depressed Classes in India*, New Delhi: National Publishing House, 1979.

Kane, Pandurang Vaman, *History of Dharamsastra*, Vols. III and IV Poona; Bhandarkar Oriental Research Institute, 1973.

Kapur, K.N. *Swami Shraddhananda*, Jullundur City: Arya Pratinidhi Sabha, Punjab, 1978.

Karunakaran, Kotta P., *Continuity and Change in Indian Politics: A Study of Political Philosohy of the Indian National Movement*, New Delhi: PPH, 1966.

———, *Religion and Political Awakening in India*, Meerut: Meenakashi Parkashan, 1969.

Kaura, Uma, *Muslims and Indian Nationalism*, New Delhi: Manohar Book Service, 1977.

Koph, David, *The Brahmo Samaj and the Shaping of the Modern India Mind*, New Jersey: Princeton University, 1979.

Kumar, Ravinder, *Essays in the Social History of Modern India, 1901-39*, Delhi: Oxford University Press, 1983.

Lannoy, Richard, *The Speaking Tree: A Study of Indian Culture and Society*, London: Oxford University Press, 1971.

Lavan, Spencer, *Ahmdiya Movement: A History and Perspective*, New Delhi: Manohar Book Depot, 1974.

Lukacs, George, *History and Class Consciousness*, London: Mertin Press, 1971.

Majumdar, R.C. (ed.), *History and Culture of Indian People*, Vols. IX, X and XI, Bombay: Bharatiya Vidya Bhavan, 1965.

Mal, Bahadur, *Dayananda: A Study in Hinduism*, Hoshiarpur: VVRI, 1962.

Malik, S.C. (ed.), *Dissent, Protest and Reform in Indian Civilization*. Simla: Indian Institute of Advanced Study, 1977.

Mathur, Y.B., *Muslims and Changing India*, New Delhi: Trimurthi Publications, 1972.

Mehra, Parshotam, *A Dictionary of Modern Indian History—1707-1947*, Delhi: Oxford University Press, 1985.

Mehrotra, S.R., *Towards India's Freedom and Partition*, Delhi: Vikas Publishing House, Pvt. Ltd., 1979.

Mehta, H.R., *A History of the Growth and Development of Western Education in the Punjab, 1846-1884*, Patiala: Language Department, Punjab, 1971.

Metraux, Guy S. and Crouzet, Francois (eds.), *Studies in the Cultural History of India*, Agra: Shiva Lal Agarwala and Co., 1965.

Minault, Gail, *The Khilafat Movement: Religious Symbolism and Political Mobilization in India*, Delhi: Oxford University Press, 1982.

Misra, B.B. *The Indian Middle Classes : Their Growth in Modern Time*, London : Oxford University Press, 1961.

Moore, Clark D. and Eldredge, David (eds.), *India Yesterday Today*, New York : Praeger Publishers, 1970.

Mukerjee, S.N. (ed.), *Administration of Education in India*, Baroda : Acharya Book Depot, 1962.

Mukherji, S., *Communalism in Muslim Politics and Troubles over India*, Calcutta: Oriented Agency, 1947.

Nagar P., *Lala Lajpat Rai : The Man and His Ideas*, New Delhi, Manohar Book Service 1977.

Natarajan, S., *A Century of Social Reform in India*, Bombay Asia Publishing House, 1962.

Nayar, Baldev Raj, *Minority Politics in the Punjab*, Princton, N.J. : Princeton University Press, 1966.

Nehru, Jawaherlal, *The Discovery of India*, Bombay: Asia Publishing House, Reprint, 1972.

Oberschall, Anthony, *Social Conflicts and Social Movements*, New Jersey : Prentice Hall, Inc., 1973.

Oddie, G.A. (ed.), *Religion in South Asia : Religious Conversion and Revival Movements in South Asia in Medieval and Modern Times*, New Delhi : Manohar Book Service, 1977.

Panday, Dhanpati and Dukhan, *The Arya Samaj and Indian Nationalism (1875-1920)*, Delhi: S. Chand & Co., 1972.

Panikkar, K.M., *Hindu Society at Cross Roads*, Bombay: Asia Publishing House, 1961.

Pareek, Radhey Shyam, *Contribution of Arya Samaj in the Making of Modern India (1875-1947)*, New Delhi: Sarvadeshak Arya Pratinithi Sabha, 1973.

Parker, Mrs. Arthur, *Sadhu Sunder Singh Called to God*, Madras: The Christian Literature Society, 1957.

Pathak, R.P., *Achievements of Arya Samaj*, New Delhi : Sarvadeshik Arya Pratinidhi Sabha, n.d.

———, *Dayanand : The Man and Hiss Mission*, New Delhi : Sarvadeshik Arya Pratinidhi Sabbh, 1969.

Picket, J., Waskom, *Christian Mass Movements in India*, Lucknow Publishing House, 1933.

Prakash, Buddha, *Studies in Indian History and Civilization*, Agra: Shivilal Agarwal & Co., 1962.

Prakash, Indra, *A Review of the History and Work of the Hindu Mahasabha and the Hindu Sangathan Movement*, New Delhi: Akhil Bhartiya Hindu Mahasabha, 1952.

———, *Hindu Mahasabha : Its Contribution to India's Politics*, New Delhi : Akhil Bharat Hindu Mahasabha, 1966.

Prasad, Ishwari and Subedar, S.K., *Hindu-Muslim Problems*, Allahabad: Chugh Publications, 1974.

Prasad, Rajendra, *India Divided*, Bambay: Hind Kitabs, 1946.

Qeyamuddin, Ahmad, *The Wahabi Movement in India*, Calcutta: Firma K.L., Mukhopadhyay, 1966.

Rafiq Zakaria, *Rise of Muslims in Indian Politics*, Bombay : Somaiya Publications, 1971.

Raghuvanshi, V.P.S., *Indian Society in the Eighteenth Century,* New Delhi: Associated Publishing House, 1969.

Ram Gopal, *Indian Muslims : A Political History 1858-1947),* Bombay: Asia Publishing House, Reprint, 1964.

Rao, K.L., Seshagiri (ed.), *Hinduism,* Patiala : Punjabi University, 1969.

———, *The Concept of Sradha,* Patiala: Roy Publication, 1971.

Rao, M.S.A. (ed.), *Social Movements in India,* Vol. II, New Delhi: Manohar Publication, 1979.

Ray, Rajat Kanta, *Social Conflict and Political Unrest in Bengal, 1875-1927,* Delhi Oxford University Press, 1984.

Rose, H.A., *A Glossary of the Tribes and Castes of the Punjab and North-West Frontier Provinces,* Vols. I & II, Patiala : Language Department, Punjab, Reprint, 1970.

Sachau, Edward C., (ed.), *Alberuni's India : An Account of the Religion, Philosphy, Literature, Geography, Chronology, Astronomy, Customs, Laws and Astrology of India about A.D., 1030,* Vol. II. Delhi : S. Chand & Company, 1964.

Sahni, Ruchi Ram, *Struggle for Reform in Sikh Shrines.* Amritsar : S.G.C.P., n.d.

Saini, B.S., *The Social and Economic History of the Punjab, 1901-1939* (Including Haryana and Himachal Pradesh), Delhi : Ess Ess Publications, 1975.

Sarasvati, Svami Satya Prakash (ed.), *Dayanand Commemration Volume.* Ajmer : Paropkarni Sabha, 1983.

Sharma D.S., *Hinduism Through the Ages,* Bombay : Bharatiya Vidya Bhavan, 1973.

Savarkar, Veer Vinayak Damodar, *Six Glorious Epoches,* Bombay : Veer Savarkar Prakashan, 1950.

———, *My Transportation for life,* Bombay : Veer Savarkar Prakashan, 1984.

Sen, N.B. (ed.,) *Punjab's Eminent Hindus,* Lahore : New Book Society, 1944.

——— (ed.), *Social and Religious Reform Movements in the Nineteenth and Twentieth Centuries*, Calcutta : Institute of Historical Studies, 1979.

Seunarine, J.F., *Reconversion to Hinduism Through Shuddhi*, Madras : The Christain Literature Society, 1970.

Shamlal *The Bhangis in Transistion*, New Delhi : Inter-India Publications, 1984.

Shan Muhammad, *The Aligarh Movement* : *Basic Documents 1864-1898*, Meerut : Meenakshi Prakashan. 1978.

Sharma, B.M. *Swami Dayanand*, Lanknow : The Upper India Publishing House, 1933.

Sharma Diwan Chand, *Makers in the Arya Samaj*, Bombay : Macmillan & Co., 1935.

Sharma K.K., *Life and Times of Lala Lajpat Rai*, Ambala Centt : Indian Book Agency, 1975.

Sharma Satish Kumar, *Social movement and Social Change* : *A Study of Arya Samaj and Untouchable in* Punjab, Delhi : B.R., Publishing Corporation, 1985.

Sharma, Sri Ram, *Swami Dayanand and Social Reforms*, Delhi : Sarvadeshik Arya Pratinidhi Sabha, n.d.

———, *Mahatma Hansraj* : *Marker of the Modern Punjab*, Jullundur : Arya Pradeshik Pratinidhi Sabha, 1941.

———, *Convention and Reconversions to Hinduism During the Muslim Period*, Delhi : All India Shuddhi Sabha, n.d.

Shastri, A.V., *Vedic Caste System*, New Delhi : Sarvdeshik Arya Pratinidhi Sabha, 1967.

Shastri, Vaidyanath, *The Arya Samaj* : *Its Cult add Creed*, New Delhi : Sarvdeshik Arya Pratinidhi Sabha 1967.

Shraddhnand, Swami, *Inside The Congress*, New Delhi : Dayanand Sansthan, 1984.

Singh, Bawa Chhajju, *Life and Teachings of Swami Dayanand Saraswati*, Delhi : Jan Gyan Prakashan, 1971.

Singh, Harbans, *The Haritage of the Sikhs*, Bombay : Asia Publishing House, 1964.

Singh, Jodh, *Caste and Untouchability in Sikhism*, Amritsar : S.G.P.C., 1936.

Singh, Khushwant, *A History of the Sikhs*, 2 Vols. Princeton : Princeton University Press, 1966.

Singh Mohinder, *The Akali Movement*, Delhi, Macmillan Company of India, 1978.

Singh, Yogindra, *Modernization of Indian Tradition (A systematic Study of Social Change)*, Faridabad : Publication Devision, Reprint, 1977.

Smith, Donald Eugene (ed.), *South Asian Politics and Religion*, Princeton : Princeton University Press, 1966.

Smith, Welfred Cantwell, *Islam in Modern India*, Princeton N.J. : Princeton University Press, 1977.

Sriniwas, M.N., *Social Change in Modern India*, New Delhi : Orient Longmen Ltd., 1982.

Stokes, Eric. *The English Utiliterians and India*, London Oxford University Press, 1959.

Suda, Jyoti Prasad, *The Indian National Movement*, Meerut: Educational Publishers 1973-74.

Tondon, Prakash, *Punjabi Century, 1857-1947*, London: Chatto & Windus, 1961.

Tuteja, K.L., *Sikh Politics*, Kurukshetra : K Vishal Publications, 1984.

Upadhyaya, Ganga Prasad, *The Light of Truth, English Translation of Swami Dayanand's Satyarth Prakash*, Allahabad : The Kala Press, 1956.

Uprety, Prem Ram, *Religion and Politics in Punjab in the 1920s*, New Delhi : Sterling, 1980.

Vable, D. *The Arya Samaj : Hindus Without Hinduism*, New Delhi : Vikas Publishing House, 1983.

Webster, John C.B., *The Christain Community and Change in Nineteenth Century North India*, Meerut : The Macmillan Company of India, Ltd., 1976.

——— (ed.), *Popular Religion in the Punjab Today*, Delhi : I.T.P.C.K., 1974.

Williams, L.F. Rushbrook, *India in 1923-24*, Calcutta : Government of India, 1924.

Williams, Sir Monier-Monitor, *A Sanskrit-English Dictionary*, Oxford : The Clarendon Press, 1872.

(b) Hindi

Gautam, Niranjanlal, *Bharat-Varsh Mein Jati-Bhed*, Delhi : Vigyan Kala, 1956.

Prabhakar, Vishnu, *Nishikant Samajic and Rajnineetik Upniyas*, Delhi : Atma Ram & Sons, 1955.

Shastria, Srinivas, *Veda Tatha Rishi Dayanand*, Kurukshetra : Kurukshetra University, 1979.

Sidhanlankar Dina Nath, *Arya Samaj ki Uplabhdiyan*, Delhi : Sarvdeshik Arya Pratinidhi Sabha, 1975.

Singh, Lakhan, *Shuddhi Ek Purai Karya*, Aligarh : Bhartiya Nedic Siddhant Parishad, 2030 Vik.

Vidyavachaspati, *Arya Samaj ka Itihas*, 2 Vals. Delhi : Sarvadeshik Arya Pratinidhi Sabha, 1957.

(c) Punjabi

Nath, Jagan, *Dayanand Hirdayia*, Amritsar: Wazir Hind Press, n.d.

Sharma, Ralia Ram, *Arya Samaji Lokan De Gor Na Karne Yog*, Amritsar: Updeshan Sabha, n.d.

Singh, Jagit, *Singh Sabha Lahir*, Amritsar: Lahore Book Shop, 1974.

Singh, Mohan (tr.), *Dayanandi Dharm ka Namuna*, Lahore: Kala Press, n.d.

Shuddhi arthat Khalsa Patit Pawan, Amritsar: Karya-Sadhak Dal Bir Khalsa Biradri, n. pub. n.d.

(d) Urdu

Ahmadi, Qasim Ali (ed.), *Shuddhi ke Ashuddhi*, Delhi: Afzal-al-Matabai, 1909.

E. RESEARCH JOURNALS AND PERIODICALS

American Anthropologist
Indian History Congress Proceedings
Indian Journal of Social Research
Journal of Indian History
Journal of the Pakistan Historical Society
Journal of Social Sciences
Punjab History Conference Proceedings
The Illustrated Weekly of India
The Indian Antiquary
The Indian Archieves
The Indian Economic and Social History Review
The Indian Year Book
The Journal of Asian Studies
The Journal of Religious Studies
The Modern Review
The Political and Economic Weekly
The Panjab Past and Present
The Sikhs and Sikhism

F. UNPUBLISHED THESIS

Blue, Irvin Frederick, "Some Factors of the Hindu-Moslem Tension in India: A Study of the Political, Economic, Social and Religious Causes of the Communal of Difficulties" Ph. D. Thesis, California University, 1941.

Choudhry, Devendra Kumar, "Arya Samaj in Punjab 1877-1901." M. Phil Dissertation, Patiala: Punjabi University, 1978-79.

Ghai, R.K., "Religious Conversions in the Punjab 1849-1914." M.Phil Dissertation. Patiala : Punjabi University, 1980.

Graham, James Reid, "The Arya Samaj as a Reformation in Hinduism with special reference to Caste," Ph. D. Dissertion, Yale University, 1942.

Gupta, Shiv Kumar, "British Attitude and Policy Towards Arya Samaj (1875-1920)," Ph. D. Thesis, Chandigarh: Panjab University, 1984.

Jones, Kenneth W., "The Arya Samaj in the Punjab: A Study of Social Reform and Religious Revivalism, 1877-1902." Ph. D. Thesis, Berkeley: University of California, 1966.

Kansal, Megh Raj, "Development of Educational Administration in Punjab Since 1854." Ph. D. Thesis, Patiala: Punjabi University, 1973.

Mehra, Lal Chand, "The Arya Samaj as an Educational Movement." M.A. Thesis, Berkeley: University of California, 1925.

Sharma, Satish Kumar, "Role of Arya Samaj Movement in the Uplift of Untouchables in Punjab." Ph. D. Thesis, Chandigarh: Panjab University, 1983.

Singh, Bakhtawar, "Social and Economic History of the Punjab, 1901 to 1939." Ph. D. Thesis, Chandigarh: Panjab University, 1962.

Thursby, Gene Robert, "Aspects of Hindu-Muslim Relations in British India: A Study of Arya Samaj Activities, Government of India Policies, and Communal Conflit in the Period 1923-1928." Ph. D. Dissertation. Duke University, 1972.

Author Index

Ahmad, Imtia, 1, 14
Allchin, B., 5
Allchine F.R., 5
Archer, John Clark, 14
Azad, Prithvi Singh, 37

Bai Parmanand, 84, 104, 105, 107
Barrier, Narman G., 145
Bawa Chhajju Singh, 27, 39
Bhatia, Shyamlal, 122

Dass, Charu, 72
Desai, A.R., 6, 12, 29
Diwan Chand, 44

Farquha, J.N., 2

Gandhi, Hiralal, 102
Gandhi, Mahatama (*see* subject index), 101-202
Ganga Ram, 72
Ghai, R.K., 5, 10, 103, 116
Ghasiram, 33, 39
Ghose, Sankar, 112
Ghurye, G.S., 10, 12
Gopal, Ram, 15.,
Graham, J.R., 33, 38, 49, 54, 62, 72, 120, 123-124, 132-133, 138, 139

Ibbetson, Sir Denzil. 71
Imam, Zafar, 114

Jambunathan, M.R., 63, 84
Javed, Ramchander, 127, 132
Jones, Kenneth, W., 2-3, 5, 2-3, 24, 28-30 35, 40, 42, 49, 54, 58-61, 123-125, 133, 146, 159
Jorden, J.T.F., 27, 29, 31, 35, 39, 132, 138, 145, 149
Joshi, Lalmani, 6
Joshi, P.C., 23
Joshi, V.C., 149

Kani, P.V., 34
Kaura, Uma, 147
Knock, A.D,, 4
Rrishan, Gopal, 117
Kumar, D., 12

Lala Charu Dass, 127, 138
Lala Ganga Ram, 127, 138
Lala Lajpat Rai, (see subject index), 1, 32, 43, 48, 11-63, 115, 123-124, 141
Lannoy, Richard, 26, 34, 121
Lekhram, 37

Mahatma Devi Chand, 135
Majumdar, R.C. 13, 102, 115, 117, 141, 147, 150
Mathur, Y.B., 117
Main, Sir Fazl-i-Hussain, 115

Miller, R.E., 100
Mimamshak, Yudhishir, 27
Minault, Gail, 114
Misra, B.B., 11-12, 22

Natarajan, S., 149
Nayar, Baldev Raj, 152

Oddie, G.A. 4
Ojha, Rameshwar G., 36, 39

Pandit Ganga Ramji, 118
Prakash, Vishwa, 65
Prasad, Ishwari, 147
Prasad, Rajendra, 118, 150

Rafiq-i-Hind, 14
Raja Ram Mohan Roy, 18

Sachau, Edward C., 35
Sarda, Har Bilas, 34-35, 38
Sarkar, Sukumar, 85
Savarkar, V.D., 119, 153
Sebring, Jamesm, 127-128
Seligman, E.R.A., 3
Sen, N.B., 94
Seunarine, J.F. 26, 96, 141
Sharda, Chand Karan, 116
Sharma, Brij Mohan, 116

Sharma, B.R., 43
Sharma, R.D., 57
Sharma, Satish Kumar, 134, 136, 140
Sharma, Shri Ram, 34-35, 38, 61, 85, 100, 102, 140
Singh, G.N., 117
Smith, Donald Eugene, 6, 152
Stokes, Erie, 13
Subedar, S.K., 147
Swami Chidananda Saraswati, 93
Swami Satya Prakash Saraswati, 57
Swami Shraddhanand, 115, 118

Tara Chand, 30
Thursby Gene Robert, 2, 94, 149-150

Upadhyaya, Ganga Prasad, 13, 31, 40, 135, 138, 146
Uprety, 1

Vashishtta, V.K., 39
Vidyalankar, Haridutt, 38

Webster, John C.B., 14, 40, 65, 147
Williams, Sir Monier, 1

Subject Index

Abdali Ahmad Shah, 10
Addison, J., 78
Adi Brahmo Samaj, 19
Al Beruni, 35
Adi, Haider, 10
Ali, Maulana Abdul, 112
Ali, Mohammad, 151
Akali, Lal Singh 99
Arya missionaries, 63
Arya-Muslim classes, 142
Arya Samaj, 3, 21-24, 49, 58, 61-64, 74, 78-79, 121, 123, 133, 158
   principles of, 49, 125, 176-177
Arya Samajist, 40, 49, 51, 58, 60, 63, 104, 123-126, 127, 144
Aryan civilization, 6
Aryanization, 7
Asghari Begum, 102
Aurangzeb, 92
Aurobindo, Sir, 21
Azad, Maulana Abdul Kalam, 100
Azad, Prithi Chand, 75

Bhai Basan Singh, 52
Bhagats, 14
Bhakti movement, 10, 25
Bhangi, 40

Biradari, 49-50, 82, 157-158
Brahminical Hinduism, 3, 6-7
Brahmo Samaj, 18, 30
British conquest, 11
British policies, impact of the, 12
   divide & rule of, 143
Buddha, 6
Buddhism, 4, 6, 31

Caste system, 5-7, 9-10, 14, 19, 31, 81, 157
Chamar, 40, 92
Chatterjee, Bankim Chandra, 23
Chaudhri Fateh Chand, 168
Chaudhri Fateh Muhammad Sial, 150
Chaudhri Jaggat Ram, 169
Chaudhri Sechet Singh, 168
Chaudry Ram Bhoj Dutt, 77, 79, 80, 129
Child marriage, 19
Christian, 77, 81, 115
   relation to Hindu and Muslim, 57-58
Christian colonies, 14
Christian missionaries, 12-14, 42
Christianity, 3, 13-14, 16, 23, 35-37, 41, 60-61, 63, 122, 145, 156
   challenge of, 142

Clark, Robert, 37
Communal roit (see roit),
Communal tension, 143
Congress, 83, 83-89, 100, 106, 110, 112-113, 147, 151, 158
Conversion, 4

Dalitoddar Mandal, 91
Das, C.R., 100
Datt, Akshy Kumar, 29
Datt, Pandit Dev, 166
Datt, Pandit Prag, 166
Delhi conspiracy case, 82
Dev Samaj, 25
Dhingra, Madan Lal. 82
Dravidian, 7

Education, 32, 137
  growth of, 41
  new, 17
Education English, 17
Employment, 15

Freedom struggle, 83

Gafoor, Abdul, 78
Gandhi, Mahatma, 88-89, 147
Gayatra Mantra, 49, 69, 131
Ghadar movement, 82, 101
Greeks, 7, 34

Harappan civilization, 5
Hasting, Warren, 22
Hindu, 2, 9, 18, 33, 38-39, 41, 48, 52-53, 56-58, 61, 79, 98-99, 106-107, 118, 122, 131, 144, 147, 155
  half, 74
  mind of, 40
  relation to Muslamman, 56-57
  social life of, 49
  social structure, 5
  untouchable, 88
Hindu Muslim relation, 117
Hindu-Muslim struggle, 120, 149

Hindu-Muslim unity, 92, 109, 118, 147
  idea of, 151
  slogan of, 85
Hindu Orphan Relief Movement, 61
Hindu religions philosophy, 8
Hindu-Sikh relation, 152
Hindu social struggle, 142, 152
Hindu social system, 19
Hindu tradition, 8, 23
Hinduism, 2-3, 19, 23, 30, 34-37, 40, 48, 52-53, 65, 79, 85, 107, 120, 130, 142

Idol-worship, 19
Impurities and pollution, 8
Indian culture and civilization, 16
Indian religious, attacks on the, 16
Indian social system, 10
Indian tradition, 5, 17
Indian value system, 11
Indus valley civilization, 5
Infanticide, 19
Islam, 3, 30, 35-36, 39, 44, 59, 74, 81, 122

Jainism, 6
  emergence of, 30
Jallianwala Bagh massacre, 88

Khadi movement, 89
Khan Sir Sayyed Ahmad, 21
Khilafat movement, 83, 113
Khwaja Hassan Nizami, 116, 151
Kitchlew, Saifuddin, 114
Kuka movement, 22
Kusunas, 7, 34

Lal Bagis (*chuchras*), 65
Lala Balmokand, 106
Lala Chhajju Ram, 170
Lala Devi Chand, 75
Lala Hanj Raj, 43, 85-86, 94, 104, 129

Index

Lala Har Dayal, 117-118
Lala Labhu Ram, 168
Lala Lajpat Rai, 43, 51-52, 113, 129, 152
   leadership of, 61
Lala Munshi Ram, 43-44, 53, 129, 137
Lala Ram Dass, 73
Lala Ramditta, 169-173
Lala Roshan Lal, 136
Land revenue system, 21
Luther, Martin, 38

Macaulay, Lord, 16
Mahavira, Vardhaman, 6
Malkhanas, 92-93
Malviya Madan Mohan, 110-113, 149
Mangles, 17
Mantras, 1
Marathas, 10
Marriad couples, 45
Maulana Hasrat Mohini, 107
Maulvis, 92
Mazhabi Sikhs, 66-67
Minto, Lord, 144
Money economy, introduction of, 11
Moplah rebellion 160
Moplahs of the Malabai eoat, 83
Montagu-chelmsford reforms, 147
Morley-Minto reform, 144-145, 159
Muslim, 33, 52, 56-58, 68-69, 78-79, 97-99, 106-107, 113-115, 145, 147, 150, 156-157
   conversion programme of, 10
   half, 73-74
   relation to Hindu, 56-57
Muslim League, 78, 143
Muslim missionaries, 93, 142
Muslim movement, 21
Muslim rule, 8

Nahar Singh, 92

Naidu, Sarojini, 100
Narain, Shastri, 108
Nathuram, 47
Nehru, Jawaharlal, 63
Nehru, Motilal, 100
New legal system, 11-12
Nizams of Hyderabad, 10
Non-cooperation movement, 83-84, 89, 108, 119, 147-148

Pandit Bhagwandin, 74
Pandit Bhoj Dutt, 75
Pandit Guru Datta, 42
Pandit Lekh Ram, 43, 53, 58-59, 129
   murder of, 142
Pandit Rishi Ram, 86
Phillouri, Pandit Shraddha, 33
Pollution, 1, 37
Prasad, Ganga, 51
Pratchit ceremony, 1, 48
Punjab Hindu Sabha, 144-145
Purification, 51, 54, 128, 155
   ceremoney of, 166

Raja Ram Mohan Roy, 18-20
Ramgopal, 47
Ranade, Mahadev Govind, 35
Rationalism individualism liberalism, 12
Relegious reform, 29
Ritual purification, 33, 37
Roits communal, 109, 115, 148-150
Rowlatt Acts, 83
Roti and *beti*, 138

Sadhus, 14
Sagar, Vidya, 29
Sakas, 7, 34
Sanatan Dharam movement, 22
Sangathan movement, 104-105, 111-114, 115, 154
Sant Ram, B., 78
Sati system, 11, 13, 19, 31
Sayed Nawab Shah, 170

Sen, Keshab Chander, 19-20, 29-30
Shastrasths, 29
Sheikh Gulab Nabi, 166
Shuddhi, 36-37, 39, 54, 72, 94, 115, 124, 149, 154-155
  aspects of, 55-57
  ceremonies, 45, 74
  definiton, 1-4
  details of. 204
  genesis of, 33
  historical background, 5-16
  respective work of, 95
Shuddhi movement, 36-37, 44, 52, 57, 59, 60, 75, 79, 101, 113, 116, 119
  effection socio-religions life, 132
  origin, 30
  political dimension of, 141, 145
  social dimension of, 120-121
Shuddhi policy, 125
Shuddhi programme, 137
Sikh, 3, 52, 56, 152
Sikh, *Mazhabi*, 66-68
Sikh Shuddhi Movement, 54
Sikhism, 5, 2-5, 3, 57
Singh, Kharak, 37
Singh Sabha, 54-55
Srāddha, 60
Sufis, 14
Swami Dayanand, 3, 21, 24-25, 33-40, 44-45, 82, 126
  history of, 27-29
  philosophy of, 21-32
Swami Ishwara Nand Saraswati, 51

Swami Satyananda Saraswati, 72
Swami Shraddhanand, 88-89, 91-94, 96, 101-102, 107, 111, 116, 118, 151
Swami Vinayak Maharaj Masurkar, 107
Swami Vivekanand, 21

Tagore, Devendra Nath, 19-20
Tanzim and *tabligh*, 154
Tilak, Bal Gangadhar, 35, 88
Tipu Sultan, 10

Umar, Muhammad, 38
Untouchability, 13, 95, 149
  removal of, 114
Utilitarianism, principles of, 13

Vaisyas, 7, 49
Varna-vyavastha, 7,4 9
Violence type of, 115
Violence, political, 154

Wahabi leaders, 21
Wahabi movement, 22
War against Turkey, 82
Western culture, 12, 24
Western idea
  impact of, 12
  spreading, 18
Widows' Remarriage Act, 16
William Bentick's Council, 16
Women, Mussalman, 54
World War, first, 82-83, 147
Wyllie, Sir William Curzon, 82

Yojna, 7
Yogyopavit, 75

Zamindar, 92